A Long Hard Look at 'Psycho'

A Long Hard Look at 'Psycho'

Raymond Durgnat

bfi Publishing

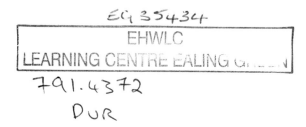

First published in 2002 by the
British Film Institute
21 Stephen Street, London WIT ILN

The British Film Institute promotes greater understanding of, and access to, film and moving image culture in the UK.

Cover design: Paul Wright/Cube
Set in Gill sans by Fakenham Photosetting, Norwich, UK

Printed in England by Cromwell Press, Trowbridge, UK

British Library Cataloguing-in-Publication Data
A catalogue record for this book is available from the British Library
ISBN 0 85170 920 6 pbk
ISBN 0 85170 921 4 hbk

Contents

Introduction

THE ARTIST PROPOSES, THE PUBLIC DISPOSES

'*Psycho*', The Master said, 'has a very interesting construction and that game with the audience was fascinating. I was directing the viewers. You might say I was playing them like an organ.' By playing the audience, through 'pure film', Hitchcock's great love, *Psycho* works through *suggestion*, through *atmosphere*, not *stating* ideas, but *generating them*, in the minds of the audience. As Thorold Dickinson, another formidable 'audience-buster', observed, 'No film ever frightens an audience. The audience frightens itself.' *Psycho* upfronts many unresolved problems, right across film theory, media studies and aesthetics. This little book must limit itself to a, by now traditional, mixture of:

1. Assumptions as to usual, or normative, audience responses.
2. 'High culture'-type critical responses.
3. The critic's own observations, with which readers may enjoy 'comparing notes', and
4. Hitchcock's intentions, declared or presumed, including his private meanings, for kindred souls to pick up if they will, and his self-expressions, sometimes inadvertent. 'What did the author mean?' and 'What ideas helped shape this discourse?' are basic, perennial, and probably instinctive, responses to all discourse whatsoever. They ought not to *monopolise* cultural history, nor stop readers using texts entirely for their own agendas and enjoyment. Nonetheless, the interaction between the man, the auteur, the text, and its 'primary target audiences', must loom large in cultural criticism, without conceding the problem of substantially different, or incompatible, audience responses.

AUTEUR THEORY VERSUS COLLABORATION THEORY

How far *Psycho*'s merits derive from Hitchcock, and how far from his collaborators, is a question beyond our scope here; our priority is the tale, not the teller. The credit sequence, so remarkable that it's rarely discussed, is surely a solo flight by Saul Bass, who more than anyone put modern(ist) visuals into Hollywood movies (which had lagged behind some popular subcultures). Bass's other credit, as pictorial consultant for the film itself, might help explain a certain visual 'wildness', unlike Hitchcock's more 'classical' tendencies (although Hitchcock would have well understood, and developed, the trend). Collaborators testify that while directing the shower sequence Hitchcock worked from a storyboard by Saul Bass, which, insofar as it influenced both *mise-en-shot* (camera angles, compositions, tonality …), and *mise-en-scène* (action in the frame), might seem to fulfil certain directorial (and editing!) functions. Nonetheless, in experienced opinion, the shower scene was Hitchcock's directorial creation; and after all it was he, not the 'illustrative sketches', who controlled the timing and rhythm, the dramatic modulations, the quality of light and all the other 'indefinables' that transform a 'grammar' into a 'poetic'.

Hitchcock selected writer Joseph Stefano, not just to write down what Hitchcock dictated, but for his rare skill at dialogue rich in 'colour' (implications about character and background), at which Hitchcock felt himself not gifted. Moreover, Hitchcock regularly left to his actors much of the character 'detail', that is to say, the substance of performance (hence the dry, blank characterology of many Hitchcock films, e.g. those with Cary Grant, a light, 'abstract' actor). That Norman, at morbid moments, nibbles a little sweetie is easily taken for a 'Hitchcock touch' (prompted by his recurrent theme of food, and akin to the chocolate factory scene in *Secret Agent* [1936]); but the idea would seem to have been Anthony Perkins', unprompted. Again, it's easy to see why Hitchcock, famously mean with praise, said to Simon Oakland, playing the psychiatrist in the film's penultimate scene, 'Thank you … you have just saved my movie.' In an earlier sequence, Perkins and Martin Balsam, acting together, hit a rhythm so fast and tight that watching technicians broke into applause; but its very speed gave the editor great problems. To give the audience time to think some dialogue implications through, he had to find some pauses, which the original continuity lacked, and then, by thorough re-editing, to *recreate* that rhythm, but at a slower pace. As for Bernard Herrmann's 'background' music – would *Psycho* be itself without it? Movie auteurs, unlike literary authors, are rarely one-man bands. Many a first-rate film has no identifiable auteur; its author is a team, an *interaction* of talents – a conspiracy of inspirations, a Platonic 'symposium'.

Admiration for *Psycho* needn't imply equal admiration of Hitchcock's films in general. In *Hitchcock: The Making of a Reputation*, Robert Kapsis shows just how much the Hitch 'legend' owes to his being the first, and for many years the only, director to compound his own publicity sense by retaining a permanent press agent. (It's also true that few directors have been as articulate, and open, about his artistic principles, and his personal life, when interviewed by fellow artists, like Truffaut and Bogdanovich.) Claims for his genius often focus on the moral and dramatic aspects of his films, but, as argued elsewhere, his claim to pantheon status may rest on his cinematic forms, which fuse very refined craftsmanship, love of 'pure film' and an aestheticism which, instead of being 'decadent', amoral and idly sham-aristocratic, is moral, robust and 'democratic'. *Psycho* is both conventional *and* inventive, and marvellous to study. (In this little book, we have little to say of the music – deplorably, no doubt; our excuse is, that every spectator is shaken by it, yet, its very 'language', and its relation to emotional dynamics, is difficult to discuss. Clearly, its nervous quality owes much to its being all strings, played percussively. But its quiet, reflective moments, its evocation of thought indistinctly 'stirring', are just as interesting as its shrill attacks.)

CONSENSUS OR DISSENSUS?

Impossible here to review the many interpretations of *Psycho*, which must by now be well into three figures. Interested readers may like to 'compare and contrast' this 'reading' with others akin to it in one way or another: for example, Robin Wood, perpetuating the – perhaps narrow, but healthy – spirit of 1950s 'Eng. Lit.' (some English film critics reckoned they could have talked F. R. Leavis into acknowledging Hitchcock's genius); V. F. Perkins (a liberal humanist/pragmatic formalist); Richard Griffith (who rightly attacks my apparent agreement with the 'guilt-inducing' school of movie criticism); William Rothman (a psychoanalytical moralist of great perspicuity and intolerable severity); François Truffaut (whose dialogue with The Master is sometimes telepathic, sometimes a 'dialogue of the deaf'); Claude Chabrol and Eric Rohmer (whose religious tendencies, characteristic of *Cahiers du Cinéma* in its glory years, from Bazin through the *nouvelle vague*, made them the first to look behind the 'Master of Fun Suspense' and posit a 'Master of Catholic Guilt'); Jean Douchet (another *Cahier*-ist, whose 'gnostic mysticism' is super-sensitive to strange passional surges in Hitchcock's films). As for my earlier 'run-through' of *Psycho*, its concern, which I should no doubt have defined more clearly, was, not so much what *happens* in *Psycho*, as, its *emotionalisation* of a *sufficiently typical* 'target audience'. Contrasting with (and complementing) these 'moral-literary' approaches, we especially recommend a chapter on the 'patrolman' sequence in Stefan Sharff's *The Elements of Cinema* – a micro-analysis which revivifies the Eisenstein tradition of 'pure film' for-

malism (unfettered by paradigms imported from linguistics, which of all human sciences has the least relevance to film), and applies it to the fine detail of narrative
editing and visual semantics. Useful, too, is Sharff's book-length analysis – *The Art of
Looking in Hitchcock's Rear Window*. After all, observation, a skill and an art, is not
reducible to sexual pleasure, and even less reducible to some voyeuristic or
scopophiliac tendency than the visual arts in general, or reading and writing.

QUESTIONING LOOKS

In discussing *Psycho*'s motifs, we make much of eyes, mirrors, looks direct to camera,
POVs (shots from near enough a character's point of view) and other 'optical' matters. This interest entails no acquiescence in all those academic theories which relate
film to a scopic/scoptic drive, or voyeurism, or a deplorably obsessive male gaze, or
murderous starings, or mirror-phases, or psychopathology – as if looking were
beyond the pale of rationality and somehow more libidinal than language or conscious thought. In our view (!), however, film, and visual art generally, has the same –
very high – degree of autonomy from unconscious structures as, say, poetry, music,
logic or most conscious thinking. The 'optical' motifs in *Psycho* are on a par with its
non-visual ones – like Bernard Herrmann's brutal and haunting music. (Is music The
Most Unconscious Art?) As for two ideas, often combined – first that POV shots
by themselves strengthen spectator identification with character, and second
that spectators often think of the camera as 'a pair of eyes like a person' invisibly present within the scene the principal objections are: one, that in fictions like
Psycho, camera and diegesis are logically incompatible, so that diegetic space and
camera space read as a non-continuum, and, two, that most spectators overlook (!) camera POV, much as they dis*regard* (!) cuts, which, if taken literally,
would jump them about in space, like performing fleas. The reasons are well
known in visual art theory and in scientific psychology.

Another problem: merely to pursue a motif in the film, through its various
appearances and forms, risks suggesting that each time it reintroduces the same idea,
it's a simple, static repetition. Often, however, its reappearance signals some kind of
change – a modulation, or development, or new aspect revealed. The new context
or new presentation (e.g. a different camera angle) is part of the *changes* which a
story *is*. (Story as *change* and story as *statement* are very different things; but that's
another essay.)

In academic Film Studies just now, psychoanalysis is a 'theory of first resort'. The
meanings of films, and of the medium itself, are sought in the Freudian Unconscious

– realm of the 'libidinal' (the forbidden) and the 'repressed'. Easily overlooked is what Freudians call the Preconscious – that vast domain of operations which are neither *repressed* nor articulated in consciousness. (Some *can* become conscious, as and when required; others can't, like much perceptual processing, since it's preliminary to consciousness itself.) Freudian tradition, while appreciating its existence, constantly underestimates its powers, partly because Freudian analysis concentrates on the Unconscious, partly because Freudian traditions routinely confuse 'the conscious mind' with what's rational, moral, adult and articulate. Furthermore, the Freudian, capital-U Unconscious is easily confused with 'unconscious' in the ordinary, small-u, sense, as in 'I must have done it unconsciously', where 'unconsciously' means 'absent-mindedly' – the mental operation was preconscious. With special relevance to film, and *Psycho* in particular, most body language is unconscious but not Unconscious. Its movements, and the prompting attitudes, may not reach consciousness, but should consciousness wish to monitor them, it has only to pay attention. Most of our thinking is preconscious, and its boundaries with the conscious are so fluid, that perhaps they're not boundaries at all. All that's another subject, but it helps explain why Freud insisted that the meanings which psychoanalysis can discern in art are more often marginal than central.

FEAR AND DESIRE

If, and it's a big if, Mrs Norman Bates' knife is 'phallic', that's not why it sets Marion, and the spectators, screaming. Their thrills arise from the reality principle, and from conscious thought: a knife in your stomach may seriously endanger your health. When Marion tries to avoid getting stabbed, what, in her motivation, is to psycho-analyse? Worse yet, the very diagnosis, 'phallic', represents, not an *Unconscious* association, but a conscious, educated, construction, which has *already* been censored (or should we say 'castrated'?). Even *when* 'knife' carries some hidden meaning (e.g. 'prick'), the hidden meaning is merely *accessory*, and carries negligible power. Psychoanalysis has a place, of course, but, when applied by lay persons, who dip into it, self-taught, in their spare moments, in the margins of art study, it's best offered, not as rock-solid theory, but as *speculation* (!) and *reflection* (!). In the psychoanalytic theories offered here, violence, fear, and other compulsive drives, are neither *caused* nor *dominated* by sexuality; it may *influence* them but, reciprocally, they influence it: often, indeed, more strongly since sexuality is the *repressed*, not the *repressing*, force. This general position is argued, on strictly Freudian grounds, by Jean Bergeret, in *La Violence et la vie: la face cachée de l'Oedipe*; it's long established among the 'independents' within English psychoanalysis; and well before the break with Freud it was the basis of the 'inferiority complex'. Bergeret goes on to argue that Freud's very emphasis on 'castration' is a *defence mechanism*, misattributing to the 'sexual' fears actually derived from survival/power drives, as prioritised in non-Freudian psychology, and in *realpolitik*-al theories (Macchiavelli, Hobbes, Marx). It's perhaps significant that *Psycho* roughly coincides with the spread, in and around psychoanalysis, of 'English school', mother-centred, theory (Melanie Klein, James Robertson, Donald Winnicott)[1], which many feminists, surprisingly, overlook. Their acquiescence in Lacanian phallocracy might almost persuade one that Helen Deutsch's postulation of female masochism was correct; however, alternative 'deconstructions' are easily available.

Psycho and psychoanalysis have some common interests (in Mr and Mrs Norman Bates); but, as Hitchcock lucidly pointed out, if *Psycho* were 'serious' as psychology, it would be a clinical case history, not a 'roller-coaster' thriller. Psychoanalytically, the most relevant text I know is 'La Mère morte [The Dead Mother]', a chapter in *Narcissisme de vie, narcissisme de mort* by André Green. Regarding Norman's more normal, sensitive side, Green's concept of 'la psychose blanche' – white (or blank) psychosis – seems interesting; especially as the whole film abounds in both white-ish visuals and mental *blanks*, some tiny, some gaping . . .

Žižek's introduction to *Everything You Always Wanted to Know about Lacan (But Were Afraid to Ask Hitchcock)* makes a richly stimulating read; the 'convergences' between its Lacanian ideas, other psychoanalytical schools and 'traditional human-ism' are well worth examining. Nonetheless, much Lacanian writing suggests, even to friendly sceptics, that, if you begin by reading Lacanian paradigms into Hitchcock's ambiguous patterns, the result can only be – Lacan in, Lacan out. More worrying, for theories of film form, is Lacan's own position, which explicitly denies the existence of visual metaphor in dreams (neatly disqualifying 'knife as phallus'!).[2] This blind spot for visual structures eclipses even Barthes' proposal that film studies should 'progress' from linguistics to – decoding film stills! So much for movement, the kinetic, the cinematic! The Grand Error is the wholesale importation of para-digms from structural linguistics, whose special expertise can know nothing of visual, perceptual or cognitive processes, or general semantic structures, or the structures of discourse (so that 90 per cent of textual meaning lies beyond its ken). Competent aesthetics do exist, but their application to film is beyond our scope here.

FROM SCRIPT TO FILM

Our references to 'the script' mean the shooting script commercially available. Its pages carry various dates, the last being 7 December 1959, about a week before shooting. Stephen Rebello's thoroughly detailed book on *Psycho*'s production history strengthens my impression that this version of the script is near enough the draft that lay on Hitchcock's lap while shooting (though what he had in mind was very likely rather different).

While (and even before) scripting, Hitchcock made storyboards (sketches of every shot), often precisely designed, as the chosen lens would see them. He sometimes said that, being a man who worried a lot, he liked everything prepared in advance, so that once he'd written a film, all he had to do was shoot it. Like most showbiz legends, that's true in spirit, but not letter. Certainly this script and the final film show countless changes. Some are quite minor (for example: the script has Marion hail a cab to get from hotel to office, but the finished film omits the cab altogether and cross-fades directly from Sam left alone in the hotel to Marion entering her office). Other changes, noted as we go, are substantial. In the script, Marion is 'Mary', and Dr Richmond is 'Dr Simon'.

In general movie practice, shooting scripts are written in numbered 'master-scenes', roughly akin to theatrical scenes. The breakdown into shots is never done by the writer, who can rarely anticipate the countless factors which govern them – the creative ideas of director, actors, set designers, cameramen, editors, etc., and countless production practicalities. *Psycho* credits the script to Stefano alone; but its writing involved sometimes weekly, sometimes daily, conferences with a producer–director famous for his original, and auteur-ial, vision. Though Stefano wasn't Hitchcock's glove puppet, Hitchcock's requirements lay heavily upon him. Neither man was the film's 'only begetter'. Film, like theatre, ballet, opera, etc., is a 'collaborative' art, and although it has its auteurs, they rarely if ever correspond to some literary notions of 'authors' as solitary, all-controlling, individuals (notions that overlook literary collaborations (the Goncourt Brothers, Erckmann – Chatrian …).

The script of *Psycho* has its inconsistencies. By and large, it's conventionally laid out in numbered master-scenes. Sometimes master-scene generalities do specify a particular angle or effect. Occasionally, though, master-scene numbers are allocated to particular shots, as if Hitchcock's mind's eye had storyboarded this scene from the start. The shower scene is written as six shots, though in the film it has around 70 (depending where you reckon 'the shower scene' begins and ends). Sometimes the numbering breaks down altogether, presumably to accommodate recent script changes, without having to change the scene numbering to which everyone in the unit was already working. Scene 118, headed 'The Dead Body' (curious scene description!), is clearly a shot, and, if you fully visualise it while reading, its description is 'necessary and sufficient' to stage it very exactly. Left implicit is a visual point to which most studio executives would strongly object – but which they probably wouldn't stop to visualise exactly. The shot was made, but not used; Van Sant decodes and restages it for his 1998 remake, times having changed.

Grateful thanks from the author to Rob White, Jason Wilcox, Dr Barry Salt, Tom Luddy, Stefan Sharff and Maurice Rapf.

Developing the Film

A BUSINESS PROPOSITION

Psycho reflects Hitchcock's dual career, in feature films, and in television (a chart-topping series of thrillers, *Alfred Hitchcock Presents* [1955–65]). As television took 'the family audience', to which 'Old Hollywood' (the Big Studio system) was geared, ever more cinemas resorted to hitherto 'niche' publics, including the teenage audience, revealed by *I Was a Teenage Werewolf* (1957) and a smaller, but growing, audience for 'art-house' (mostly foreign-language films). Both audiences baffled 'Old Hollywood' thinking, especially when they overlapped, and combined libidinal tastes with quicker intelligence, a higher educational level and greater moral irresponsibility. 'Old Hollywood' mostly deplored the new trends, often for entirely sincere moral–cultural reasons. Hitchcock developed *Psycho* with the teenage, 'sex and violence', audience in mind, as its 'core' audience, while hoping also to reach the wider market spread of his previous successes. From the 'teenage werewolf' angle, Norman is a 'realistic' werewolf, geared to the increasing interest in psychology. Though pushing 30, he's an arrested teenager, still mother-bound, and Anthony Perkins was popular with teenage girls. As for Marion and Sam, they too are socially unsettled, lonely, and to that extent psychologically 'marginal', and so have strong appeal for niche-market teenagers, but still interest without alienating maturer spectators. Relevant, too, was the art-house market, which, though still small, was spreading. In worldwide terms, art-house films could outgross Hollywood products, and some art-house fare had broken into the widest US markets – notably, *The Wages of Fear* (Henri-Georges Clouzot, 1954), *And Woman Was Created* (Roger Vadim, 1956, with Brigitte Bardot) and *Les Diaboliques* (also by Clouzot, 1956). Hitchcock often referred to the last, whose structural similarities with *Psycho* are spelled out in the Rebello book. In the event, *Psycho* survived considerable hostility from within 'Old Hollywood', the press and moral campaigners, and more than achieved its intended market spread. It's a woman's film but with mayhem galore for the young, especially young males; it's sensitive enough for mature moviegoers; it's libidinal and intellectual; it's Gothic adapted to a psychological age; it's emotionally literate (as not all art is); it's morally serious but not obviously moralistic; it's – pleasurable and anguished.

SOURCES OF THE STORY

The City and the Country

Robert Bloch's novel was inspired by (but not based on) one of two recent crimes which had shocked thoughtful newspaper readers, and served to epitomise threats to the 'suburban', middle-class norms looming newly large in the national self-image. The other case was a city incident. A woman was attacked in a fairly respectable street, and repeatedly, gradually, stabbed to death, over a ten-minute period. Though passers-by and neighbours must have heard her pleas for help, no one even called the police. It's sometimes thought to have influenced Hitchcock's choice of *Rear Window* (1954), the main theme of which is, not voyeurism, but, neighbourhood watch. If *Rear Window* is the 'urban myth', *Psycho* is the 'rural myth'.

Wisconsin Death Trip

Ed Gein (1904–84) lived his lonely life in a farmhouse a little way from a tiny hamlet in Wisconsin. A quietly eccentric oddjob-man, given to enigmatic mumbling, he was generally presumed feeble-minded. Then, in 1957, his house was found to be crammed with female bodies and body parts; he sat in chairs made of human bones, and wore apparel made of women's skins. He had tortured and disembowelled at least a dozen women, mostly vagrants, before killing them and also stolen female cadavers from local cemeteries. Part of his house, associated with his long-deceased mother, had been set aside, and never entered since. His own rooms were strewn with household rubbish.

Initially, local officials and newspapers couldn't bring themselves to print the grisly details; but what did emerge created a national sensation. Local gossips, and psychologists, attributed the crime to an unhealthy relationship between Gein and his mother, a grimly pious woman, who had died in 1945. Committed to an asylum, Gein applied for release in 1974, insisting that he was now normal enough to lead a harmless life. Though at least one psychiatrist testified to his sensitive disposition, he was never released. He also inspired *The Texas Chain Saw Massacre* (Tobe Hooper, 1974); by this time the norms of cinema violence had drastically escalated, partly through cultural changes, partly through the movie market's shifted demographics.

Norman Mark II

For years Robert Bloch (1917–94) made a modest living writing fiction, for lower middlebrow and 'pulp' magazines, often in the Poe–Lovecraft genre, suitably updated. Wisconsin-born, he was struck by, not the grisly details, for their own sake, but by everybody's difficulty in mentally coping with the facts. Rather like *Rear Window*, *Psycho* is a 'blind spot' story. Norman's own mind splits under the strain; and when the facts come to light, his neighbours misremember their own attitudes, crack sick jokes and make desultory attempts to exploit Norman's notoriety. Lila concludes: 'We just blundered along until we did the right thing for the wrong reasons.' (This will become a guiding principle of Hitchcock's film.) 'And right now, I can't even hate Bates for what he did. He must have suffered more than any of us. We're not all quite as sane as we pretend to be …' Wise words, no doubt, though Lila's increasing absence of indignation, about murder, may seem disconcerting: is it moral alienation?

The novel anticipates many striking features of the film, and Bloch deserves credit as a co-*auteur* – at least of structure and substance, if not artistic quality. His novel has the office situation, Mary's drive out (though it's short and eventless), her soulful chat with Norman, his problems with Mrs Bates, the shockingly premature death, Sam, Lila and Arbogast teaming up, Arbogast's untimely end, the climax in the house, the explanatory psychiatrist and Mother taking over Norman. Rarely has Hitchcock taken so much from a literary original. While respecting Bloch's craftsmanship and his modern, sensible, observations, I was surprised to find myself completely unmoved by his, merely *adequate*, characterisation. For me, the story remained words well ordered on a page. Generally, 'artistic *quality*', and its power to involve the imagination, owes little to 'structure' or 'concept' or 'correct ideas', and much more to a 'texture' of fine, richly suggestive, detail, which takes the mind by surprise, and yet has resonance.

Bloch's Norman is fat and fortyish, a soft, bookish creature, of timorous habits. Aware of Freudian theory, he understands that the Oedipus complex is his problem, but when he tries to explain that to his mother, she won't listen to such filth. When we first meet his normal, everyday self, he's quietly reading a book on anthropology. Its account of an Aztec victory dance, with drums made out of the stretched skins of the slaughtered enemy, gives him a comfortable shiver, and he imagines the details ever more vividly, until the drumming sound becomes rain pattering on the window and then the footsteps of his approaching mother. During their long conversation her non-existence is concealed from the reader by his never quite daring to look at her directly. Technically, the 'sound fade' is neat enough: we go from an *imagined* sound, through a *realistic* one, to an apparently real one. (The first two terms, suggesting a 'return to reality', help fool the reader.)

Bloch's general style derives from the Hemingway–Cain–O'Hara school: plain, fast prose mixes terse statements, which imply rather than declare their dramatic implications, and a sort of 'hard-edge impressionism' (like the 'sound fades'). It usually adopts some character's perspective, while staying in the third person. Within this broad 'POV system', the terse description and the long passages of direct dialogue read exactly as they would in non-viewpoint writing: in effect, the two modes (POV, objectivity) are fused, with deft informality. The structure is often neat. Chapter 1 consists of Norman's thoughts, as his reading is interrupted by his mother. It ends as he hears the buzzer from the motel desk. Chapter 2 consists of Marion's thoughts (including the office back-story) as she's driving towards him, and it ends as she rings the buzzer. Thus a crucial event occurs twice, each time from a different POV; and character viewpoint overrides chronology. It's thoughtful carpentry, not just textbook formulae.

The novel's genre ascription is debatable. Is it horror, crime, mystery, thriller, contemporary Gothic, or all of the above? Not that it matters much; most genres interbreed freely while also evolving the specialised forms which tempt certain theories to confuse genres with formulae. Although sensational, the novel is *not* 'pulp' culture. Its highly respectable publishers were Simon and Schuster, and it appeared in their hardback crime series. It did push that genre's then bounds of good taste, and divided the critics, but the Poe connection was recognised, and some literary critics thought it frighteningly good stuff. Its references to Freud and anthropology indicate a lower-middlebrow, not a lowbrow, cultural level. Its sales were satisfactory, though not outstanding; the film has kept it in print, and brought Bloch other work, though, unfortunately for him, he had no percentage of the film's profits.

PRODUCTION HISTORY

The production history of *Psycho*, with its artists' 'intentionality', is richly detailed in the books by Rebello and Janet Leigh. Alerted to the novel by a favourable review, Hitchcock immediately acquired the rights, for $9,000 flat. Paramount, with which Hitchcock's company, Shamley Productions, was contracted, disliked the subject, as small, sordid and nasty. After mutually exasperating negotiations, Paramount jumped at Hitchcock's offer to finance the film himself, with Paramount distributing and taking 40 per cent of gross receipts.

Quite as dismayed as Paramount's executives were some long-standing friends of Hitchcock's, notably Joan Harrison, currently Shamley's head of production, after starting as Hitchcock's secretary in 1930s England, and producing two admirable film noirs, *Phantom Lady* (1944) and *Ride the Pink Horse* (1947). However, the subject found a powerful advocate in Alma Reville, Hitchcock's wife, who had been his boss at Gaumont–British, and whose professional judgments, on subjects, scripts, casting and rushes he always took very seriously. It's said she supplied the 'woman's angle', the finer points of which his pessimism and sense of humour, left to themselves, occasionally roughed up – though by and large he thoroughly understood Hollywood's 'woman's film' theories. *Rebecca* (1940), *Spellbound* (1945), *Notorious* (1946), *To Catch a Thief* (1955), *The Man Who Knew Too Much* (1956), and *Psycho*, apply them painstakingly, in that respect.

Another supporter was Lew Wassermann, head of MCA, the powerful talent agency. It was he who first proposed the Hitchcock TV series, *Alfred Hitchcock Presents* (later, *The Alfred Hitchcock Hour*). Perkins, Leigh, Gavin and Stefano were all clients of MCA. (Miles was contracted to Hitchcock himself, though relations had turned quite sour, between two strong-minded people.) Paramount studio space being, apparently, fully occupied, *Psycho* was shot at Universal, then at a low ebb. MCA had just bought it, but had yet to turn its fortunes around.

A first script was commissioned from James Cavanagh, who imported some elements from his 1957 Hitchcock TV play, *One More Mile to Go*. (It had a corpse placed in a car boot, and dumped in a lake, and an inquisitive highway patrolman.) Hitchcock was still dissatisfied so MCA recommended Stefano, who until then had had little movie experience, although he had written Paramount's *Black Orchid* (1958), starring Sophia Loren. Hitchcock was initially reluctant, as Stefano's TV credits hinted he might just be a liberal message-monger. Conversely, Stefano was completely bored by the novel's characters, but, when Hitchcock said he wanted a livelier Norman, maybe played by Anthony Perkins, Stefano became interested.

Though *Psycho* was likely to find a large audience among libidinal teenagers, its wider prospects were uncertain, and Hitch resolved to keep costs within what the smaller market would bear. He planned a 36-day shoot (about half the average 'A' feature length), eventually stretched to 42, and used one of his TV crews who were used to working more swiftly and cheaply than movie technicians. However, 'old Hitchcock hands' were given key positions (notably photography, editing and design). Where necessary, Hitchcock spent lavishly, allowing seven days for the shower scene. In the event, some elaborate shots had the TV crew in trouble – and some *very* elaborate shots would have had *any* crew in trouble. Lighting-wise, much of *Psycho* is rough and ready, by Hitchcock's usual movie standards, especially in its earlier, high-key (light-toned) scenes. Saul Bass's credits came expensive, and Hitch finally agreed Herrmann's $17,500 fee.

Although the censors had expressed their uneasiness about the script, they passed a final print, despite, it seems, considerable confusion: apparently the censors demanded cuts, but when Hitchcock resubmitted the film without them, it was accepted all the same.

Contrary to his usual way with actors, Hitch talked long and intensely with Janet Leigh, who was more familiar with light romantic roles, and had to carry the first 45 minutes of the film, during most of which her action is 'internal' and non-demonstrative. Unusually too, he acted out for her the shower scene, to demonstrate her every move; he likewise 'pre-enacted' all Perkins' moves with the dead body. As for Marion's nudity in the shower scene, all conceivable rumours abound, about body doubles and so on. Janet Leigh insists that the figure in the shower is mostly herself, with strategically placed moleskin. An artificial torso was used in the occasional shot.

Ironically, Mrs Bates is *never* Perkins. She's a variety of doubles, including a female 'Lilliputian' (jumping onto Arbogast). Her voice is three different people's; one was provided by a man, another by Jeanette Nolan (who played Lady Macbeth in Orson Welles' film of 1948). In her final scene, her voice is a 'collage' of different voices, even within the same sentence.

Since 1954–5 Hollywood had all but abandoned the old 'Academy' screen shape for 'wide-screen' (as distinct from CinemaScope and the other special systems). There's a little mystery, however. Academic colleagues assure me that in some prints of the film, one shower scene shot exposes Marion's breasts; this might explain why, in some British release prints, this area was covered by a black band, almost as if the screen had changed shape.

As usual with wide-screen, *Psycho* uses mostly a 28mm lens, or thereabouts. The walls around the shower were 'wild walls' (or could never have been filmed: cameras must be *away* from what they film). The track-in to a dead face staring into camera may look straightforward, but focus-pulling at this micro-distance was then a finicky process, and it seems this shot took 22 (or 26) takes. Although the camera seems to make one continuous movement from the bathroom into the cabin and to show a landscape beyond, the bathroom and the cabin were separate studio sets, and the landscape was out on the studio lot. So two camera movements were designed to edit into one, while the landscape is a back-projection within the second set. (A useful reminder that the shot taken by the camera and the shot seen on the screen may be very different things; and that most screen shots have been 'topped and tailed' from a very much longer take.) All the shots of Marion 'on the road' are process shots, using back-projection in the studio; Hitchcock was proud to have devised a contraption fitted with lights to give him finger-tip control of the headlights of the other cars.

PUBLICITY AND PRESENTATION

Normally, publicity and presentation were delegated to distribution departments, after discussion with the producers. In this case, Hitchcock wished to devise and control the whole campaign, and Paramount was doubtless relieved to let him take over.

Those who saw the first rough cuts recognised an exceptional film, but feared hostility generated by quality press objections to 'bad taste', campaigns by moral pressure groups and bad 'word of mouth' via the better-class audiences in first-run halls. Proposals were made for a 'saturation release', the strategy devised for an earlier 'bad taste' film, the Selznick–Vidor *Duel in the Sun* (1946). Instead of the usual release pattern – press shows geared to first runs, with staggered release to ever less important cinemas – press shows would be replaced by heavier, cruder advertising, and the film given near-simultaneous release to a wide range of cinemas, to reach the mass of moviegoers with bad or no taste before middle-class put-downs could discourage them from going to see it. This strategy was double-edged, however. Quite apart from requiring more prints than phased release, it cut out the 'grapevine' – the word-of-mouth recommendations from enthusiastic spectators to their friends, which, once they get going, which takes a few days, can have 'landslide' effects, such as no publicity campaign can match. *Psycho* looked to be a 'grapevine' film, and needed the usual, slower release.

The press advertisements were designed to attract the 'youth' audience, but not so grossly that staider spectators would be repelled. They did show Marion in her underwear – a far cry from the dignity of Ingrid Bergman or Grace Kelly – but the names of the stars were reassuring. The cinema previews (what British English calls 'trailers') pursued a different line, for more 'mainstream' audiences. Very unusually, they showed almost no scenes from the film, but 'starred' Hitchcock, a household presence thanks to his TV series; he addressed the audience in his whimsical-macabre mode, but with more weight and edge. One preview was a 'conducted tour' of the Bates abode, in which unspecified, but evidently special, events were going to occur. This sense of 'the house' was astute; the *Psycho* house remains a highlight of the Universal studio tour.

Psycho presented another problem: its heavy dependence on a final twist, which word of mouth, left to itself, might well have revealed. This pushed Hitchcock to his greatest risk. Not only did publicity urge spectators not to tell their friends the ending; but exhibitors were pressured to admit no spectators once the film had started. This went right against the 50-year-old practice of 'continuous performance', to which the whole industry was geared. Working hours being what they were, spectators could, and very frequently did, drop in whenever convenient, maybe halfway through the film they wanted to see, watch its last half first, then stay through the 'B' flick and other matter, watch their chosen film round to the point where they came in, and then depart. This did indeed play havoc with films' narrative and aesthetic structures, but so many spectators found the practice satisfactory that most exhibitors clung to it. By 1960, however, patterns of leisure were changing, and Hitchcock could turn the problem into an advertising attraction. Already, in France, Clouzot had taken that tack, successfully, with *Les Diaboliques*, which would help explain why Paramount went along with Hitchcock's policy.

Apart from losing the 'drop-in' trade, which traditionally was substantial, exhibitors and moviegoers were not accustomed to being told to turn up on time, or get locked out. Hitchcock's advertisements were admirably tactful. 'Please don't tell the ending; it's the only one we have.' And: 'We won't allow you to cheat yourself ...'

All in all, *Psycho* was quite a risky prospect. Just how risky is shown by the case of *Peeping Tom*, released in Britain a few months earlier, by Hitchcock's old colleague and friend, Michael Powell. Both films have a serial sex-killer, sensitively portrayed, who murders women nastily, amidst mirrors; and they must have been in preparation simultaneously (a case of 'Great Minds Meet'?). Powell was well regarded in the trade, and the production company doubled its normal budget for what they hoped would be a prestigious film. In the event, it provoked such hostility, from middle-class highbrow reviewers, that the distributors rapidly withdrew it.[3]

FIRST FORTUNES

Hitchcock didn't show *Psycho* to the press. The critics immediately paid to see it, as he must have anticipated, but at least they would see it along with a normal audience, whose responses might influence theirs away from their ideas about 'good taste'. However, he could only hope that this influence would overcome critics' resentment at exclusion. In the event, most critical notices were hostile including those in the *New York Times* and *Esquire*. The Roman Catholic Church decreed it 'Objectionable in part for all.' *Variety*'s assessment was: 'Shock meller, with a couple of particularly lurid scenes. Unelaborate production. Well done, doubtless will succeed.' Hitchcock, said its reviewer, was 'up to his clavicle in whimsicality', and implied, more quietly, that he was indulging his libido. In the emphasis on whimsy, readers-between-lines may perceive a concern to deflect moralistic ire. Summarises Rebello: 'No amount of explanation could have prepared anyone ... for the firestorm the film was creating ... [or] have predicted how powerfully *Psycho* tapped into the American subconscious. Faintings. Walk-outs. Repeat visits. Boycotts. Angry phone-calls and letters. Talk of banning the film rang from church pulpits and psychiatrists' offices ...' By 1990, *Psycho* was the second most profitable American film ever made, maybe 'second only to *The Birth of a Nation*'.

PSYCHO THE FIRST TIME

'*Psycho came out just before my 14th birthday. Everybody wanted to see the movie, and there was a real sense of, er, anticipation, and we were all going to see something very special.*'

'*This wasn't a movie that you went to with your parents. There was always a big debate – would you be allowed to go see* Psycho? *You'd have to sneak out of the house ...*'

'*In America there was a big teaser campaign about* Psycho, *and the teaser campaign had to do with the ending, and it was, 'Don't tell the ending, whatever you do, don't tell the ending.*'

'*It was the first film where you could not just walk into the theatre ... which was very novel, because moviegoing was a very casual experience in those days ...*'

'*I'd seen other Hitchcock movies, I was expecting a, a good scare, and some really good film-making ...*'

'*I do remember turning to my wife and saying, "It's okay, but there's not very much happening", and then the shower murder came and the rest of the movie to me was pandemonium ...*'

'*The screaming of the audience, and the shrieking of the music, sort of combined itself into this howl, that just kind of rose up and bounced off the walls ...*'

'*I was a bathtub person from that film forward.*'

'*... we were really in shock from that, I mean, there was absolute silence in the rest of the film, people were in total mourning for the loss ...*'

'*I think Hitchcock broke probably every rule that the Hollywood film industry had been going along with.*'

'But the most chilling was at the end, with no murder, with just Perkins in the blanket ... and ... that's what stuck with us as we were filing out, and that's why we were so silent.'

Moviegoers' testimony in Psycho – The First Time

A Long Hard Look at 'Psycho'

THE CREDIT SEQUENCE

The Paramount logo fades to a black screen, which turns light grey as music starts: chunky staccato chords under keening violins. From the right-hand edge, black stripes stretch across the screen; more appear, at unpredictable heights, till they block the screen like a window-blind. Against the last bands, streaking across at middle height, white angular flecks appear, like enigmatic signs, and turn out to be the tips and tails of letters, slashed laterally and vertically disaligned. The 'window-blind' breaks up as more black bands thrust in, pushing the last grey strips off left. The bits of letters click together, to read, bold white on the all-black field: 'Alfred Hitchcock's'. Uncompleted syntax holds the screen for a full two seconds, until the letters' middle stratum skids left, pursued by more grey bands, which amass in a tight, though still staggered, formation. They rebuild the 'window-blind' striation, but this time from grey on black (reversing the earlier construction process). New shards of letters slide in, but before any words can crystallise, the blank grey bands scud back the way they came (surprise reversal of directional thrust). On the now black background, the scattering of broken letters slide and snap together, spelling 'Psycho', for about two seconds, until that word, too, cracks into three strata. They slip a little notch sideways, but in opposite directions, so that each letter, vertically misaligned, seems to jerk and tug against itself. The word disintegrates – not, as the generally lateral kinetic has led us to expect, laterally – but, instead, the letters' top halves fly up and away and off the screen, while their lower halves plunge off the bottom of the frame. Since each half of a letter implies the other half, and it all happens so fast, it's as if our word-world suddenly doubles and splits and speeds in opposite directions, like a 'troubled reflection'.

This vertical split begins a second, mainly vertical, phase. From mid-screen level, like a virtual horizon, columns stretch upwards and downwards unevenly, and simultaneously, like a restless graph. Various lines split into groups and rove in block formations.

The last phase, or 'movement' (to borrow a musical term), is more leisurely; it leaves time and space for areas bearing credits. Whether single names, or blocks of *names, they zip in, abruptly stop, abruptly scud off. The conjunction of names, which we try to read along the line, with shiftings in non-linear space, which patterns and pictures use, disconcerts our perceptual scanning processes. On the final credit, to Hitchcock as director, the music quietens, while the grey upright columns retract, upwards and downwards, into a suggested 'horizon', and continue moving slowly, quietly, as if stealthily. They gradually disappear, through a cross-fade, into a photographic landscape: a city skyline, sun-bleached and torpid, with desert mountains beyond.*

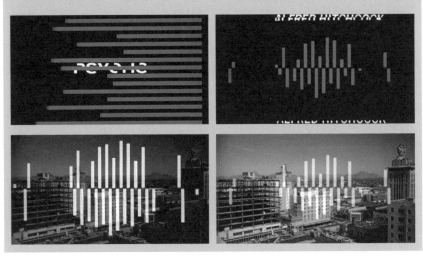

MOTION PAINTING IN GREYS

The credit sequence was designed, and hand-made, by Saul Bass, using animation, pixilation and live-action photography. The stripes were rods painted the 'colour' required, and pushed across by hand; however, they're so featureless, so flat-on, that they register as 'pure pattern', as non-representational forms, as abstractions. The music, too, is abstract. This little film-within-a-film deploys the idioms of avant-garde abstraction, and extends the tradition of Eggeling, Ruttmann, Lye, MacLaren. It also qualifies as 'concrete' art, since its moving kinetics, violently disturbing the mechanisms of human perception, emphasise the *actual physical presence* of the graphic patterns.

The bands and columns imply some cold, geometrical order; its thrusts, shifts and vectors are unpredictable. Brutally rapid changes disorganise us. The images, without the music, would be *softly* unstable, slithery; but the pistoning music gives them its impact. The 'lettrist' scraps and flecks add another, wayward chaos, like the fitfully fluttering 'angel' in Borowczyk's *Les Jeux des anges* (1964). Both films are exercises in 'structuralist' grid-forms as madness. Here, everything resembles hypnagogia (the 'break-up' of gestalts and forms, well-known in the states between sleeping and waking). Its driving energy, its streams of cognitive dissonance, don't just *metaphor*, they *inflict* perceptual disintegration. Some unseen activity keeps imposing rigid pattern and then disintegrating them, like obsession and hysteria. By 1960 the structures and modes of schizophrenia were being re-explored by, among many others, 'existential' psychiatrist R. D. Laing, whose *The Divided Self* (1960) was poised to become a radical cult. Herrmann's music uses stringed instruments only, but its counterpoint of chugging chords and skeetering violins evokes Stravinsky's *The Rites of Spring* (1913), whose modernist neo-primitivism asserts the stunted compulsions of the mad animal, man. Narrative-wise, the credits of *Psycho* are entirely meaningless; yet, like an 'abstract overture', in visual kinetic, they presage its theme – disintegrating thought. (Do the striations suggest a window-blind, therefore voyeurism? Do the flecks evoke bird claws? Or a flock of birds? Whose screaming is the violins?) As the columns subside, and fade into the city, the suggestion is not that they've stopped operating, but that their sinister energy continues, quietly, invisibly, 'behind appearances'.

◆

SCENE 1 PHOENIX, ARIZONA: EXTERIOR

The camera moves slowly around a white-ish cityscape. Mid-screen subtitles scud abruptly in, from alternate screen edges, then whizz off, brief reminders of the credits' spirit of panic: 'Phoenix, Arizona/ Friday December 12/ 2:43 p.m.' The camera drifts forward, slides around an imposing building, and finds a shabby part of town. It dives towards a high rear window, sneaks in under the blind, and discovers Marion (Janet Leigh), in her underwear, flat on a bed, a man in dark trousers standing beside her.

FROM GOD'S EYE VIEW TO CROTCH-HIGH VIEW

White was an occasional convention for oppressive heat. The overall 'scene', though continuous, comprises four different 'zones': a high-angle cityscape, a zoom-in to and through a window, the abruptly dark room (relative to the sunlight) and the room lit normally, as befitting gradually adjusted vision. The camera starts high in the sky, and ends down by a man's groin. The script treats all this as one continuous scene, and Hitchcock originally intended one long shot from a helicopter, from where a zoom would look in through a window, and then, being seemingly inside the room, become an interior, shot from the exterior! Since 1949, the 'ten-minute takes' of *Rope* held the record for the movie shot with the longest running time. Now *Psycho* would bid for the longest continuous distance travelled by the camera. Its along-the-way ingenuities would renew the admiration of Hitchcock's Hollywood peers and help offset his stooping to a low-budget production, whose sex and violence many 'Old Hollywood' people would abhor. That apart, Hitchcock, like many Hollywood craftsmen, loved solving technical difficulties, as a personal private challenge, as craft for craft's sake, art for art's sake.

In 1960, the new zoom lenses were just about up to all this, but other problems were probably insurmountable. Would any American city allow a helicopter so close beside a building? And wouldn't its hovering flight adjustments make the extended zoom jerk unwatchably? As things are, the succession of separate shots is of interest: they make up one, virtually continuous trajectory in space, and, in that sense, they're 'all one scene'; yet they're also several separate scenes: an exterior, and an interior; a landscape very long shot and, miles from there, a close shot low in a narrow room.

FROM WYSIWYG TO WYSILLTYG

Movie technicians, watching with gimlet eyes for craft practicalities, would much admire Hitchcock's cunning paraphrase of his Plan A. What looks, to the layman, like a 'flight across the city' is three separate shots, from three different fixed points, each combining a pan and zoom, and so suggesting 'onward travel'. The separate shots are fused by cross-fades (from which we're slightly distracted by both the sudden titles and briefly conspicuous buildings). The last zoom over the city ends in a downwards and sideways shift (a sort of side-slip) towards a wall of rear windows; in mid-dive a cross-fade introduces a steeper shot, and then a last cross-fade introduces a near-horizontal track-in, from closer in, and from the *other* side of the window. This last cross-fade is so quick it's virtually a cut, and the changed angle makes a little visual 'jolt' – what some editors call a 'hard cut' and what Eisenstein called a 'montage collision'. This particular cut *enlivens* but doesn't *disrupt* the sense of a long, long camera movement. It's just – an early tremor …

The film forms revealed by a 'close reading' don't invalidate the 'layman's impression'; they're intended to suggest it. Non-technical spectators normally 'overlook' the *exact* forms of films, and with good reason. They're looking for other things: the story, its 'human interest', its moods, its 'atmosphere' (a hot, white, dry city), its 'poetic'. The text itself is one thing; its intended reading isn't 'literal' in the least. Form is the spectator's springboard to an *idea*: but the idea is only *part* of the meaning; the *full* meaning is the overall movement of his mind: it's A to B, not just B. Meaning exists, not in the text, but in the mind of the spectator. In that sense, it's 'only subjective', but insofar as it's *shared* between spectators, and therefore *consensual*, it's an objective social fact. By and large, a film is like an iceberg: What You See Is a Lot Less Than You Get. ('Get' in the American sense – 'to intuitively understand' – 'D'you get it?', in English, 'D'you see?')

THE HIGH WINDOW

Probing camera + hard-to-reach window + blind may well imply voyeurism – but this flying, diving camera is no ordinary peeping Tom: it's hardly human – more like a bird's-eye view, or a God's-eye view. After those 'shifting abstract forms', the camera's destination suggests a secret event astir, that we earthbound creatures can't see, but that somebody up there can.

THE SYSTEM'S EYE VERSUS THE NAKED CITY

Surveillance/omniscience, of a shabby, chaotic city, was a 'social realist' focus. It loomed large in the post-war cycle of 'documentary thrillers', like *The Naked City* and *Call Northside 777* (both 1948) and persisted through TV 'police procedurals' like *Dragnet* (filmed 1954). Often, it balanced 'liberal social authority/responsibility' against the unruliness of real life and criminal subversion of society. These time-place subtitles suggest a great precision – yet, their skidding on and off unsettles us.

LOOK IN ANY WINDOW

A different attitude entirely inspires the interest in city windows in another 'social realist' genre: movies about the 'little lives' of 'ordinary people' (as against glamour and escapism, Hollywood's stock-in-trade). Cameras rove around windows in a 'populist' cycle *c* 1930 (*The Crowd, Street Scene, Sous Les toits de Paris, 42nd Street*). In 1954, *Rear Window* harks back to it, as a crippled photographer inspects another 'cross-section'; about this time, the 'populist' genre makes a little comeback, with, notably, *Marty* (1955) and *The Wrong Man* (1957).

For *Psycho*, Hitchcock sought a 'documentary' quality (in a very loose sense of the word: critics then spoke of 'semi-documentary', meaning, 'social realistic fiction with much location work and documentary trimmings'). This film's first third is steeped in 'everyday realism', in the grey details of ordinary life – unsatisfying love-making, mean-minded point-scoring in a dreary office … Its protagonists are all 'ordinary people', 'little people' – a secretary, a hick-town storekeeper, a passive youth in a moribund motel. They're all losers, locked in sad lives. To be sure, the stars imbue them with beauty, charisma, energy and style, which from one angle is escapism. But if other things are right, these qualities may claim 'poetic licence', as metaphors for qualities, or potentialities, or 'soul', which 'ordinary people' often feel they have but can't live out except in their imaginations (or at the pictures). Much of *Psycho* pursues Hitchcock's on-and-off interest in 'ordinary people', in 'little people' – in people *like* the cinema audience of those days – as in *Blackmail/A Woman Alone* (1930), *Shadow of a Doubt* (1943), *The Wrong Man* and the first third of *Rear Window*.

Without claiming *Psycho* for neo-realism, is Marion's plight-and-flight so very different from some Rossellini movies with Ingrid Bergman on a spiritual journey? Or Chabrol's 'poetico-realistic' *Les Bonnes femmes* (1960)?

SCENE 1 (CONTINUED) PHOENIX HOTEL BEDROOM

Marion Crane (Janet Leigh), in her white underwear, lies on a hotel bed, smiling up at Sam Loomis (John Gavin), who mops his bare chest with a handy towel. Pleased with himself, he remarks that she forgot her lunch (quick cut to a sandwich). They fall to kissing (again?), her body sloped forward as urgently as his. Yet, even as they caress, she talks about leaving: it's time overdue she returned to her office and dyspeptic boss. Sam complains he'll be at a loose end until it's time to catch his plane. He runs a hardware store in Fairvale, a rural town in northern California; he's burdened by his dead father's debts, and alimony to his ex-wife. He can only afford a cheap hotel, and trips that are tax-deductible. He fears that a decently comfortable marriage is out of the question for at least two years. Marion offers to share his poverty, in marriage; but he seems to prevaricate, and she all but breaks off the affair.

SEXUAL TYPES OF AMBIGUITY

What are they up to, half-undressed on that bed?

In 1959 Hays Office morality still dominated movies, despite social trends epito-mised by, notably, the Kinsey reports on sexual behaviour (in the human male, 1948, in the human female, 1953), Broadway hits like *The Moon Is Blue* (1951, filmed in 1954) and bestsellers like *Peyton Place* (1956, filmed in 1959). By and large, Hollywood preferred a certain reticence, partly to dodge the 'X' certificate, but also because it allowed considerable ambiguity: Old Morality and New Morality specta-tors could read the love-scenes as they liked. A kiss, especially if followed by a fade-out (like three dots in a novelette?), might or might not be more than just a kiss. The Hays rule was that, given two lovers embracing on or about a bed, each must keep one foot on the floor. Hitchcock breaks it right away, with Marion's upper body flat out on the bed as if she'd just been pressed right down into it. But then again, in this particular shot, Sam isn't actually touching her. And with the camera winding round rolling faces in close-up, who can say which of all four feet is where? A few years earlier, the censor would have cut all this, as overly suggestive; but little by little, he'd been making concessions, and was now unsure where to draw the line.

A LIKELY RANGE OF MORAL POSITIONS

Back in the 1950s, many spectators, habituated to Hollywood's *overt* morality, at least on the screen, could suppose that Marion and Sam have booked a lunch-hour bed-room just to be alone together, since being seen together might start unseemly gossip. (Dialogue confirms they're reluctant to be seen together, without saying exactly why. However appropriate in small towns, as per *Bus Stop* [1956] and *Picnic* [1955], it's less appropriate in even a relatively small city, as Phoenix had been until fairly recently. But the general idea was familiar; it inspires the very title of *Strangers When We Meet* [1960], a 'modern American' variant of the *Brief Encounter* 'genre'.) For spectators for whom Sam and Marion not sleeping together is a natural, and moral, assumption, perhaps they just want some privacy while passionately kissing, and if they're half stripped-off, it's only to keep cool, in this hot, close, un-air-conditioned room. Other spectators again, young teenagers perhaps, could reasonably assume, from the evident 'flesh contact', that they're indulging in 'heavy petting', a common compromise between vice and virtue, especially among the young. Very worldly, very adult minds might presume that Marion and Sam have just 'made love', and are in a mood to start all over again. Sam towels his manly chest, which might suggest he's been exerting himself.

From one angle these readings are separate and distinct – and importantly so, morality-wise. Nonetheless, they all point to the same idea: 'morally controversial sensual pleasure' (and the setting suggests heavy self-indulgence). As important as the distinctions were between 'heavy petting' and 'going all the way', the line between was famously thin, and by 1959 more teenagers than ever were crossing it (and trusting to birth control, or luck, or whatever – the pill was not available until 1963). As morally fraught as all this is, Marion 'going all the way' would not have transformed her from 'good girl' into 'bad girl', or from 'virgin' into 'vamp', or from 'Madonna' into 'whore' (the last quite foreign to the Bible Belt). The enormous success, in 1957–8, of Bardot in *And God Created Woman*, arose from its paraphrasing 'advanced' teenage behaviour (which Hollywood left at 'beach party' banalities). Consider that supposedly 'rebellious' movie, *Rebel without a Cause*, (1955). When James Dean and Natalie Wood spend a night together, in a romantically empty house, they're not even *tempted* to misbehave; instead, they practise 'mutual respect' (and what's wrong with that?), and they behave like parents to Plato. Instead of the sex act, adult and neighbourly responsibility. When 1950s sex-dramas indicate a copulation, it remains rather abstract, more like a plot-point (focused on conse-quence) than an act of pleasure sensually described. But here, Hitchcock's camera, hugging the lovers close, brings the touch of flesh alive. (Realism-wise, one might criticise the lack of sweat-drops, but that might well have upset 1950s hygienism and, anyway, Sam's towel makes the point.)

In *Psycho – The First Time*, a woman recalls that Marion's bra and half-slip were as big a shock to her as the shower scene. Until then, all female stars wore full slips over their bra (as specified in the script). Hitchcock, talking with Truffaut, wished he could have showed Janet Leigh's bare breasts rubbing against John Gavin's bare chest (tac-tility again). His wish chimes in with Jean Douchet's waggish remark that, by showing Gavin but not Leigh stripped to the waist, *Psycho* left half its audience unsatisfied. What's disquieting is that, as Marion's lips nibble Sam's, she murmurs words of dissatisfaction, of edgy negotiation, of despair. (This links with *Notorious*, where the lovers never stop necking, while also scheming.)

Marion and Sam being both half-undressed rather favours the idea that they're only heavy petting, and that Marion is still a *demi-vierge* (everything but penetration). Heavy petting worried some socio-sexologists, who feared that protracted self-control might eventually induce a sort of orgiastic impotence and that 'halfway house' orgasms could weaken the impact of the first full sex act, which was very important for bonding. Often, too, heavy petting (widely supposed to be an American speciality) stopped short of climax or release. Thus each lover teased the other and himself or herself. The irony would have appealed to Baudelaire, and probably to Hitchcock, perhaps as a Catholic moralist ('sin and human nature punishes itself; sexual desire is sexual misery'). In pop Freudianism, all this sexual teasing and frustration would help explain Marion's compulsive drive to get to Sam. Has she yet to *consummate* her sexuality – to know a man, in the biblical sense?

The film is a bit of a tease about her past. Sam, admiring her dry *savoir-faire*, says, 'You sure talk like a girl who's been married' – so perhaps she has been. Four pages later, she counters his alimony complaints by remarking she's not been married once. Though cut from the film, a script innuendo hints at some other, disabusing, sexual experience: 'I've lost my girlish laughter.' Sam, gallantly: 'The only girlish thing you have lost.' ('She lost her girlish laughter' was an ironic idiom, from the 1920s I believe, though I haven't found its origin.)

All this talk about morality and sensuality risks making the scene just salacious (and this aspect did have to be *judged*). In fact, the loving has an urgent tenderness. Visually, it's dominated not by *anatomies*, but by hands, his as much as hers, feeling with tender, restless speed the other's shoulders, neck, face and mouth, while eyes lock on eyes. Hands, eyes, embracings are all questing for the mind within the other, not focusing on their own sensations. An unsympathetic spectator might suppose that s/he's being made a voyeur, but if you're half-identifying with either of the lovers, and half-sympathetic towards the other, the scene is about tactility, about palpability not just as 'sexual stimulus' (though a streak of that is there), but as communication. It's the *other, fonder* half of their negotiating talk. It's the half that expresses 'togetherness' and 'the Oceanic feeling', as Freud called it.

After the lovers pull apart, vigorous movements sustain the scene's nervous energy – Sam fondling the bed-linen Marion has vacated, spreading both arms wide in his gesture of full surrender; snapping open the window-blind; Marion shooting her arms around his neck (like a lariat?).

STAR VERSUS CHARACTER

Lana Turner was considered for the role of Marion, but Leigh thought Hitch preferred a softer personality. Doris Day, a theoretical possibility, was too big a star for this half-part and, in her case, early death in the shower might well have been too much; it might have not just shocked people, but turned them against the film.

Janet Leigh's usual screen persona was lively, clean-living, with a decisive streak and a lively watchfulness in reserve. Even in her medieval romps, she struck me as a fine identification figure for young women, especially of the 'office secretary class' – a conspicuous subculture, before its decimation by social change. Marion, in the script, is to some extent a 'blank' for spectator identification to fill in (in art, usually a defect; in entertainment, often a desideratum).[4] Leigh finesses her into life, with pencil-sharp emphases. Here, at calendar age 32, she embodies that especially American combination of an ever-youthful prime but with stonier, more scared thoughts creeping in, fixing the eyes, and at serious moments lengthening the heart-shaped face around thinned-out mouth. She's briskly efficient, fully trusted. Her 'commercial' culture, clear-headed, practical and often supposed, by highbrows, to be 'blandly superficial' was as prone to complicated passions as more educated subcultures.

John Gavin, star of many a plush romance, was a male star for women – a handsome hunk (hence the bare chest here), smoothly well-mannered ('beautiful manners', even in a heel, were a major pleasure for female spectators) and redolent of wealth and 'class' (he later became US ambassador to Mexico). In *Imitation of Life* (Douglas Sirk, 1959) he partnered Lana Turner and Susan Kohner, as women who love 'not wisely but too well', and in *Midnight Lace* (1960) he unnerves the unsinkable Doris Day. Hitchcock found him disappointingly wooden. Perhaps his natural style suited those glossier, slower 'women's films', which dwelled in leisurely fashion on reaction shots, thus reversing the 1930s cult of fast pace, to which lovers of film art were still very attached.

Sam in the film and Sam in the script are quite different characters (though, narrative-wise, they're functional equivalents: they'd work equally well). The script describes a stolid, cheery, smiling chap, trying to half-dream, half-laugh his problems away, without quite facing them. Nonetheless Lila finds him reassuringly relaxed and solid. John Gavin as Sam is more brooding, passive, enigmatic. Hitch, it's said, thought his love-making too listless and asked Miss Leigh to 'take him in hand'.

CONVERSATION AS NEGOTIATION

Their conversation, which is admirably written, has six main 'move-and-counter-moves'.

1. Even while sensually enlaced and kissing, Marion expresses her discontent.
2. Getting dressed, she states her terms: from now on they meet in her home (since he can't afford good restaurants? to re-domesticate him?), with her sister there (as chaperone?); together they'll broil a steak (good, simple meals for busy people). He promptly surprises her, and us, by agreeing to everything, almost with relief, and confessing he needs her on any terms at all.
3. She's warm and tender, virtually proposing to him, and yet, he turns away.
4. She promises to share his life, and if most of his money must go to his ex-wife, so be it: 'I'll lick the stamps.' Perversely ignoring what she's just said, he asks, with almost contented jealousy, if she's looking for someone else.
5. Dryly she warns: 'I'm thinking of it.' When he makes no response, she prepares to walk out.
6. He asks to accompany her; she points out he's still barefoot. (He's like a child, shirking responsibility, yet clinging to her; she's like the disapproving mother, but, since she *noticed* his shoes, she's his mother still.)

Interest in child, parent or adult personality types was in the air. It's all but spelled out in *Blind Date/Chance Meeting* (Joseph Losey, 1959), and was already inspiring Transactional Analysis, whose long-running bestseller would be *Games People Play* (Eric Berne, 1964).

THE DRAMATIC LINES

Though seeming to wallow in sensuality, Marion's restless desire is for respectability. Is she using sex as 'the tender trap' (as in *The Tender Trap* [1955])? The script says she is: 'girls are so often surprised when they discover men will continue to want them even after the sexual bait has been pulled in.' Were it *only* a bait, perhaps she'd be a 'semi-vamp', but she seems to genuinely like him, although he's strapped for cash and prospects and she's very likely caught in the sensuality trap with him. 'I'll lick the stamps' – a brilliant line – speaks volumes: she accepts their humiliation, by The Other Woman, the woman who got Sam first and financially crippled him. In Freudian terms, she's The Mother, as triumphant rival (like the eponymous *femme fatale* of *Rebecca*. Many films about imposing, sinister ladies in portraits, who once 'owned' the hero, are 'women's films', and metaphor tensions between women and their mother figures rather than between vamps and men).[5] Marion's 'baiting the hook' is normal premarital play. Her fast switches between manipulation and devotion, sensual sex and renunciation, and her restless movements, like her sudden jack-knife rise from the bed, generate a heavy instability.

Sam's ideas about marriage are one big mess. They're like odds and ends from psychology articles in popular magazines (like the masseuse's 'peeping Tom' theory in *Rear Window*). When Marion regrets these shabby brief encounters, his cheap-shot reply is that bored married couples get kicks from things like this. He switches between rat-pack terms like 'swinger' and ingratiating spiel about working really hard at a mature relationship. Is hunky Sam an overgrown teenager? A small-town low flyer? A local Casanova, ducking and diving if marriage rears its head? Or a bit of a bird-brain, pecking at scraps pulled from shallow reading? Or an obstinately passive stick-in-the-mud? Or depressed by his father's death, and scared off marriage by divorce, badly in need of firm and friendly female guidance? We can't be sure, and that's the interest. But the scene's last shot drops a pretty broad hint: abandoned by Marion, Sam just stands there, head drooped in utter dejection, in a near-Expressionist posture. Confused love hurts all concerned.

No wonder that his sudden surrender provokes in her, not only a 'romantic' response, but also something between dubiety, suspicion and ironic dryness.

HITCHCOCK'S UNCERTAINTY PRINCIPLE (1)

What matters, in any scene, but especially in a mystery thriller, is not just what it establishes *in the end*. Just as important, in the spectator's experience, is the flow of uncertainties, the questions, the possibilities, in scenes *as they go*. A film is a time-based experience, not a concise summary in retrospect. It includes our wondering: Who is Sam, at heart, really? Is he worth the hopes she's lavishing upon him? What's behind his slippery turnabouts? Such questions wouldn't trouble a voyeur. They loom large in our dramatic involvement with people whom we can like and admire and identify with and criticise – and in whose hopes, experiences and errors we recognise our own and those of our friends and acquaintances, and through which we can easily start reviewing our moral codes, our culture and our 'ideology'. This scene, like the opening moves of a chess match, is an 'envelope' of possibilities, teasing, promising, unnerving.

SCRIPT VERSUS FILM (1)

The written word makes nothing clearer. There's an extra page (about a minute) of conversation, which lumbers Sam with yet another dead-end notion – he dreams of a far-off island where love comes free of complications. (As even Hollywood knew it never did: cf *Bird of Paradise* [1932, 1951], *Pearl of the South Pacific* [1955] and *Enchanted Island* [1958], based on Herman Melville's *Typee*; the worm in the island paradise is cannibalism.)

A FEMINIST MYSTIQUE

Many Brand X feminists write as if Hollywood, traditional morality and 'patriarchy' all agreed that only wicked women entertained sexual desires for men. Women were either 'good girls' or 'bad girls', Madonnas or whores, docile helpmeets or *femmes fatales*; and Marion's murder was in some poetic way 'punishment' for her sexual goings-on with Sam. But the American media were one thing, American life another. In real-life negotiations, Marion's 'tender trap' was a ploy as old as the hills, and well known to occur between basically decent persons. Silent movies could wonderfully convey the heroine's sexual desires, in myriad *verb. sap.* ways, for instance, a certain 'female gaze' – shining, eager, unguarded, of which most Hollywood ladies had versions. That few heroines *mentioned* sexuality *as such* by no means implies 'repression' or 'suppression'. It was certainly tactful avoidance, but sexual self-expression hardly needed to spell everything out: a gentle hint, a tacit prompt, or not saying 'no', might suffice. In some celebrated cases, prostitutes die (e.g. *Destry Rides Again* [1939] and *Butterfield 8* [1960]; but in other cases, they enjoy a happy end (e.g. *Her Man* [1930], *Stagecoach* and *My Little Chickadee* [both 1939] and *The Brothers Karamazov* [1958]); and sometimes they shame the virtuous (*Rain* [1928, 1932, 1953]). When they die, it's not because death is a 'traditional' punishment for promiscuity (it never was); it's more often a fantasy punishment, involving Superego (Unconscious) fantasy, with weepie accompaniment *(Waterloo Bridge* [1931, 1940], *Camille* [1936]). In Hollywood movies, the principal function of such a death was to *avoid* challenging a highly specialised censorship code, designed by rearguard Victorians for 'the family audience' (i.e. children). By the early 1950s other, semi- popular media, e.g. the bestselling novel, freely ignored any censorship code. And, anyway, Victorian morality never thought death the appropriate fate for sexual misbehaviour. In *Psycho*, Marion's death makes no moral sense at all: her fate is in every way 'absurd'; that's part of the film's heavy punch.

By 1960, Christians who thought sexual desire *as such* was wicked were well outnumbered by others who thought it forgivable without extravagant repentance, and by those who (like some old-fashioned puritans) thought sexuality was God's gift to both the sexes, to be used with discrimination and responsible concern for 'the other' as a subject like oneself not a pleasure-object. When Hitchcock was asked if the priest in *I Confess* (1953) had slept with the heroine, he replied – 'I hope so. Far be it from me, as a Jesuit, to condone such behaviour' – which is close enough to a 'worldly common sense' about 'moral dissonance' as a condition of life.

Sexually, Marion may be calculating (affectionately). But she doesn't seem repressed; her flat-out smile seems as conscious of joy as Sam's grin down at her is of prowess. No doubt her sexuality is often frustrated, as she seems to live alone, but frustration and repression are entirely different things. Equally frustrated are her other female desires: to enjoy her sexuality respectably, and with assured companionship.

Insofar as Marion's sin has unintended, unpredictable and disproportionate consequences, her fate is *tragic*. The idea, that *the person merits better than the sin*, so that even due 'punishment' for sin is *not* deserved, is familiar enough; in 'tragic flaw' theory in drama, in the story of Faust, in *An American Tragedy* (1931) in such films as *They Live by Night* (1948) and *Du Rififi chez les hommes* (1954) – another European hit in the US – and in *The Exorcist* (1973), where the little girl, left lonely, finds an imaginary playmate, 'Captain Howdy' – who could blame a little child for not recognising the devil?

HEROINE AS TRAGIC HERO

Spectators of all sexes and genders would, I think, take Marion as their principal identification figure. Compared to the only alternative, Sam, she's more straightforward, positive and desperate; she makes the stronger moves dramatically, and the stronger moves visually; and as the scene proceeds, she's steadily more favoured by the camera. She's the protagonist and our primary (though not our only) dramatic concern. Sexually, she and Sam seem nicely matched: they roll around pretty freely, through him on top and her on top, to side by side. Some teenagers then would note such things: improvements on the missionary position were on popular agendas. In England, the leading marriage counsellor, Dr Eustace Chesser, advised that though the woman on top was more delicious, it might, if it became a habit, induce passivity in the male and so should be reserved for special treats.

Most of Hitchcock's leading men were 'male stars for women'. Gavin and Perkins (and, of course, Cary Grant) were 'romantic' stars, i.e. stars largely for women, though perfectly acceptable as identifications for men (unlike some male stars for women, such as Zachary Scott or Liberace). *Psycho* is very much a 'woman's film', like many a thriller about ladies in distress, e.g. *The Spiral Staircase* (1945), *The Naked Edge* (1961) and *Midnight Lace*. The formula, if such it is, allows all kinds of variations. (In *Phantom Lady*, the hero loiters passively in prison while his lady secretary does all the hard-boiled sleuthing in sleazy clubs and mean streets: she's both the 'damsel in distress' *and* the active hero. A similar duality applies in *Psycho*, where *each* sister is *both* endangered *and* active – Marion tragically, Lila successfully.

WHEN IS A MELODRAMA NOT A DRAMA?

From a certain angle, Sam is a 'male vamp' (sometimes romantic–erotic for women, like James Mason in *The Wicked Lady* [1945]). He's a 'dark handsome man', who plays with Marion sexually, while moodily refusing to be possessed. He keeps her on ten-terhooks and his thing about money drives her to crime. But really he's neither 'wicked' nor intentionally selfish; he's a 'weak lover', a common type of man in 'women's films', especially insofar as they tended to *drama* rather than *melodrama*. In a traditional sense of these words, a drama emphasises the relatively finessed emotions and attitudes at play *within* a usual social framework, whereas *melodrama* emphasises the grosser and instinctual drives, with a relatively 'soot and whitewash' morality (pure heroes, vile villains). Applying this terminology, *Psycho* is something of a hybrid. It's a melodrama insofar as it's a suspense thriller, with 'orrible murders, shrieking surprises and nail-biting panics; but often, as in this bedroom scene, it's built on dramatic finessing. Often its very suspense turns on nuances, uncertainties, under-tones, in fairly ordinary negotiations between morally nuanced people. In a sense, it *magnifies* the tensions *subtending* quite ordinary transactions, for instance the uneasy little quiver that *everybody* feels when questioned by a policeman. One might even say, that *Psycho*'s 'home key' is the *intertwining* of melodrama, drama and everyday experience *as read by* our 'irrational' (but sometimes justified) fears. It 'works through' the background anxiety in apparently ordinary transactions.

STYLE NOTES: FACE VALUES

Hitchcock treats Marion's story in an *opposite* style to many 1950s women's films. Their slow, 'plush' style generally preferred luxurious-looking settings, glossy faces, ponderous dialogue and long 'chains' of close shots which glorified the feminine face, especially in full-face or three-quarters-front views, which best display those reservoirs of emotion, the mouth and eyes. Within this general 'glamour' style, one might schematise four main 'idioms':

1. The super-sumptuous – *Imitation of Life* (1958), *Pal Joey* (1957).
2. The sumptuous and gloomy – *Possessed* (1947).
3. The bleak, almost noir – *Tarnished Angels* (1957), *The Loves of Jeanne Eagels* (1957) and

4. High-life crimes – *Mildred Pierce* (1945), *Casablanca* (1943).
    Hitchcock was master of them all, as with *The Man Who Knew Too Much* (1),
    Suspicion (2), *Rebecca* (3) and *Marnie* (4) in 1964. But *Psycho* is the least lux-
    urious and glossy of them all, the most brisk, oblique and unsentimental.
    Marion with Sam is often in near-profile, or shares a two-shot with him. Even
    the 'turning-point', when she first gives up on him, denies her a full-face close-
    up, and substitutes a sudden body-swerve, her face away from camera.

HITCHCOCK'S GRAND STRUCTURE

This 'de-emphasis' reflects the 'marginal' status of the Marion–Sam affair. It's no
sooner established, as a motive for theft, than it's dropped. As Hitchcock said, it's a
false trail, narrative-wise, a red herring: it serves to establish Marion as our heroine,
to give her and us something to think about, and to foreshadow the flight *without*
foreshadowing the eventual shock of her sudden death. All the same, Hitchcock and
Stefano do it proud. Moreover, Marion's and Sam's abrupt U-turns and the *hidden*
thinking thus implied establish an 'unexpectedness' principle, which will make the *big*
surprise seem, not an arbitrary contrivance but 'part of this dramatic universe', and
link it with a theme of 'gaps-and-splits in consciousness'.

FORM NOTES: DYNAMIC INTERVALS

Until the window-blind goes up, the half-dark room accentuates the whiteness (and
heat) of flesh, bed-linen and underwear; afterwards, it's a drab whitish-grey. Entering
the room, the camera passes dark indistinct areas of, presumably, furniture, before
settling into the crotch-height shot. (It's all quite unlike the usual establishing shot –
more of a disorienting shot!) The camera perches in odd positions (now groin level,
now just beneath the ceiling). The angles are steep, the compositions unstable. The
shots include distractions (the window is now blocked by a blind, now shows a vast
ornate building with rows of windows like blank eyes – looking at the sleazy lovers?
Or *not* looking at them – just windows staring at this window – blind reflections?)

  Between restlessly displaced shots, cuts generate unsettling 'intervals'. 'Intervals'
was Dziga Vertov's term for the *graphic differences* between adjacent shots. They're
a principal source of visual 'contrasts' and 'collisions' and a mainspring of Soviet montage theory. Directors should so plan their shots, even before shooting, that strong
hard cuts generate subliminal shocks on the spectator's visual perceptions and, by
knock-on effect, on his thoughts and emotions. 'Dynamic' cuts are the *sine qua non*
of film art, propaganda and agitprop.[6] 'Intervals' include, not only 'differences of

graphic forms', but also 'jumps between camera positions'. Normally, Hollywood preferred to *minimise* collisions, shocks and jumps, and keep cuts as soft and smooth as
reasonably possible. Hence the traditional distinction, summarised by Thorold
Dickinson, between 'montage editing' (aka 'Russian editing', 'dynamic editing', 'visible
editing'), and 'continuity editing' (aka 'Hollywood editing', 'narrative editing' and 'invisible editing'). Hitchcock understood both schools, and *Psycho* achieves some remarkable trade-offs (and syntheses!) between montage kinetics and continuity flowings.
(Saul Bass may have had something to do with it, for modern graphic design often
made a point of juxtaposing strong hard forms – in collage, photomontage, comic
strips, etc. – and a thoughtful craftsman could switch from juxtaposing static forms
side by side in space to juxtaposing moving forms successively in time. But many
Hollywood traditionalists were so used to setting up smooth cuts they couldn't or
wouldn't adapt their ideas of 'good style' to achieve a degree of expressive dynamic.)
A virtuoso segue starts with a close shot of the lovers' profiles on the bed. A cut to
a second close shot, at 90° to the first, favouring the back of Marion's head, makes
an eye-boggling 'collision', quite as disruptive as any jump-cut. Its dynamic seems to
launch Marion upwards, her back to the camera, which pulls back fast to show her
long back as she jack-knifes up to her feet, at the end of the bed, and then turns
about to march back beside the bed, on which Sam sits up and swivels around to
keep looking at her. The camera, having pulled back and up, is as if perched high up
on the wall, looking down at her, as she looks straight ahead, as if into a mirror, and
dresses again. While gazing off-screen left, she talks to Sam behind her screen right.
Her uncompromising words and posture unnerve him; he crosses behind her and
sits beside the window, which is on her left in real space, but on her right in screen
space. Both complicated and smooth, it's highly unsettling – very elegant, very disturbed. Later, when Sam *almost* agrees to Marion's terms, comes a very simple effect:
their profiles in close two-shot, close behind them, the lowered window-blind. It's
tight, close, stable, but – too brief, close, shallow, perhaps, after the 'tearing apart'.

THEMES AND VARIATIONS
Windows

The camera dives in through a window; as Sam and Marion kiss, the window-blind is
closed behind them; until Sam, recalling his divorce, raises it angrily and reveals the
building 'with a thousand eyes'. A voyeurism theme? Conceivably, but more relevant
to this particular dramatic situation is its *secrecy*, the need for which unsettles the
lovers' intimacy and privacy (unfashionable notion?). As, briefly, marriage looms, the

lowered blind implies it. The building opposite appears as Sam wonders bitterly where his ex-wife is now and, in relation to that, the 'many enigmatic windows out there' echo her disappearance (with his money), his 'lost intimacy', his *betrayal*.

Food

Pointless, narrative-wise, is a quick shot of the sandwich Marion forgot, amidst a mucky litter of a meal. It's an 'atmosphere' shot; almost, indeed, a metaphor, an emblem, for lunch-hour love as … fast food. (It's punched in, its visual mess half-snags our eye, and it's whisked off. The 'double jolt' and drastic speed contrast with the traditional idea, that symbolic details should hang about on-screen, to 'sink in'.)

Appetite and Forgetfulness

Marion only nibbled at *this* food, but looks forward to a respectable family meal. Sam gleefully spots she forgot to eat; she reminds him he's still barefoot. He's scoring a sexual point: 'I make you forget yourself.' He's scoring a childishness point.

Foreshadowings

Sam fondling bed-linen anticipates Norman's daily linen-changing. As one or two critics remarked, Sam, advancing to stand over Marion, briefly looks like Norman, with the same black glinting eyes (and from certain angles Gavin and Perkins are the tall dark type). Come to think of it, both men are low-income stick-in-the-muds, hamstrung by past women, unable to escape dark, stifling homes, and psychologically unstable. And both men, talking to Marion, make a long, strong movement with their hands – Sam spreads both arms wide to agree with her, Norman's right arm will reach to a small, stuffed, nocturnal bird.

Eye-lines

As Richard Roud noted, Antonioni's movies abound in shots where A (usually a man) looks at B (usually a woman) who gazes out of frame, elusively, and as in passive search for she knows not what. Hitchcock's 'off-screen mirror' shot has something of that quality, though Marion's 'horizon' is near, firm, forceful and decisive.

THE QUESTION OF INCIDENTALS

It's hard to know when such 'incidental details' – whether recurrent, like motifs, or local within a scene – are meant to carry some meaning, or are merely circumstantial. But even when irrelevant, they may nonetheless contribute a *visual restlessness*, a sense of the 'roughage' of lived life, of its *non*-signifying 'texture', the 'openness' through which we move. They indicate the 'randomness' (or pseudo-randomness) of our existence, *between* meanings. Many dramas, especially realistic ones, need such details in order to 'breathe'.

However, Hitchcock being a master-craftsman, with a degree of Soul, might he not endow his film with subtle details – for his own satisfaction? For kindred spirits and 'unknown friends' out there in the dark? For the 'happy few'? For 'the ideal reader', should one exist? For connoisseurs who love *maximising* meaning in artistic texts? And if a text is rich enough, we tend to accept effects which any of the artists (including Leigh, Gavin and the rest) contributed, even unconsciously; nor do we fussily reject serendipity. Furthermore, Hollywood theory and High Culture theory both agree that spectators and readers respond to far more than they realise, and that little details can escape conscious notice but still have some unconscious, preconscious or subliminal pay-off.

If *sensed*, the similarity of Sam and Norman might suggest the currently fashionable idea that as Laing used to say, sanity in our society is just another form of madness, and that Sam, Norman and the normative spectator are three of a kind – all 'Guilty! Guilty! Guilty! (to cite *The Phantom Tollbooth*). Hitchcock would, I am sure, agree – but he might also insist that the similarities between sanity and madness don't abolish the differences. In which Hitchcock would include the 'conservative, reactionary' defences – sexual taboos and repressions, prudent fears of punishment and of ruining one's life, including even the need to be hypocritical (*because* we live in society). Sam's ambivalence and unconscious cruelty to Marion are radically, systemically and forever alien to Norman's.

◆

SCENES 3–5 MARION MEETS TEMPTATION IN LOWERY'S OFFICE

Marion rushes back into the office, enquiring if anyone (tacit: Sam) telephoned for her. Her fellow-secretary, Caroline (Patricia Hitchcock), a plain, self-centred girl, supposes Marion has a headache, and offers her a tranquilliser. Their anxious, sharp-faced boss, George Lowery, returns late from his lunch with a client, Tom Cassidy, a grizzled, tightly swaggering oil man. Cassidy, perhaps a touch tipsy, produces $40,000 in cash, to pay for a house, a wedding present for his teenage daughter. Spotting Marion's glum look, he boasts of 'buying off unhappiness', almost as if propositioning *her, though perhaps he's just boasting about his wealth. He bustles Lowery into the latter's inner office, to close the deal with a drinking session. Lowery, worried about so much cash on the premises, bids Marion take the money to the bank forthwith; next Monday morning, he'll ask Cassidy for a certified cheque instead. Marion, pleading a headache, asks if she can go straight home to bed from the bank. She puts the money in an envelope, and the envelope safely deep in her bag, and departs.*

A NEW DRAMATIC PATTERN

Sam's debts gave Marion a motive; the office grants her the opportunity. Half an hour ago, she renounced pleasure for respectability; now, respectability proves spiritually hollow. She teased a man (and herself) sexually; now, men tease her, sexually and financially. Cassidy and Lowery lead her into temptation, one by teasing her, the other by trusting her (opposite attitudes work together). It's another temptation scene, but also an aggravation scene: office chat rubs salt into her wounds. Two rather selfish people, Cassidy and Caroline, have the family lives they want. Cassidy's joke about tax-evasion has the ring of truth, and makes Lowery some sort of accomplice, technically. Dishonesty being all in their day's work, why should she not take their money and run? Cassidy's boast, that he never carries more than he can afford to lose, assures her, and us, that she'll do no great harm.

SCENES FROM OFFICE LIFE

A drama written according to the textbook would show Marion's reactions, quietly gathering strength, until the moment of decision. Normally, Hitchcock is conventionally emphatic about such things. Not here. The dramatic issue all but disappears, as Marion 'rises above' these petty provocations, seeming not even to notice them. The scene becomes 'a slice of office life', as Hitchcock and Stefano lavish tender loving care on characters who will never appear again.

CITIZEN CASSIDY

Cassidy, looking at Marion, the pretty one, begins, 'My sweet little girl'; love-starved Marion looks up, only to get, 'Not you – my daughter!' The nastily canny redneck has zeroed in on the unhappiness she didn't show. His pseudo-jovial chat celebrates his family happiness – as a function of money–power. His teenage daughter will have home and husband while Marion, pushing 30 – rather late, for the 1950s – has neither. Cassidy's generosity towards his departing daughter mimics fatherly unselfishness, and its fond melancholy; but he strongly smacks of the domineering tycoon (vide Lionel Barrymore in Duel in the Sun, Burl Ives in Cat on a Hot Tin Roof [1955, filmed 1958], Ives again in Desire under the Elms [1924, filmed 1958] and eventually, Dallas. Or imagine Citizen Kane with a sweet little daughter – how he'd indulge and dominate her for ever … In the script the patriarchal theme is stronger still: Cassidy calls his future son-in-law a 'penniless punk'. On the one hand, he lets his daughter have her wilful way, but on the other hand, won't a worthless husband ensure dependence on Daddy?) This well-satisfied father knows just how to taunt

Marion: first, he hints at a demeaning proposition and then he lets it drop. Finally, he's in Lowery's inner office, enacting a 'good ol' boy' ritual with a reluctant colleague. The spiritual dregs ...

Men who bully women also bully men. Cassidy embarrasses Lowery in front of his female employees. He 'accidentally' reveals that Lowery has a liquor stash; he notes that the girls' outer office lacks air-conditioning. His description of its air, as 'hot as fresh milk', implies his own experience milking cows (as a country redneck, before striking oil?).

'MOTHER'S LITTLE HELPERS'

Caroline's friendly chat bristles with little barbs, some unintentional, due to self-centredness, some 'accidentally on purpose'. Asked by Marion if anyone phoned for her, she starts by remembering all the calls for herself. Assuming Marion has a headache, she offers, not the normal thing, aspirins, but – a tranquilliser! The new-ish popularity, and routine abuse, of tranquillisers was much deplored, as a cheap-shot response to life's problems – instead of facing up to them, one dopes oneself. As Caroline's chat implies: 'My mother's doctor gave these to me on the day of my wedding. Teddy was furious when he found out I'd taken tranquillisers.' Her careless, almost gleeful tone completes the picture: fear of the bridal night, sneakiness about it, matriarchal interference, a husband deceived and disappointed, triumphalist chat to other girls ... 'Momism', and female dominance, was a topic of the time (of which more anent Mrs Bates). But for all her – frigidity?, Caroline is jealous of Cassidy's quasi-propositioning to Marion. She calls it 'flirting' (she euphemises it, because she wants some), and then consoles herself with 'I expect he saw my wedding-ring'. The lighting, unkindly, makes her face doughy, puddingy (like her father's).

TAKING A RISE OUT OF THE BOSS

Lowery's panic about keeping big cash in the office smacks of avarice, a deadly sin. The result is paradoxical – he thrusts the cash on Marion – who robs him. Is this poetic justice – punishment for foolishness (as with another Hitchcock boss, Strutt, in *Marnie*)? Maybe, but then again, the cases are different. Marion has been honest for ten years, which is reasonable grounds for trust. And trust, as a form of respect, is important in Hitchcock (Rutland [Sean Connery] seeks trust, *not* love from Marnie). Optimists about human nature expect everybody to love everybody; but for pessimists, like Hitchcock, love is rare and unreliable. It's trust that makes the world go round.

The office scene is almost a little 'playlet' on its own. As a 'slice of office life', it's comparable to the work of some 'realist' novelists, such as J. B. Priestley in *Angel Pavement* (1930) or Graham Greene in *It's a Battlefield* (1934), and the oblique *implicationism* of Harold Pinter. Its concision demonstrates the opposite strategy to Mike Leigh's fecund sprawl. It's far more elaborate than 'narrative structure', as such, could require.

STRANGE DRAMATURGY

This 'realist' description both *carries* the plot, and *veils* it. As Cassidy brandishes his money, all the office people react, but in different ways. Caroline marvels, Lowery worries; but Marion's calm, polite cool shows class. You can study this scene for ever, yet never know if, or when Marion decides to rob and run. Pleading a headache, her hands are clasped twistily in front of her, like a nervous schoolgirl, age nine. A sign of guilt? Or just strain after a difficult day? A strong, capable woman, uncomfortable when asking favours? Is it a real headache, or did Caroline give her the idea? We'll never know. Her exit line, 'You can't buy off unhappiness with pills!', rings like old-fashioned wisdom, renouncing 'shallow materialism'. But does she speak too jauntily, thus belying her crippling headache? And doesn't triumphalism, so early in a story, *invite* reversal? Is her moralising a form of hubris? The little uncertainties pile up. Like dissonances in music, they say nothing definite, but they spark little tensions in your nervous system.

HITCHCOCK'S UNCERTAINTY PRINCIPLE (2)

Why this 'opacity'? The logic, I think, runs something like this. Many spectators will concentrate on the overt action, on the 'shock' of 'naked cash', Cassidy's boorishness, etc. It's interesting in itself and at this early stage in the film audiences are patient with quiet exposition. *Not* 'pre-telegraphing' Marion's envy and temptation – by edgy looks etc. – makes its eventual revelation all the stronger. Many other spectators, however, will suss, *from their own reactions*, that she might really, desperately, desire that lovely bankroll. (It's a basic problem in all discourse whatsoever: ideas which spectators will quickly think of for themselves need no sign in the text. Omitting signs for what the spectators already know makes texts faster, subtler, richer. So, basic key ideas may have no signifiers.) These suspicious spectators, anticipating her desires, will scrutinise her reactions closely – but to no avail: *nothing* says she'd die for it. So the scene preserves the uncertainty, the *suspense*, of '*Does* she want to steal it?' which is *less* familiar, *more* novel and more interesting, than 'Will she steal it, and what then?'

(which a lesser *auteur* would never fail to seize on). Another advantage: Marion's moral dignity will make her downfall more sudden, more poignant.

All the way through *Psycho*, uncertainty is Hitchcock's little game. This may seem odd, for his usual watchword was, 'Clarify! Clarify! This very watchword may ring oddly, when you consider that his stock-in-trade was *mystery* (plus MacGuffinry). But mystery works on *controlled implication*: you have to clarify what it is that you're being mysterious about, and what sort of thing might count as clues, hints, suggestions, suspicions (or red herrings). Here, Marion's impenetrably innocent behaviour keeps the audience *uncertain*. More important still: when, eventually, we discover her decision, we realise that seeing everything, we knew nothing; that unspoken thoughts are always brewing ... like those 'mental shapes' working away within the cityscape ... The hotel scene uses ambiguity of the *alternating* type (Sam blowing hot and cold). The office scene uses ambiguity of the *parallel* type (spoken versus unspoken).

Howard Hawks noted another factor. Discussing the script of *Rio Bravo* (1959), he said, 'Television has come in and ... [has] used so many thousands of plots that people are getting tired of them. They're a little too inclined – if you lay a plot down – to say, "Oh, I've seen this before." But if you can keep them from knowing what the plot is, you have a chance of holding their interest. And it leads to characters ... [i.e. meaning: more *detailed* characters.]'.[7] The Marion story is very low on plot, very high on *detail*. Indeed, 1959 was to be the year of the vanishing plotline: in *Psycho*, *L'Avventurà*, *La Dolce vità*.

In both *Psycho* and *L'Avventurà*, a woman disappears, a third of the way through, and then a couple look for her, in vain.

BUYING WITH PILLS?

Two verbal-mental slips from Marion presage imminent confusion. Her grand exit line is a mixed-up metaphor (confusing pills with money). (It's not in the script, it smacks of inspired improvisation. If it's an actress's blooper, she was right to make it, and Hitch to leave it in. Leigh confessed to repeatedly stumbling over 'Not inordinately' – a nice line – it's just the sort of slightly unusual word that would have stuck in the mind of a 1950s secretary which she then found herself using – not pretentiously, but *because* it's a bit stiff.) More subtly odd is, 'Headaches are like good resolutions, you forget them as soon as they stop hurting.' (If you tease out the logic of that, good resolutions are a useless pain, to be gotten rid of. Her Unconscious has spoken.)

THERE AIN'T NO JUSTICE

When Cassidy says 'My sweet little girl', words which suggest a fond father figure, Marion looks up – and trips the machinery of fate. Was her catching his eye blind chance? Or the natural reflex of a lonely woman? Or linked to some sin by her (the dissatisfactions of premarital sex-play? Or female, or human, frailty?) In the 1960s anthropologists used to say that The Savage Mind attributes every misfortune to some evil intent, and Freudians drew parallels with the Superego, which, left to itself, induces damnable guilt for every little accident. Maybe it's this pre-moral guilt that Hitchcock taps – whether or not it happens to have some moral sub-component. Is the photographer of *Rear Window* guilty of voyeurism, or is voyeurism the false guilt that caring about your neighbour must outface? Back in 1935, the 'inciting incident' of *The Man Who Knew Too Much* is a little girl letting her dog slip its lead. Does this misadventure reveal some deadly sin – disobedience, carelessness, imprudence? – which makes her morally responsible for what follows – kidnap, shootings, parents in danger … Or is the moral that there is no moral – that life is unjust, unpredictable, chaotic? It's a very traditional and perennial opinion: as the jokey rhyme used to go, 'The rain it raineth every day/ Upon the just and unjust fella/ But mostly on the just because/ The unjust stole the just's umbrella.' It's the usual point of view, among worldly people; it's not cynical and it often coexists with strong moral principles. It's a – if not the – Christian tradition. True, some Christians practise goodness as insurance against acts of God, but what Jesus said was, 'Pick up thy cross and follow me', and Christians know what is meant by 'having a cross to bear'. The fact that Marion's downfall has an odd combination of 'causes' – including Lowery's *trust*, which she *earned* – is, perhaps, a hint that *Psycho* is not about 'sin' and 'punishment', and that its moral pattern is not sado-moralistic but dramatic-ironic. (I don't mean there's no sadism in Hitchcock, presumably there is; but its expression isn't moralistic; it's in his skill at inflicting enjoyable suspense – a socially admirable sublimation.)

ESOTERIC CONFESSION OR JOKEY COINCIDENCE?

Just outside the office Marion passes a stranger in a Stetson who, turning round, proves to be Alfred Hitchcock. Cowboy headgear makes an incongruity joke. Some critics, determined to find Hitch guilty of everything, link his Stetson with Cassidy's, as a token of spiritual affinity: Hitchcock like Cassidy sexually harasses female employees (Vera Miles, Tippi Hedren and so on). Come to think of it, Cassidy talks about his daughter, and Patricia Hitchcock plays Caroline. Mix a little gossip with a Freudo-structuralist logic of 'substitutions', and this scene has a secret theme: it's

Hitchcock's Unconscious confession of incest and paedophilia. The latter is about the only mental crime he hasn't been accused of.[8]

A WHITE SPECTRUM

This sedentary, potentially static scene is kept mobile by brisk camera follows of short 'walkabouts'. Unlike the bedroom scene, angles and compositions are stable, though the 'shot dissection' beats nine films out of ten.[9] The general tonality is greyer than the bedroom scene, but still quite light (and well within TV's tonal range). This 'white-end' palette continues the theme of 'heat', of *sensual* strain, working on Marion; its shrill, blank spaces conceal 'hidden depths'.

Amid the pallid greys, Marion's skin shines white. White, too, a large desert landscape, of furrowed dunes, just behind her desk. 'Hot as fresh milk' is a vividly white *idea*; its sensuousness sticks in the mind, and may well refer, in Hitch's sly way, to Marion's bra. The 1950s were unprecedently breast-conscious, as per the briefly famous joke in *The Girl Can't Help It* (1956), where Jayne Mansfield clutches a fat milk-bottle against each breast, and on sight of her a tradesman boils over. Cassidy's mentions of first milk and then whisky make a classic pair of 'opposites'.

THE WILDERNESS

Profiled against the desert, Marion speaks her moralistic exit line. Strutting off, she passes a second landscape, of similar size, but very dark in tone. As she sweeps out of frame, the camera stays, to linger briefly on this second scene; a river, or a long lake, reflecting the quiet clouds above it, amid dark trees and narrowing away into the distance. Especially after the bleached, heaped-up desert, it's refreshing, calm, melancholy perhaps. Maybe a photograph, maybe a painting, it evokes unspoiled nature — even, perhaps, a 'virgin continent'; the great American forest, silent, withdrawn — a vision, perhaps, of a *pre-American* past — like the strange time-shunt in *Vertigo*. Desert and forest — two faces of Nature, both void of man? Stranger thoughts have occurred, in dreams, in poetry, in the settings of fictions....

After Marion's exit right, escorted by her shadow, which has suddenly appeared on the wall behind her, this dark landscape cross-fades into the next scene. Here, after the briefest of pauses, Marion will resume her movement in the same direction. But the movement's character will be completely different: from a bright momentum, to a dark sidling drift. The whole 'trope' is a structure, of pace and time. The master of 'cross-fade painting', Joseph von Sternberg, would have admired this one. (There's no mention of pictures in the script, from which, indeed, it's impossible to visualise *any* scene in the film. From these written words, every *auteur* could make *his own* film. Even when word-perfect, scripts are not blueprints, they're not even rough drafts. They're just a foreseeable aspect of a text which is undefined, unforeseeable, even in the *auteur*'s mind's eye.)

◆

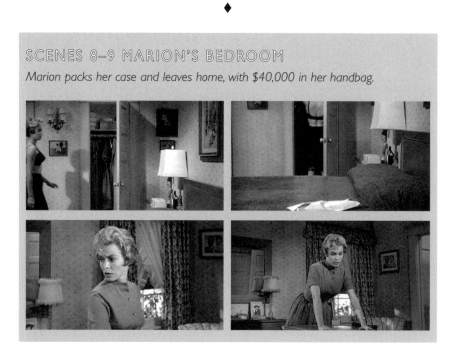

SCENES 8–9 MARION'S BEDROOM
Marion packs her case and leaves home, with $40,000 in her handbag.

CRIME AND CASUISTRY

So far as 'the text itself' lets on, Marion may be taking the money for herself alone. However, context assures us she's stealing to marry Sam. Maybe in that order. But her crime is for *their sake*. It's selfish *and* unselfish; like a decent marriage.

Far from alienating the audience, Marion's crime enhances our sympathy and concern. 'There but for the grace of God go I.' As ultra-'Victorian' as Hollywood morality was, it well understood heroes with moral flaws, and villains with redeeming virtues. As Hitchcock said of *Marnie*, spectators are quickly drawn into empathising with screen characters attempting hard and risky tasks, even if it's in conflict with their own moral principles. Here, as often, ambivalence intensifies audience interest and involvement.

As hard as it tried, Hays Code morality couldn't make all crimes unsympathetic. In the first place, most spectators know, or sense, the differences between legality, morality, ethics, generosity and prudence. The Hays Office rule, that crime must be shown not to pay but to suffer punishment, is not, in itself, a *moral* argument, it's a pragmatic, amoral one, but it's *conducive to* moral behaviour, so 'moral' in that sense. It stacks the odds against Marion's enterprise, but, since we have some sympathy for her, it makes her, already, a sympathetic victim, a brave underdog.

Even within Hays rules, Marion's theft could have been done as a crime comedy, a romantic escapade, a caper – as in *Trouble in Paradise* (Ernst Lubitsch, 1952), or Ealing's *The Lavender Hill Mob* (1955 with Alec Guinness), or Hitchcock's *To Catch a Thief* with Cary Grant. Grant's character, by profession a jewel-thief and cat-burglar, is a confirmed recidivist; but his only victims are the super-rich (who, like Cassidy, can afford to lose it); he seems to others very romantic, though he's prudently selfish, and his apparent destiny is a comfortable retirement. Marion's far lesser crime, during an emotional lapse ('while her balance of mind is disturbed'), is ominous because Hitchcock tunes his lyre to the key of anxious dread. It's not *what* a hero does; it's *what tones and values a particular film* invests it with. At the cinema, your 'typical spectator' was not some goody-goody citizen, but 'l'homme moyen morale', the *moderately* moral person – with the stress on 'moderately'. The gap between censors and the *only moderately* moral (but still *basically* moral) spectator is just one reason why most movies are *bad* guides to *real* social attitudes – even though they represent a limited consensus. In the privacy of their own hearts, many Mister Nine-to-Fives would agree with the Surrealist view that Marion's desperate defiance of society is rather fine – even if it's desperate – it's a *noble risk*. Even if it's *also* foolish and wicked and a bad case of *hamartia* (tragic error) plus *hubris* (a challenge to the gods, whose modern dress is society). You don't have to be Surrealist to see Marion's flight as a dream-like state – a semi-trance – fuelled by *l'amour fou*.[10]

A conventional drama would have felt obliged to 'explain' her folly, or at least describe her change of mind. But what's to explain? Everybody understands how low, immoral desire can just 'come over' you, and suddenly you're a different person, in a different world. It's a normal degree of schizoid split. The Old Adam (or in Marion's case, the Old Eve) creeps up on the Upright Citizen, and takes over; there's no Jekyll-and-Hyde contortion, just a smooth cross-fade in consciousness (that trope is both mysterious and exact). Marion's folly is quite short-lived (Friday afternoon to Saturday/Sunday round midnight) and it acts out a kind of fantasy many a law-abiding clerk has consoled himself by thinking through. It's the omission of conscious decision, the intensity of the mood and the haphazard nature of her planning that make her appear as one 'possessed'. Her slightly alienated state is more than a mere 'impulse' and it might be called a 'compulsion', except that it's conscious, willed, rational and deliberate; might it be called an 'impulsion'? A strange word for a strange mental state. It's partly involuntary, partly voluntary – the hybrid condition which makes moral judgments so difficult. For the Jesuits, from whom Hitchcock says he learned analysis, sin may lie less in the initial impulse, than in active assent to it, by the 'rational will' (a saint can have temptations, St Jerome being famous for them). The very idea of a 'rational will' may seem absurd, if, like so many modern materialists, you're absolutely sure that all human thoughts arise from training and conditioning, that no human mind is free, and that no individual is morally responsible for his own thoughts or actions. Nonetheless, the idea of a conscious effective will was culturally widespread among Hitchcock's target audience (and is still maintained by many rationalists, humanists and elastic-minded materialists). The father of psychoanalysis often spoke as if the rational ego had some significant margin of autonomy, and could be freer still, if more of the Id were open to the ego. For 'l'homme moyen morale' a general idea that rational decision may *tip the balance* between contending passions makes a useful shorthand for – well, exactly what is another question.

'SHE'S LEAVING HOME'

The twelve-word narrative point of this long and roundabout scene was easily containable in one swift, simple shot. Hitchcock lavishes on it two quite baroque constructions, plus a 'woman's walkabout', in the class of Max Ophuls' 1953 *Madame de …* (that shrine of *Cahiers du Cinéma* and its spiritual pleasure in *mise-en-scène*).

1. Through the fade itself. Marion and her shadow, having left her office screen right, re-enter this scene, from screen left – suggesting one continuous movement (it's the age-old continuity rule for doing so). But the office wall gives way to another wall, and the dark picture to a dark dress-closet. But Marion's walk is soft, quiet and she wears a *black* bra and slip. She's preceded by her quiet shadow (leading her?).

2. Cash on the bed. As the fade completes, she looks towards the camera, then turns back to the closet. Now the camera tilts down to discover, close to us, a fat gleaming white envelope, laid on a grey-toned bed. A quick glide into close-up reveals (or, if we guessed, confirms) there's money inside it. Having got down to bed level (another 'bed-height' shot), the camera pans left to show a packed suitcase, its upraised lid almost looming over us.

3. Marion's walkabout. From more normal viewpoints, Marion finishes dressing

and packing, gathers her documents together, puts the money beside them in her handbag and leaves the apartment.

4. A brief garage scene, with Marion driving off, was scripted but omitted.

Phase 1 is 'Marion through the Looking-Glass'. As in a dream, 'everything has changed'. The cross-fade was a soft, melting figure; it segues into a hard, steeply angular close-up one. Two unlike styles, jammed together, feed the one ellipsis. Moreover, confronted with this blank envelope, we're puzzled at first, but from it we *deduce* what *already* happened. We don't just *read* the story; we have to *construe* it. We must shift from narrative mode – the story carrying us along – to a retro-deductive mode.[11] An awkward gear-change – and meant to be so. Although within a rough consensus, different minds will tackle it rather differently. In my case, the new sexy-sleazy-stealthy atmosphere mixed with perplexity – at 'the riddle of the envelope' – then one by one the clues kicked in – the packed suitcase clinching it. Michael O'Pray remembers wondering if Marion had laid the envelope out like that to display it to herself while making up her mind whether to steal it or go to the bank with it after all. Another colleague followed a 'third way'. Before seeing the envelope: oh, now she's in a woman's bedroom, probably her home, has she been to the bank already, and going to bed for her headache – but wait, strange bed-wear for a headache – has she not been to the bank? In mainstream movies, a perennial problem, so familiar that it's rarely stated, is finding forms that lead along converging paths the many different kinds of mind, background, knowledge of the world, etc., that exist among spectators. Moreover, the succession of clues must gear in with some sort of *thinking speed*. (In the final analysis, artistic form is ergonomic.)

Phase 2 implies 'fatality'. The camera starts with a figure shot of Marion *over there*, and its downward tilt reveals something *behind her*. It's hidden very close to us, under the camera's very nose – in the 'unseen zone' *between* the camera and the scene. Literally *overlooked*, the ominous fact lay in ambush.[12] Its appearance *negates* both previous scenes. In one, she rose above sex, in the next, she rose above money. But now, they've both got her. The trope weaves neatly together, in one bold visual construction, three earlier motifs: bed-level shots, objects of desire, things overlooked. Sex displaced food. Now cash rules bed. It's a lot more sordid than the black underwear (to help seduce Sam or to encourage herself?). In her suitcase, however, the lingerie and shoes are satiny-white – *respectably* smart, womanly, even wifely. They're what she intends to become, they're her real self.

Phase 3. Her 'walkabout' is all brisk, taut looks and walks, this way and that, around and across, with unquiet pauses. Its time-space design is strong but not too simple: it's 'a circle with radii'. She works her way around the room – first the dress-closet, then a dressing-table with mirror, then a low drawer in some off-screen piece of furniture, then back past the closet. After each hasty pause she steps back to the bed (with shining envelope) in the centre of the room. From various spots around, she looks back at it, and most of her looks are 'answered' by a shot of its blank white form, dominating the screen, at a sharp visual 'interval'. Even while it's off-screen, and she's doing something else, it's an invisible, obsessive force, and keeps her in its orbit.

Her actions are prosaic – pulling on her dress (while walking), topping up the case, sorting documents, taking a quick last look round – but they give the actress *things to do*, efficiently, calmly, yet with scared face and tense body language. The business of *putting things together for a trip* invokes a familiar experience, strengthening audience involvement in this unusual, melodramatic instance.

Form-wise, the scene is rather beautiful. In a respectable grey dress, she stoops over the suitcase, as if leaning on both arms, stares at the off-screen object of desire, breaths nervously (and fetchingly), half-deciding on action, half-surrendering to it. When she sits on the bed, beside the fatal attraction, she's sideways on to it, as if to mitigate its power, before scooping it into her bag. Appropriating it is obeying it. Her quick exit is 'walked choreography'. On our side of the bed, she steps right to left, her left hand crosses her body to lift the suitcase from her right, she makes a quick U-turn round to behind the bed, and, stepping left to right, plucks a coat with her right hand from the closet on her left and, without stopping, slips through a doorway not expected by us – and a cross-fade closes this action before its completion.

Her first 'orbit', with its last turns inwards, sketches a tightening spiral, a 'winding up'; after taking the money, her departure is a fast unwinding (in the contrary direction). As often, in 'well-constructed' scenes, the closing shot 'reflects' the opening shot – or, more exactly, it resembles yet reverses it. Marion entered left and drifted along a wall. Her exit right resumes the same line. One might say that the two shots 'rhyme'. Like rhymes, they combine similarity and difference. The similarity is: 'Marion moving past the wall.' The differences are, dress, position, speed, mood, entry/exit. The meaning is not *in* the difference (as Saussurean paradigms might lead one to suppose); it's in the *combination* of difference *and similarity*. (Is difference definable, except alongside similarity?)

Mise-en-scène apart, the scene is a *soliloquy without words* – it's thought 'spoken' by restless movements, body language and 'business' with objects (as pioneered by Chaplin and prescribed by Pudovkin). It's also a 'dialogue', between Marion's silent looks and the blank envelope.

It's often said, not without good reason, that a movie should have some stylistic unity, and the style of *Psycho* can seem very consistent. All the same, are the soft cross-fade and the hard down-tilt one style, or contrasting styles jammed together? How do you distinguish variations *within* 'a style' from different styles?

PIECES OF PAPER

Marion's graceful fingers tuck the blank envelope beside her bank-book, driving-licence and other documents. They're emblems of ownership, status, legal 'identity' (and, perhaps, 'social self-respect', as distinct from her '*inner* self-respect' – her private, personal and *subjective* 'identity'.[13] This scene's closest shots – the envelope and Marion's documents – introduce the theme of *pieces of paper* (a scrap of paper, with calculations on it, will be a last little clue to her presence). A woman's handbag is a related 'fetish', and if women proverbially keep their handbags close by, it's not for their sexual meanings (like, say, vagina, womb or supportive Mother), but for reasons of social potency, which pertain to ego-psychology. Its contents are precious, because they're not only *signs*, but also *agents* of 'social power/identity'.

'AND UNAWARES MORALITY EXPIRES'

Spectators with consciously strong moral principles may note that Marion, gripped by obsession and apprehension, gives herself no moral or spiritual arguments. She thinks hedonically – about pills and happiness – and she thinks about being respectably set-tled. With Norman she will discuss, not morality, but contentment. Though she's a smart, strong, worthwhile person, is there here some moral, therefore spiritual, void?

Her apartment seems agreeable but impersonal and very orderly. We probably spot a picture of two quietly serious people, her righteous parents no doubt (they're the only ornaments to be mentioned in the script). Unlike the office pictures, they're small and briefly glimpsed. Another odd detail: the mirror reflects two doors, both flat on to camera, but they're slightly disaligned, in such a way as to signal to our sub-liminal perception that one is a closed door, while the other stands open from a doorway at right angles to the first. This symbolises absolutely nothing, but some-times mirror-disalignments hint at alienation and, somehow, I don't know why, they signal, to me at least, emptiness, nothingness, and whatever existentialist 'Nothingness' and Lacanian 'lack' might be about *really* – some hollow at the heart of things. Marion's impeccable, melancholy bedroom – and Norman's empty life – links *Psycho* with a little cluster of films about empty lives of a lower middle-class, 'suburban ticky-tack' level: *The Prowler* (Joseph Losey, 1950), *A Cold Wind in August* (Alexander Singer, 1960), Jack Garfein's remarkable *Something Wild* (1961), Kubrick's

Lolita (1962), *The Honeymoon Killers* (L. Kastle, 1969) and, eventually, another *Something Wild* (Jonathan Demme, 1986) and perhaps *Misery* (Rob Reiner, 1990).

◆

SCENES 10–25 LATE FRIDAY: MARION LEAVES TOWN

Marion drives slowly in a busy shopping street. In her imagination, Sam's greeting sounds very worried. She stops for pedestrians to cross; among them are Cassidy and Lowery, who nods at her briefly. She smiles back, almost gratefully. He pauses and frowns perplexedly, before walking on. Easing her car forward, she's dismayed as well as relieved. She drives on through the dusk; night falls. She winces away from oncoming headlights; the background music slows, the image fades to black.

THREE MENTAL LAPSES

Marion's getaway might have been filmed as an optimistic caper; she's bringing her lover her loot, to start their life over, free as a bird. But all is ominous. Sam says, 'Of course I'm glad to see you', but his tone is more perplexed, and 'Of course' suggests she's just told him he seems not pleased at all. But then Lowery distracts her. Forgetting her new status, big-time thief, she smiles at him. *Her* mental lapse is can-celled out by *his* (drink and 'Thank God It's Friday' drowsiness?). Beside him, Cassidy, drunker still, barges along, head in air, unseeing. All three minds are out to lunch. (In *Sabotage* [1936] already, mental lapses were a running theme. A wife stabs her hus-band without quite meaning to, driven by her [morally decent] compulsion [and his unspoken death-wish]. A detective with a bandaged head can't remember whether she incriminated herself or not. A terrorist's bomb signal starts, 'Don't forget. The birds will sing at 4:15.')

CROSSING THE BAR

The bank will be closed until Monday; Marion can still turn back. Lowery's appear-ance is a scare, but is it a salutary one: a last warning, from God, or Providence, or whatever moral powers may be? Or does it distract her from her own 'inner voice' (intimating Sam's displeasure) — so letting her drive on, deeper into trouble? The pedestrian crossing becomes an invisible boundary, between 'Office Community' and 'Moral Wilderness'.[14] Alas, she's on moral automatic …

SEQUENCE DESIGN

This first of Marion's three long drives has five 'phases', or, maybe, 'paragraphs'.
1. Sam's voice is an *internal* prompt.
2. Lowery's silent look is an *external* prompt.
3. Marion's drive through the afternoon.
4. Marion as night falls.
5. Marion's mind shuts down.

FULL FRONTAL FIXITY

Paragraphs 1 and 2 are dominated by nearly identical camera set-ups: close-ups of Marion full face, at the driving wheel. She looks ahead, sometimes directly into camera, sometimes just off it, and sometimes her eyes move in wide arcs around it. Her strong face has a 'triple frame' (front windshield; upholstered interior; rear window). The rear window is small, but it's centrally placed, and, from our POV, it's right next to Marion's face, so visually it's quite strong. The rigidity (which lesser directors would have felt obliged to vary) dominates the shots, and locks us on to Marion's full face – the angle of strongest expressiveness – and onto her eyes – 'the windows of the soul'. It also allows, or rather *strengthens*, a series of 'little' changes – in light, in size of close-up, in Marion's fixed or roving gaze (sometimes like a trapped animal's), in bodily tensions – her fingers on the wheel, her body stretching diagonally forward or slumping abruptly back, or resettling in her seat. As often in good 'head and shoulders' shots, breathing, and stirrings of the body, even below the frame, become cinematically 'palpable', as the shoulders shift, the head re-balances itself and spectator kinaesthesia kicks in. Many such shots will subsequently recur; they're a dominant 'trope' of Marion's long lone drive.

THE LUST OF THE EYE

Some theorists suppose that something called 'bourgeois language' forbids looks into camera, as somehow breaking 'the illusion', or intercepting the spectator's voyeurism, and making him feel guilty. Either way it's an alienation effect. As research very quickly shows, looks into camera, though carefully controlled, are not uncommon in 'bourgeois' movies, and tend to occur at moments of character *sincerity*. (For much the same reason that people associate sincerity with 'look me in the eye'.) As for guilt: 'people-watching', when encouraged by the very fact of a film, is neither a furtive nor a morbid act – unless, of course, *all* the visual arts, pictorial or performance-based, boil down to morally dubious sexual indulgence.

A SILENT SCENE, WITH MUSIC AND A VOICE

Between Lowery and Marion, the 'speaking looks' make another 'silent dialogue'. Marion's face is a 'silent soliloquy', but when her face responds uneasily to Sam's imagined voice, that's a 'pseudo-dialogue', with her thought distributed between her mind and her face.

No sooner has the frontal *fixity* settled in, than it's broken up, by the fourth paragraph, a burst of 'dusk roadscape' shots, with a travelling POV of wild and beautiful clouds tipped by a band of sunset light. Then headlights charging forward sabre-slash across Marion's eyes. Such 'free' spaces might suggest 'free at last!', but the movement is relentless, the cuts hard, we can't relax, and the strangest trope so far concludes the sequence. After Marion's strained face, the screen is black, the background music slows down. Very slow fade into early morning, a distant view of a black car parked on a desolate highway. Here's another deft ellipsis: *non-diegetic* music, slowing unnaturally, over a black screen, suggests the car stopping as a tired mind 'crashes out'. It's a subjective impression of (another) mental lapse.

THRIFT, THEFT, GIFT

On the one hand, Marion's action is unselfish, devoted; but on the other hand (and in *Psycho*, there's always another hand), she's thrusting her gift on Sam, trying to force his hand. Is she, in her way, 'matriarchal'? not, like his first wife, by legally extracting his money, but by giving him *illegal* money. Is it, in a way, control by gift – as Cassidy controls his daughter? True, it's more impulsive than controlling (and impulsive she often is, as Lila will confirm, when the script spends two pages discussing the problem of gifts, generosity and sacrifice all generating resentment). Marion seems impulsive, not only about sexuality, but also about its opposite, *respectability* (abruptly she jack-knifed up off the bed).

LOGICS AND POETICS

1. 'The first thing I throw out is logic', Hitchcock declared. The bane of his life was 'the plausibles' – spectators who want their plots convincing, when Hitchcock wanted them poetic, Surrealist, absurdist, Alice in Thrillerland-ish. A plausible might ask: 'As Marion's behaviour seems so businesslike in the office, surely she'd try to phone Sam, to tell him she's on her way, with a nice surprise?' And so on. But even the plausibles, if they *enjoy* a film, keep their demand for logic within limits.

2. Freudian 'pansexualists' may see the $40,000 as 'phallic' – Marion, having stolen Cassidy's patriarchal 'power', has become a phallic female, so there may be trouble ahead, with her virile though wobbly man.

3. The Phoenix street had Christmas decorations up, infuriating Mr Hitchcock, since his script had no Christmas references. However, Christmas, season of gifts, might be said to chime in with a theft–gift for Sam. Marion is Mother Christmas, bearing gifts. So maybe 'serendipity strikes again' – as often happens, once a text achieves a certain level of complexity. Strange, too, for many spectators, is oppressive heat at Christmas.

4. A scene in the script, deleted from the film, has Marion stop for petrol, but when the attendant answers a ringing telephone, she gets scared and drives off again. Is this fear rational or not? Hard to say, I'd say not very, but it's not irrational either. Rational/irrational – we-ell, you know …[15] As things are, the film suggests a more gradual descent into nervousness. Might her early fearfulness, under no real pressure, have lost her a little audience respect? Or was Hitchcock just shortening his film?

♦

SCENES 26–38 SATURDAY MORNING: A COP
INTERROGATES MARION

Lonely hills, low shadows; on a highway hard shoulder a car is parked, apparently abandoned. A Highway Patrolman draws up and finds Marion lying asleep on the front seat. Startled awake, she's confronted by his hard, unsmiling face, eyes hidden by black sunglasses. Her reflex action is to start her car, which he forbids. Her nervousness turns his routine enquiry to concern for her, until her light sarcasm provokes his irritation. He asks to see her licence, which she must dig out from right beside the stolen money. After noting her number-plate, he lets her drive on. But his car sticks behind her, until at last he swings away along a, briefly parallel, road.

PHASE 1: THE WASTE LAND

Here, for once, is an almost normal establishing shot. It's another 'landscape painting': *Desert Hills with Empty Automobile*. Beyond the car, dwarfing it, is a mass of dark hills, their shadows made turbulent by early morning sun; close to camera are a few spindly weeds. (Two more sorts of wilderness.) Though context leaves no doubt that it's Marion's car, we've never seen its exterior before, so there is a touch of, not 'mystery' exactly, but 'vagueness'. Coming after the 'sudden sleep' ellipsis, it prolongs a sort of 'blankness', through a different turn of style.

Still in long shot, the patrol car creeps up behind Marion's, passes it, stops, reverses, and stops again, close behind her. Pictorially, he has 'bracketed' – surrounded – her. The cars are like two insects, one creeping up on the other. To attack, or to mate?

PHASE 2: THE INTERROGATION

The cop is a fourfold threat.

1. Narrative-wise, it's vague and distant; he suspects no crime, and why should he find out?
2. But, as Hitchcock said, cops make even the innocent uneasy (normal paranoia aside, laws have become so complicated that you're *always* guilty of something, often through honest ignorance of some point of law, or some natural 'human error'). In the Arizona of 1959, is sleeping on a highway hard shoulder, miles from anywhere, legal? Uncertainty again.
3. In visual terms, this cop is a *heavy* threat – a burly, vigilant male, endowed with virility, authority and very likely mental brutality, for the round black glasses concentrate his impenetrable gaze. He's a centaur, or a sphinx. Of his uniform, more anon.
4. We've seen Marion *give herself away* to Lowery: will she give herself away to a cop, as focused as Lowery was vague?

Most dramatic conversations are *duels*, in one way or another. Marion's first reflex, jerked from sleep, is to start the car, thus putting herself in the wrong. He's stonily polite; and his tone implies reproach (a standard cop tactic, or maybe their 'second nature'). However, she acquits herself very well, justifying her actions (her explanation of her actions around the 'music/black-out' is another bout of 'retro-narration-after-ellipsis'). Now his enquiries, still stonily deadpan, imply *concern* for her: 'Is anything wrong?' The word 'wrong' bats back and forth between them. From him it means, 'Have you a problem, do you need help?' From her it means, 'I've broken no law, so mind your own business.' Unexpectedly, he says just 'Please', and she turns dismissive. Is she over-reacting, from nervous strain – as per her moral triumphalism about pills? From his point of view, it's rather sharp, since saying 'Please' cast aside his authority – perhaps to be sincerely nice, perhaps because he fancies her. Either way, her ingratitude irritates him so he takes her number, for no real reason except to reassert his authority, and perhaps because 'A little revenge is more human than no revenge' (Nietzsche). This trivial by-play will push her deeper into trouble. Her sin? His? Both their sins? No sin at all, just life's little ironies?

But a double disappointment is in store; one right away (he tails her), the other deferred (later in the film, he will reappear). After this relief, the renewed anxiety is worse, like in the French phrase, 'torture by hope' – a paradoxical plight, guaranteed to dement you.

As the cop interrogates Marion, the big question in our minds might be 'Will he stop her going on, and joining up with Sam?' I suspect it's rather 'Marion, you should *turn back*!' – as the tone of the film is so ominous, so pessimistic. Her whole project feels wrong. Now, she drives off; having defeated Sam, Cassidy and Lowery, she defeats The Law as well. (All for nothing, we later realise.)

THE LAW AS NECESSARY BULLY

Marion acts as if the cop had bullied her. She's not entirely wrong. A main function of The Law, in all its majesty, is to *frighten*, not just criminals, but also *potential* criminals, although they're still quite innocent. The duties of The Law include *deterrence*, that is to say *bullying the honest* into *remaining* honest. The Law (like the Lord, and the sphinx ...) is all about *fear*, and fear is good for you. That once seemed plain common sense: in Judaism, in Christianity, and in atheistic *realpolitik*, from Macchiavelli through Hobbes to Clausewitz and to Hitchcock, I have little doubt. (In *To Catch a Thief*, why is rich Grace Kelly so difficult, so spoiled? Because, says her mother, when you were a child, I didn't spank you enough. She's not in favour of child abuse; she reckons a degree of healthy fear, well-placed, is a necessary protection.) This by no means rules out a tragi-ironic awareness that The Law and sadism may go together – as with the English judge in *The Paradine Case* (1946). *Murder* (1930) is pessimistic about British juries (i.e. 'ordinary people', 'the little people who feed the birds'). So much for English justice, allegedly the best in the world. As for *Blackmail* – its perversion of justice is absolutely scandalous, *if* you follow the logic of the plot. Our hero, a Scotland Yard detective, saves his girl from due process of law, by bullying her blackmailer and having him hounded to his, conveniently accidental death. When his stressed-out girlfriend goes to Scotland Yard to tell the truth, she sets the whole audience screaming at her, 'Don't do it! Shut up! Keep schtum!' In the nick of time, the detective turns up and stops her confessing. Four years later, the Hays Code would have banned it outright. (Though Hitchcock, like Lubitsch, had the gift of moral slipperiness.) *Sabotage*, too, ends with The Law confused, thank God. Hitchcock's position, I think, is that we need The Law, to save us from our neighbours, and from ourselves, because they and we are very easily wicked, but also that The Law, even with good intentions, is sometimes an agent of Chaos (and so is everything else). In *Psycho*, too, The Law means well, yet has a perverse effect: the cop frightens Marion, but only so much that she *compounds* her crime. By failing to *deter*, The Law *aggravates* her crime. (That's a challenge for liberal penal theory.)

ALL THAT HEAVEN ALLOWS

God works in ways so mysterious that it's hard to know where providence begins and chaos leaves off. That may prove that there is no God, but then again, it may only prove that we rarely know what's really going on. (Just as Cary Grant has no idea in *North by Northwest* [1959]) Either way, 'Be afraid, be very afraid'. *Fear* is the key. (Fear, as distinct from guilt. They're different things, though the popular imagination routinely confuses the two, for whatever reasons.) You need The Law to bully you, but the good news is, you can bully people back … play them like an organ … remain aloof and in control … like the stony-faced presidents on Mount Rushmore. Meanwhile, prudence is all … moral prudence especially, as there *might* be Somebody Up There … who, though he probably likes you not at all, may, in his infinite mercy, let you hang on by your fingertips … like the saboteur from the Statue of Liberty … but he certainly won't, if you're down in his script as a villain …

THE SEXUALITY OF DETERRENCE

According to the script, the cop keeps on at Marion because he fancies her. (Nowadays, it might count as sexual harassment; dark glasses are ocular rape, etc., but then again, she'd be less anxious were she innocent.) In the film it's not clear that he fancies her, perhaps because of the pitch-black glasses. Not foreseen by Hitchcock, they were suggested, on set, by the actor. Perhaps they change the balance of friendliness and threat. Morally, he stands for *being honest*, as, at heart, I think she is (and as Lila certainly is); is he a *social* form of her *inner* self? Her inner voice in outer-directed form? From the 'woman's film' angle, his 'unstable mixture' of threat, virility, authority and vulnerable 'Please', altruistic and/or amorous, might be attractive (or is he not quite good-looking enough?). His uniform, glasses and the sense of high-way encounter might explain why, in 1960, I associated from this 'highway centaur' to an outlaw centaur, Brando in *The Wild One* (1955). In 1959, Brando's uniform-like rig-out still loomed large in movie legend, in images you remembered. By 1965 it loomed in gay iconography (*Scorpio Rising*) where it kept on going, e.g. *Cruising* (1980). In many films (*Electra Glide in Blue* [1973], *Strange Days* [1995]), cop patrols make a kind of poetic: The Law *as* brutality, The Law *as* disorder.[16]

A QUESTION OF CONTINUITY

The film gives the interrogation 35 shots; where the script gives it just six (for iden-tical dialogue and narrative). Script shot '27b' becomes 16 screen shots. Stefan Sharff analyses the shot sequence thus. The establishing shot lasts 22½ seconds (it's the longest by far), while the others vary between 1½ seconds (the cop's close-ups) and 11½ (Marion's). The shots fall into six successive groups. In Group A, shots 1–3, the cop approaches Marion. In Group B, shots 4–8 'alternate' their faces, giving each its own shot, though they're close together with only the window between. In Group C, shot 9 is an objective two-shot; showing the cop change his position, from just *aft* of Marion to *forward* of her. In D, shots 10–27 constitute another 'alternation', which is sustained through most of the conversation. Group E, shot 28 is another objective two-shot, and a climax of tension. In F, shots 29–35 cover the cop's moves to note Marion's front licence-plate, return her driving-licence, and walk away: she then starts the car. It's a 'mixed bunch' of shots (including a licence-plate shot).

The 'dramatic rationale' of this breakdown goes something like this. The opening shot is of long duration because it explains what went before and adds new infor-mation; it's geared to audience thinking-time; it also catches an 'early morning country timelessness'. As Sharff explains, the cop gets only brief close-ups, since his face presents a fairly simple threat; Marion's shots last four times longer than his because they show a 'nervous flow'. The cop's face comes *at* us, Marion's reactions *engross* us. The phases may correspond to dramatic 'paragraphs'. Group A establishes *physical location* as the *topic* of conversation. (*Topos* indeed!) Group B registers 'con-tact impact' between the 'duellists'. In Group C, shot 9, the cop 'blocks' Marion's 'premature' forward impulse.

Group D, shots 10–27, covers most of the conversation; mostly they're an 'alter-nation of opposite faces'. Often in Hitchcock this becomes a 'ping-pong' of close-ups: face A looks *right*, at approx 45°, face B looks left ditto, to and fro a bit monoto-nously. Here, the speeches are so short that left-right flip-flops might become more obtrusive than 'invisible editing' liked to be. A possible solution was the use of two-shots – these faces are inches apart. However, *alternating close-ups* add, not only their cutting dynamic, but a special 'intimacy of *connection*' between the faces. Each person having his own space, we 'sense' each in turn more exclusively, more strongly, than in two-shots shared with an adversary. This fuller 'awareness' (not necessarily identification) then *collides* with the other (hence a 'duelling dynamic'). In any case, the shortest distance between two points is a *cut* (for in a sense it's no distance at all!).[17] Thus, *separating* faces, formally, *collides* them psychologically! So, Hitchcock opts for 'alternation', and here he avoids monotony, by 'big, little differences' between the compositions. (The cop's *dark* face *fills* the window-frame; Marion's pale, very lightly shadowed face is a little further from camera, with a little space around her delicate neck and head. Sometimes the single window-frame 'cuts against itself' in adjacent shots. Marion looks up, or uncomfortably upwards and behind her; the cop is hunched down. As Michael O'Pray pointed out to me in conversation, their eye-lines meet at 'wrenched' angles.)

Shot 28, a striking two-shot, marks 'the point of maximum danger'. Marion, nearer the camera, keeps her back turned to the cop, hiding her handbag, should its contents spill out; her cramped arm dips awkwardly into the papers, slightly like a claw. It's a 'co-planar' shot, both characters facing the camera; as she looks downwards one way, the cop, further off, runs his gaze over the back seat (the wrong way). We can't see his eyes (and never do), but the movement of his head says a lot; his formidable gaze is shrewd yet idle. (There are several such 'co-planar' shots in the film, all quite striking – e.g. Marion looking in the unseen hotel mirror or at the envelope.) Moreover, Sharff points out, the camera-position has 'jumped' to the *other* side of the *entire* scene and of 'the action line'. In other words, it's a *true* reverse angle – unlike most cuts between 'alternating POVs', which keep to the same side of the line. (The *true* reverse works like a mirror: it reverses the scene's left and right, whence many confusions, compounded by other problems, which mirrors don't introduce, though they cause their own confusions.) Graphically, it's a quietly tense event.

The cop having shifted from slightly *aft* of Marion to *alongside* her, Group E 'continues' his forward movement, to the front of her car (to note its number); this makes a *second* 'peak' of tension. He stalks off without a word.

THE SMALL PRINT

A close-up shows Marion's number-plate; it reads 'Arizona 59, ANL 705, Grand Canyon State'. A-N-L, some critics believe, spells 'anal'. It's possible. By 1959, Freudian ideas of oral, anal and genital stages in child (and adult) sexuality were just entering 'general educated knowledge' in America (in England, this happened about ten years later). *But*, A-N-L is just as likely a random series, like 7-0-5, which no one ever offers to decode. *But*, Hitchcock was famous for practical jokes, and why not play a joke on Freudian decoders (and all those educated idiots who feel compelled to interpret every scrap of print they see)? Marion shows none of the anal characteristics listed in Freudian catalogues, so the 'anal' tag on her car tells us nothing at all. So perhaps it's an 'empty' signifier. *But* perhaps its 'meaning' is, the 'frustrating tease' into which it lures you. *But* 'anal' hints at something quite nasty – and something which Freudian theory *would* think deeply 'anal' *will* indeed happen to Marion. So perhaps it's an ominous presage, that soon 'her number will come up'. As for 'Grand Canyon State', a colleague insists that a canyon is a *split*, and that Freudian dream interpretation might very well treat 'Grand Canyon State' as unconscious awareness of a 'Seriously Split Mind' (Marion's 'impulsion', and, of course, Norman's). So – OK Hitch, you win, I'm teased …

PHASE 3: ON THE ROAD AGAIN

Released, but tailed, by the cop, Marion is often seen in 'front windshield' shots, as the day before. But now they're much looser. The rear window view is very conspicuous, partly because it shows the police car, still a source of anxiety, and partly also because it is itself an ever-changing vignette: in it the road flows ever backwards, winding, twisting, sloping, amidst whitish-grey grassland, studded with thin, dry, faintly skeletal forms (telegraph poles and metal-staked wire fences). The cop car appears in slightly shifted positions (*little* shifts being edgier than *decisive* ones) behind her – and sometimes in the rearview mirror in front of her. (One shot of the mirror *and* the window *behind* and *around* the window, so the road moves in different directions, is even stranger than that sounds – it's almost too short to notice, which is just as well, as your eyes have to glaze over, if they stray away to the surround – I suspect Hitchcock loved it.)

In a mirror shot, a third car appears alongside the police car, apparently overtaking it. This leads to a certain suspense: why does the cop stay back behind her? A moment later, the police car moves into that position, and also starts to overtake. (Normal continuity prescribes that the first car complete its overtake, to avoid confusion with the second, which, as things are, suddenly replaces it in its position, and risks confusion with it. But later on there'll be another intrusion, at the car dealer's, which rather suggests a pattern.) When, at last, the cop car leaves Marion's horizon, it's by overtaking, i.e. by *first coming up closer*, before speeding along a roughly parallel road, which then slopes gently upwards. It gradually pulls ahead and up, exiting left while the camera stays with Marion. After this visual climax (*two* speeding cars, in parallel, pulling apart), Marion's car slows to a crawl, past messy-looking commercial lots, and makes a leisurely right.

CONTINUITY AT A DISTANCE

Continuity craftsmen (and continuity pedants) will admire the fine detail of this separation. Seen by a camera looking back at it, the cop car swings off, screen left. Seen by a camera going along with it, Marion's car swings off, screen right. The opposite directions express their separation. But, as pedants will note, in *real space*, both new roads are going in the same general direction. And the two cars will meet again, on the road outside the car dealer's, the cop arriving a few minutes after Marion. How can it be, that *the same direction* in 'real' space appears as *opposite directions* on the screen? It's because the cameras with the cars have *turned around*: one looks *back*, within the line of travel, the other looks *forward*. So, the camera has 'turned around' in space. So, left and right must reverse as well. Just as, when *we* turn around in space, what was on our left is now on our right, and vice versa. A mirror-reverse is just the same. When you look in a mirror, you're facing your own image; the image is you, turned around in space. Mirrors reverse left and right, just as we do every time we turn about. Yet, the *reverse-angle* discombobulates perceptions, boggles minds, generates a certain 'poetic', fascinates film directors, bedevils film continuity and commands film syntax and 'grammar'. (Linguistic structures know nothing remotely like it.)

Further refinements:

1. Marion jerking up from the driving seat may remind us of her jerking up from the bed.
2. The two roads look like *a new highway* and a *more local road* – thus anticipating Norman's point, about an old and a new highway.
3. The cop reproaches Marion for not finding a safe motel. She'll find a safe motel all right.

♦

SCENES 39–51 MARION TRADES HER CAR

Marion turns into a used-car dealer's, California Charlie's. While waiting, she strolls along a line of cars with California registrations, buys a Los Angeles newspaper from a vending frame and doesn't see, although we do, a patrol car stop outside the lot and that same patrolman emerge and stand there, looking in her direction. The dealer suggests she relax and take her time to make her choice, but her nervous haste prompts his wry comment, 'First time I ever saw a customer high-pressure the salesman!' When she accepts his first, low price (her car plus $700), he's taken aback. When at last she sees the watching cop, he follows her glance and gets rattled; but as her papers are all in order, he hurriedly closes the deal. To count out her money, she retires to the ladies' room. The patrol car drives right into the lot; re-emerging, the cop saunters towards Marion, as she starts her new car hurriedly, only to be halted by a shout from behind. A mechanic brings up her suitcase and coat, forgotten on her previous car's back seat. Still panicky, she jolts off into the road, leaving three men staring after her.

PSYCHO AGAINST FORMULA

Hitchcock was famously unfaithful to his literary sources and might easily have reshaped Marion's story around his favourite narrative form: basically, the hero chases a MacGuffin as crooks *and* cops chase him. He's both hunter *and* hunted. There's a three-way pursuit (by our hero, by the police and by the forces of chaos). Maybe Marion's story *is* a variation on that theme. She hunts Sam, she brings him the MacGuffin (the cash), she only imagines pursuit by The Law and those who should pursue don't (until after she's dead). Instead of a chase, her long drive is an introverted limbo. The men she meets are just 'echo-chambers' of her fears. She thinks about Sam only once, very briefly, and thereafter hears only the wrath of her victims. Though she keeps driving forward, she keeps thinking back. Her journey is less quest than flight, less hope than fear. Hence, I think, it's more a 'she should turn back' story, than a 'will she reach Sam?' story.

CLOSING THE DEAL

California Charlie's long, twisty-serious face suggests WASP or Scandinavian farming stock. His well-oiled spiel is folksy-tricksy. It starts, 'I'm in no mood for trouble' (a deadpan joke that jolts Marion), and flatters female willpower. In his salesmanlike way, he urges her to relax, take her time, yet his fast patter bustles her along. But she's so anxious, she hurries him along, until he protests,' First time I ever saw a customer high-pressure the salesman!' They've switched roles. The easier the sale, the more worried he gets. Finally their minds meet – in mutual hostility.'I must get out of here!' – 'I must get her out of here!'

THE LONG LOOK OF THE LAW

We see the patrolman long before Marion does and his reappearance inspires anxiety in us, directly. (It's a sign of our sympathetic concern for her, akin to identification; we react *as if* we were her; we don't need to be prompted by seeing her reaction – to which few but the Hollywood masters [William Wyler perhaps] would *prefer* the more 'distanced' relation.) Shocked, we wonder: 'Has he been following her?' (even though we saw him turn off first). As the scene goes on, our fear modulates to: 'Even if it's just blind chance, and even though she won their last encounter, he's still dangerous'. Worse yet: *merely by reappearing*, is he … Blind Fate?

His behaviour is slightly anomalous; he stands there, for a while, beside his car, out there on the street. Visually, it's a very 'distantly assertive' position. (I doubt that even 'plausibles' would wonder why he doesn't just drive into the garage, though perhaps Marion's old car blocked the 'IN' lane for a while.) We never find out if he has even seen her, or just likes resting his eyes upon her, from a polite distance, or is only looking out for signs of her impending departure, so that he can drive in. His look is not a 'male gaze', it's a *legal* gaze – the eye of The Law. He's inexpressive, silent and does absolutely nothing. One can't even say that just by being there he makes Marion too nervous to negotiate a decent price, since she's nervous enough already. Yet he registers as Marion's main antagonist. His dark glasses reflect back her fears. He's her mirror without a face.

FEARFUL SYMMETRIES

The salesman and the cop make an 'opposite pair', a bit like 'the good cop and the bad cop'. The salesman seems to say, 'I must and will oblige you'; the cop asserts punishment. The salesman is quick, talkative, testy-affable, wily-snaky and rich in local colour; the cop is burly, slow, silent. The salesman's moral culture is dishonestly folksy capitalism (like Lowery's and Cassidy's); the cop's is The Law (whose 'good neighbourliness' Marion rejected). The salesman tries (at first) to hold her back, the cop (who *had* tried to hold her back) now sharpens her nervous hurry. They're 'opposite' characters – like Laurel and Hardy – and so they exactly correspond to what Eisenstein meant by a 'montage of attractions' – and yet they combine to worsen Marion's state of mind. Here is a 'collusion between opposites' – a favourite device in non-naïve kinds of drama; it's easily ironic, it frustrates schoolmarm moralism and it apprehends the complexity of real-life interactions.[18]

HITCHCOCK'S UNCERTAINTY PRINCIPLE (3)

In an 'action story', Marion's *three* getaways from the cop would give her and us relief and confidence. Yet her third escape is very ominous, for the film's mood responds instead to her mental lapse – the 'inner story', in two senses. One, her inner psychology, and, two, the story theme: *mental absences*/madness. The second sense is the more important, however, for though Marion's state of mind, and mood, is most lyrically conveyed, much of her psychology is left out. Through the last scene, she kept her nerve (just), and was nervously cocky enough to reject the cop's friendliness. Yet, as this scene *starts*, she's *already* too nervous to haggle with the salesman. *Between* the two encounters her confidence has ebbed, almost disappeared. The disappearance is unnoticed by us, as she drives on (and, perhaps, unnoticed by her). Here's another ellipsis, retrospectively revealed. The first ellipsis was signalled by 'pure cinema' (the very fancy optical). This one isn't signalled at all; her drive from there to here reads as continuity.

Some other points are only vaguely construable, when an 'action story' would make them the main emphasis. Hitchcock's Uncertainty Principle leads him to blur, or soft-pedal, the clear succession of story-points so common in 'action narrative'.

1. How *clear* is it that, *because* the cop took careful note of her old car, she's buying this new one – but that the whole transaction *may well* be futile, since the cop *may well* remember the new car *and* the trade?

2. How *clear* is it that she goes to the ladies' room because there neither cop nor dealer can see the great wad of money that would ensure they remembered every detail about her?

3. How *clear* is it that she's just crossed a state line – by tradition, a symbolic act (for reasons of legal jurisdiction), with which Hitchcock slyly plays (the name 'California Charlie', the line of cars with California number-plates (shown in close-up, not for anality reasons) and Marion buying an LA paper. Eventually, we get confirmation that she's *over* the line, not just *near* it: the harassed dealer mutters, 'Out-of-state number-plate and all.'

4. Marion's purchase of an LA paper gives us a prettily filmed *temps mort*, but is it another 'little' anomaly? She turns to an inside page – looking for news of her crime, perhaps? (This implication would be much stronger had Hitch retained the earlier scene, when she flees a gas station because its telephone starts ringing.) But isn't it too soon for news of her crime, in this paper from another state?

5. The male 'trinity' which stares after her is neatly disparate – The Law, a folksy trickster and a bestubbled, virile mechanic.

ABSENT-MINDED

In the office, briskly efficient Marion mixed a metaphor – so what, never mind. But face to face with the salesman, she can't haggle (her nerve has gone), and now she forgets her belongings – is her mind falling apart? What she forgets is not her hand-bag with the money (an *extremely* alarming plot possibility, which Hitchcock very likely pondered, before deciding on the subtler mishap), but her case and her coat (emblems of her respectability with Sam?). You don't have to be a Freudian to wonder if forgetting them means she's beginning to forget what she wanted the money *for* (obsessed with the *means*, she's forgetting the *end* … as easily happens, with money and power).

Some narratives look like 'a chain of events', with each action prompting the next, in a manner akin to 'cause and effect', of a loose kind at least. Marion's 30-minute story is nothing like this. The cop and the dealer make no difference to the plot at all. Eventually the storm will drive her off the right road, onto the old, deserted high-way and so to the Bates Motel. The cop and the dealer are there to describe Marion's state of mind. Their form is narrative, but their function is descriptive (not analytical, but lyrical – that is to say, synthetic).

Psycho upfronts, not 'chains of causality' but 'the web of uncertainty'. The drama is not set out in 'clear alternatives'; with 'the right thing' versus 'the wrong thing', and 'the wrong thing' leading to a 'consequence'. There *is* a feeling of impending or poten-tial doom, but it's not 'consequentialist'. It's 'indeterminist', in the sense that Chaos Theory is indeterminist. That is to say, cause and effect no doubt exist, but the struc-tures and outcomes are unknowable by anyone less omniscient than God. Every effect has so many causes, direct and indirect, most of them necessary but insuffi-cient, etc., that what we find useful to isolate as cause is a purely pragmatic selection. Indeterminism can be as fatalistic as determinism, in ascribing a certain helplessness to man. Hitchcock's 'indeterminist fatalism' is very different from, say, Fritz Lang's. Fate in Lang is grimly inexorable, it's a complex trap closing slowly: Hitchcock's jokey humour, his hopes in defensive order, his Jesuit streak, allow a sort of *inconsequen-tiality* – and even allow a merciful providence – as in *The Wrong Man*.

The first half of *Psycho* is really a 'lyrical drama of uncertainty', a description of a mood, of deteriorating morale. It's a mood painting, in cinematic form, with a few symbolic figures, who do little more than touch off mood-change in Marion herself. The cop and the salesman could be taken out entirely, for Marion might, and in Bloch she practically does, drive from Phoenix to Norman and encounter nobody at all. Her drive is built, less from plot, than from *Stimmung*, and less from narrative, than from narration (the control of information, e.g. retrospective detail after ellipsis). Marion's story is a very 'perverse' construction – wrong for most stories, right for this. That is to say, it's an exceptionally well-constructed film: it disregards the formulae, every last detail is custom-made.

THE LADY IS A NERD?

Leigh's charisma, and Marion's businesslike *persona* forestall a potential problem. The Hollywood wisdom says that by and large audiences prefer heroes who are 'wish-fulfilment' improvements on themselves, 'superior' to themselves, not in all, but in certain ways, such as *energy*, *beauty*, *poise*, *presence*, *confidence*, *audacity*, *style*. Faced with Marion's great nervousness, might many spectators lose interest in her – and therefore in the film? *Psycho* follows a cluster of Hollywood experiments with 'inferior' – ordinary, ugly, weak, nervy, – heroes. The best-remembered is the Oscar-winning *Marty*. Significantly, its producers intended to combine a labour of love, and a prestige picture, with a convenient tax loss, though in the end its Oscars put it in profit. *The Night Holds Terror* (also 1955), an essay in 'realistic suspense melodrama', was a surprise success. In Hitchcock's *The Wrong Man*, Chayefsky-type realism met Bresson prayerfulness – and did a box-office nosedive. Its hero (Henry Fonda) and his wife (Vera Miles) were too sad, passive, unhappy – too crushed, for too long. It got the balance wrong, between wish-fulfilment 'superiority' and identifiable-with weakness. Marion's story gets it right. The balance is always precarious.

As a 'petty-bourgeois' tragedy of status and morale, *Psycho* belongs with Murnau's silent classic, *The Last Laugh* (1924). Murnau's old doorman cracks up the moment he loses his uniform; Marion starts cracking up the moment she turns dishonest (perhaps *because* she's a basically honest person). In both stories the follies, sins and crimes of the protagonists intensify audience sympathy; we hope things will go well for them.

A DIGRESSION ON HUMAN ERROR

Chabrol and Rohmer popularised, or perhaps invented, the idea that, in Hitchcock, the suspense the hero gets into represents punishment or purgation for sins that are minor versions of the villain's. *Apparently* minor – but just as deadly to the soul. *North by Northwest* is Cary Grant on a 'Pilgrim's Progress'. Sometimes, indeed, the suspense is *punishment for the audience*. The thrills and spills of *Rear Window* give us the punishment we richly deserve for coming to the cinema. Hitchcock speaks of suspense as roller-coaster fun; for his earnest young admirers, then deeply interested in

Catholicism, roller-coasters are really punishment apparatus, except when they're cream separators (separating our hero's virtues from his vices). Moral severity was a Paris fashion in those days. On the left, J.-P. Sartre proposed 'commitment' to Communism as the only alternative to nihilistic noir or bourgeois 'bad faith'. On the thoughtful centre-right, the new wave cohort of *Cahiers du Cinéma* applied *auteur* theory to Hollywood, thus challenging the dominant leftism, and reasserting an apolitical aestheticism and individualism. Hitchcock's films lent themselves very well to traditional, conservative moralising – worldly, ironic, not naïve, and yet severe and principled. For example, in *I Confess*, the priest, bound by the rules of the confessional, keeps silent about the murderer, thus incurring a lesser (but sufficient) degree of legal guilt and/or sin, and in *Strangers on a Train* (1951) the tennis player's weak reaction to the playboy's 'murder bargain' makes him 'complicit' with his wife's murderer. Agree or disagree, they're fascinating ideas.

Fashionable in the 'literary Catholicism' which Chabrol and Rohmer knew well was Jansenism, a movement which, though eventually deemed heretical, represents a recurrent tendency within it. The gloomy ideas of its intellectual champion, Pascal, are lengthily discussed, between two Catholics and a Communist, in Rohmer's *Ma nuit chez Maud* (1968). Tireless antagonists of the Jansenists were Hitchcock's mentors, the Jesuits – Buñuel's *The Milky Way* (1968) depicts the intellectual duelling between aristocratic supporters of the two factions. Jansenism, like its 'Bible Belt' cousin, Calvinism, stressed the 'total depravity' of human nature: a tiny sin can damn your soul for ever, just as 'a man can drown in two inches of water'. The Jesuits were relatively lenient: they invented the idea that not all pagans and savages are damned, and that 'invincible ignorance' of the faith might get you out of Hell and into purgatory, and that although Hell must exist, maybe there's nobody in it. They had a little more patience with worldly mediocrity, a little more hope in the 'rational will', in habits of careful moral analysis, in thoughtful self-examination. The rigorous analysis of individual cases became that Jesuit specialty, 'casuistry'. As it often justified, or went easier on, what the (Calvinist) Puritans condemned, the word often connotes 'logical hair-splitting in defence of sin'.

Although more lenient in their theories than some of their fellow-Christians, the Jesuits shared the, then usual pessimism among Christians about human nature in itself. This isn't so far from most versions of Freud, whereby everybody's Unconscious has committed all the sins that flesh is heir to – oral, anal, genital, incestuous, parricidal, matricidal, suicidal, you name it, and they're all simmering away down in the libido, which leads the rational will by the nose. As Hitchcock once said, 'A beautiful woman is a force for evil.' She may not be evil in herself, but male sexual desire is, and she can't help provoking it. She's the innocent cause of evil in others. Even today many Christians, Muslims and feminists think like this. In Hitchcock's day, Jesuit education thought guilt and fear necessary motivations to piety; Hitchcock ruefully recalled the brutality of his school-day punishments.

Maybe Hitchcock's religious education straddled a four-way split. His parentage was partly Irish, and Irish Catholicism was harsher and more puritanical than English Catholicism – in some ways, indeed, more puritanical than most English Puritanism. Where 'London Irish' had the reputation for ferocity and roughness, Hitchcock's lower middle-class parents applied that ferocity to their *respectability*. Doesn't having a child locked in a police cell for hours count as 'cruel and unusual punishment'? Around them, lower middle-class English piety was more restrained, fearful and dif-ferently destructive. Orwell thought lower middle-class homes were 'cells of fear', which is exaggerated – many were smugly contented, and many were happy – but it points to something in Hitchcock, which he renders exactly in the politically sub-versive households of *Sabotage*. Hitchcock's family were poulterers (hence birds?) and greengrocers (hence *Frenzy* [1971]?) and dealt with East End market traders – a shockingly foul-mouthed class (the phrase 'Billingsgate language', which refers to a London fish market, means gale-force-10 obscenity). Some contradictions in Hitchcock's behaviour – a sort of aloof respectability, a delight in shocking people – may be as sociological as sexual. As a child, he obsessively studied foreign maps and timetables, meticulously planning imaginary journeys, which he didn't yearn to actu-ally make. It sounds as if he was often left alone, perhaps through long gloomy Sundays, such as pious English homes observed, thinking of escape, as, not 'happiness' (like Sam's sloppy island), but as a sort of limbo, a moving limbo, a state of pure movement (like pure film), in no particular world. Many of his films are long, ram-bling journeys that go astray; mostly, the itineraries are thriller-jokey-picaresque, though *Rich and Strange* (1932) is bitterly ironic; and *Psycho* is the most inward.

THE BIG PICTURE

Marion moves through a messy series of messy spaces: a brick office, frilly pennants, a line of licence-plates, a narrow alley with long-shadowed people, a corner with a mirror in a ladies' room. *Crooked* spaces, might one say? The mirror, far from *enlarg-ing* the ladies' room, cramps it further, by inserting a second Marion, awkwardly joined to the first, like the Siamese twins in *Saboteur* (1942). Their two right arms, not quite joined, are prominent. Marion and Mirror Marion are at different angles to the camera: Mirror Marion seems more papers/bosom/arm than face. As Marion counts the money, with cashier-like expertise, her left index finger flicks in and out between the bills, like a woodpecker. She folds the newspaper in her bag in such a way that from now on, it shows the ironic word 'OK'.

As Marion wanders through the messy labyrinth the cop's look, and his car, cut straight across it. He's always in long shots, but visually dominates them (being carefully surrounded by spaces; and though cars pass to and fro behind him and the camera, they only make his steady presence stronger). He arrives *twice*, and in opposite directions. First he noses in from screen left (on the *near* side of the mid-screen road). Having stopped and shown himself (mounting suspense), he drives off again (to our great relief), in the same direction, screen right – with just a hint of going into an off-screen turn. He then re-enters screen right (on the *further* side of the road, but *further* goes with *more* dramatic). Marion hasn't seen him yet; it's *we* who suffer first relief and then disappointment – the 'torture by hope' pattern. Later, his automobile lumbers heavily towards us: it's not just a *shape*, it's a dark glinting *mass*. Still trundling towards us, it slides off-screen right – it *exits towards us*.

Now Hitchcock cuts to a 'panorama' shot – a more-or-less reverse-angle shot, looking *from* the road into the lot, downwards over the top of an empty car, which is big in the foreground. Beyond the lot, a white fence runs across the screen; and an empty space beyond that – it's 'activated', laterally, by extras strolling back and forth (it roughly 'mirrors' a space beyond the cop in the previous shot). The cop's car slides in from screen left (a reverse-angle match with its exit screen right) and parks at an angle between lanes and fence. The cop emerges and starts walking (not hurriedly, but still worryingly, for cops sometimes move unhurriedly on purpose), towards the right, where Marion would be; and promptly Marion and the dealer walk on screen right, no doubt making for the empty car nearest the camera. Is the cop coming for Marion? Will he see her? His gaze shifts idly away from her as a *third* car hurtles in from screen left, passing between his car and the fence, and rounding sharply in behind the other. Meanwhile Marion, stepping quickly 'down screen', slides sideways into the empty car's driving seat, and jerks away in panic. The camera executes what looks to me like a simultaneous crane, tilt and pan leftwards and downwards, till it's roughly eye-level to her side-window, with her profile in medium shot, as an off-screen shout jolts her to a stop. Cut to a further, wider view: Marion peers out and back, she's at the intersection of two looks, one from the cop mid-ground left, the other from the dealer mid-ground right. It's a 'triangulation', such as Bazin admired in *Citizen Kane*, but much deeper (1960s cameras enjoyed much deeper focus) and much tighter (the triangle is squeezed into the right two-thirds of a crowded screen picture). This 'acute' geometry is no sooner set out than it's broken up by the third car, from which a mechanic emerges, behind the salesman, and hurries forward with Marion's forgotten belongings (so his car was Marion's old one). Shaken by her forgetfulness, which ensures all three men notice her, she speeds off, leaving them in line abreast, at a loss, but alerted to her.

Just as the cop might have seen Marion, his gaze is pulled 'the wrong way' (again!), just as an anonymous car appeared (again!), almost as if to bump Marion's car out and away. The human figures, their movements, their turning looks, are very precisely 'sited', like moving architectural units. It's a tensely organised space-and-motion nexus. Long sight-lines stretch across this wide vista (which contrasts with the messy little spaces through which Marion has been moving). The three cars are 'moving architectures' – *kinetic* architecture, as it were (their overall movement is a U-turn). 'Architecture is frozen music' (Schelling, 1809); film is 'unfrozen architecture', as this sequence demonstrates. Like the credit sequence, it's 'visual music' – played on different 'instruments' – the credits played it on abstract/concrete shapes, this sequence plays on narrative/pictorial ones. One might almost compare the cars to long chords by the brass, mixed in with lighter 'masses' and smaller 'shapes'. Avant-garde composer Cornelius Cardew liked ending lectures by getting his audience to 'play' on kazoos some handy visual space – for instance, a wall with a line of windows – and what's amazing was that we spectators-turned-scratch-orchestra would respond to the architectural details with almost synchronous, semi-analogous notes and sounds. Architectural 'events', musical 'events'.

It's the *pictorial* events that make this scene so *heavy*, dramatically. The visual events give to Marion's dread visual tension, weight and momentum – though only because the characters are strongly positioned, strongly acted, in a 'big picture' strikingly removed from Marion's POV. All too often 'big architecture' *dwarfs* a film's characters; makes them small, remote and cold: hence 'big architecture' scenes slide with notorious ease into academicism.

The actual outcome of this scene isn't all that important (she loses money on the deal), and even the visually big climax has an unclear consequence (*should* one of these men hear of Marion's crime, he could describe her new car). Its real 'kick' is, that the 'big' outward scene conveys the enormity of Marion's distraction, about her mental lapse. (Which, again, is much less serious than it might have been: supposing she'd forgotten, not her coat and case, but the handbag with the big money.) Oddly enough, Antonioni, almost simultaneously, was finding new ways to relate 'architectural' long shots, mental states, micro-events and uncertainties. (Or not so oddly: for broad cultural changes can easily affect quite disparate minds.[19] The new developments revealed that Hitchcock and Antonioni, seemingly poles apart, had more in common than you'd expect, in how their minds linked with their eyes.)

HITCHCOCK'S GRAND STRATEGEM – WHEN LESS IS MORE

As the first-time spectator noticed, 'Well, it's all right, but there's not very much happening.' As Hitchcock put it, he redoubled the shower shock, by 'boring them first'. 'Boring', of course, is an ironic word, like 'torturing' the audience (for thrills, spills and chills are pleasure). A fine psychoanalysis of the *healthy* delights in danger is Michael Balint's *Thrills and Regressions* (1959). Better than 'boring' is 'lulling' or 'hypnotising' (an effect often attributed to cinema). Better still would be 'engrossing', as the big picture palace screen, all in darkness, commands our full attention. (Attention, as distinct from 'illusion' or 'belief' – whatever they may be – do we believe in King Kong? – well, enough, but, no. Maybe *most* beliefs are *half*-beliefs ... working assumptions, context-limited, just pro tem and strictly ad hoc.) *Psycho*'s narrative minimalism, its 'little things', helps make us *sensitive*; and, then, out comes the razor. That's Buñuel's strategy in the opening shots of *Un Chien andalou* (1928), a passionate moon precedes the slicing of an eye. As Georges Franju put it: 'Some directors try to knock the spectator's head off. That's not right. You should *twist* it off.' Twisting is softer, gentler, it goes the long way around; a strangulation can start like a caress.

HITCHCOCK'S UNCERTAINTY PRINCIPLE (4) – SUSPENSE VERSUS SURPRISE

Hitchcock often expounded his theory that suspense was far superior to surprise. Consider a bomb exploding under a restaurant table. If no one, not even the audience, knows it's there, the explosion is a big surprise, but over in a moment. But if you first show the audience the ticking bomb, and intercut it with the diners chatting away, the suspense lasts, and builds (and you can still insert some surprise: who's killed, who isn't, and so on). And yet, Hitch repeatedly declared, that his *only* reason for making *Psycho* was the sheer *surprise* of the shower murder. To break his own rule, he made the necessary adjustments. First, he pre-mobilises your dread, by Marion's nervousness, working on 'minimal' threats, which are magnified by lyrical *Stimmung*. It's suspense all right, building up to the surprise. But, the *terms* of the suspense leave us unprepared for the nature and severity of the surprise. But once spectators have been surprised, in defiance of every Hollywood rule, convention and protocol, they'll be in continuous fear, in continuous *suspense* – and so a certain 'min-

imalism' can resume. (In some film theories, *auteur*-ship is *repetition* of themes, attitudes, 'messages' and stylistics. But many artists *like* breaking their own rules (or
habits and think the differences between films more interesting than the similarities.)

A NOTE ON THEORY OF SUSPENSE: OPTIMISM STRIKES AGAIN

Suspense, of course, is fear with a thread of hope. In most Hollywood suspense, optimism acknowledges tragedy (of a sort), only to then negate it. But the darkly ominous suspense of Marion's journey establishes the possibility of deep unhappiness.
The sheer *surprise* of the shower scene shatters optimism entirely — and if 1960
American audiences became hysterically bewildered, it was not only on account of
shock sex-and-violence, but the shattering of a moral-philosophical co-ordinate.
(English culture is less ardently optimistic, and English audiences didn't become hysterical.) *Psycho* takes its place in the thin brave line of Hollywood movies which, one
way or another, challenged that optimism. (Most films with 'unhappy endings' didn't;
their conclusions were worthwhile, or redemptive, or punitive, or sacrificial, or soap-
weepie, or heroic. Between 1930 and 1960, very few movies, even when culturally
critical, had a true tragic tone (pain plus subverted values plus stoic — or no — consolation).[20] Marion's story is one; others include *The Ox-Bow Incident/Strange Incident*
(1943), Wyler's *Carrie* (1952) and, perhaps, Wilder's *Double Indemnity* (1943, even
though it's punitive).

TELLING DETAILS

Magic Mirror Lore. The camera looks downward to Marion standing beside the
mirror. Her face and her reflection both look the same way, which may seem odd,
since our usual idea about mirrors is that they always reverse left and right.
Explanation: this mirror reflects the *other* side of her face; it gives us the *reverse angle*,
i.e. the profile hidden from us. (In other words: when our two profiles are seen sideways-on, each from its own side, as from true reverse angles, one of our profiles
looks left, and the other profile looks right. But here, the mirror reverses the reverse,
so, both her profiles look in the same direction; and since her countenance is pleas-
ingly symmetrical, her 'opposite' profile looks like this profile twice.) Another oddity
in mirrors, often overlooked, is conspicuous here: mirrors reflect scenes back to
front. In the *real* Marion, her right arm, the busiest one, is closest to the camera; in
mirror Marion, it's furthest from the camera. I can't think of any symbolism, about
splits, doubles, doppelgängers: on the contrary, it's strangely beautiful, even though
context makes it quietly uneasy.

The theory that Sam and Norman are 'lookalikes' gets a boost here. The mechanic in overalls makes a third; he too is tall, dark, handsome, helpful, sexually appreciative. That strange overtaking edit has a sequel here – another unexpected, anonymous car lurches in between the cop's and Marion's. This time, though, it's visually 'big', and its precision deployment must have complicated an already elaborate scene.

As Janet Leigh points out, Marion first wears white underwear, and then, after her crime, black; it's like going from good to evil. Let's try a riff on that: If a woman's underwear is her sexual mood, Marion, on a bed with her lover, is still *good* Marion – if only because she's still got the willpower to get up off it. Her sexual thoughts only turn noir once her marital instincts make her dishonest. However, the envelope, emblem of sin, glares white. Is that what evil does – *confuses* all moral signs, as your mental polarities reverse? Neither white nor black, the grey coverlet, the greyish dress, are – a grey life, not wicked, but only negatively good – morally empty. When Marion changes her car, it's *conversely* from her underwear: her first car is black, she trades it in for a white one. (The cinematic reason is, of course, that since a night swamp will be black, the car it engulfs should be white.) Meanwhile, the police car is black *and* white. Pure coincidence, very likely. But sometimes, with artists, there's sly design, or serendipity. So, if only for the heck of it, let's try glossing it: 'The Law exists because we're *all* part-good, part-wicked; and so, of course, is The Law itself. Cops, judges, juries, they're all a mixed lot … Justice is usually imperfect, The Law is one big moral irony – but that's better than nihilism and chaos.' If Hitch is morally conservative, with law and order a *sine qua non*, it's because he understands what noir unchecked can lead to. His conservatism isn't 'idealism versus anarchism'; it's prudent fear versus chaos. Marion personifies Hitchcock's fears, of – anybody, everybody. Fear of *the others* is a basis of 'common sense', and philosophically respectable (Sartre: 'Hell is other people'). Whether or not such rigorous fear is wise, it's logically rigorous, and it's how much of the Unconscious works.[21]

◆

SCENES 52–87 MARION DRIVES ON, ARRIVING AT THE BATES MOTEL

Having resumed her long drive, Marion imagines various voices talking about her. Late afternoon: patrolman and salesman discuss her suspiciously. Late afternoon:

next Monday, in his office, Lowery asks Caroline if Marion has come in yet. At dusk: Lowery instructs Caroline to contact Marion's sister. Caroline answers that she has already spoken to the sister, who promised to check Marion's apartment. Night: on the phone to Marion's sister, Lowery suddenly remembers his last sight of Marion, and worriedly tells Caroline to phone Cassidy. Night with oncoming headlights: Cassidy is irate, Lowery tries to calm him. Night with glaring headlights: Cassidy rages impotently, Marion smiles meanly. Rain stipples her windscreen, then floods down. Marion can't see clearly and steers round a gentle descent in darkness until a lonely, neon sign rearing up ahead proclaims, 'Bates Motel. Vacancy'. She glides along a line of cabins to the motel office.

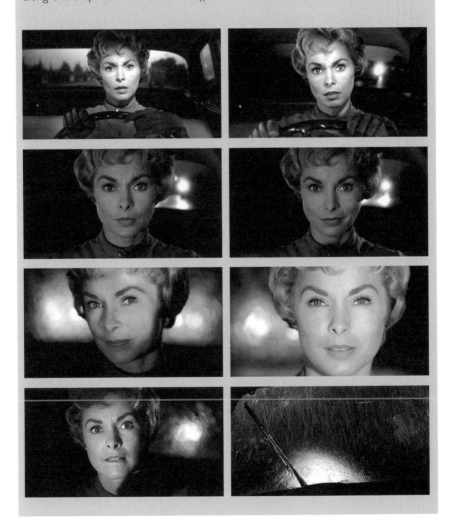

MARION'S MORAL DRIFT

Marion's drive evokes a mythic form, the 'moral journey': some original sin triggers a time of spiritual drift (unlike a quest or pilgrimage). Two famous examples are Coleridge's *The Rime of the Ancient Mariner* and *The Red Shoes* ballet sequence. In Powell and Pressburger's 1948 film, a woman plunges downwards through space, and traverses spectral landscapes; in Coleridge's poem, a sailor is lost on a strangely controlled ship.

WHEN THE DEVIL DRIVES

The sequence modulates through four 'visual movements': a 'solo face', a 'duet with storm', 'the slippery slope', 'eerie quietness'. First the close-up camera is locked on Marion's tense full face, responding to inner voices; then, as if at her sly smile, external forces take command (the oncoming headlights lance at her eyes, rain blurs her view). Then her car quietly glides downwards round a winding road, and then she drives alone as if in a ghost town.

Marion's 'impulsion' resists the voices within, and defies the storm ahead. The previous night, she drove until sleep stunned her; tonight, nothing stops her, and, confused, she takes the road to Death. Is the storm some kind of spiritual force: The wrath of God? The wrath of her moral Unconscious (the Superego)? Or is providence telling her to stop and think (cop and salesman having failed, providence tries force)? Or is chaos playing its treacherous role? Alas, neither the gods above, nor the Unconscious below, speak clearly – and if they did, would we listen, and if we listen, why trust them? On a more earthly plane of irony, Marion, in sunny California, hits a flash flood.

TOUCH OF EVIL

The 'voices' shots recap the earlier sets of full-face close shots of Marion at the wheel (with 'wider' variations: ever darker, or darker *and* more glaring tones, more strained body movements). This 'soliloquy' is a medley of 'voices', none of them hers. The expressions on her silent face 'reply' to them (she gloats about Cassidy, but not about Lowery). Her 'voices' are not wildly persecutory (she's realistic, and though badly scared, not paranoid – and vis à vis Norman, not paranoid enough). Her colleagues are neither malign nor benign, merely concerned. Cassidy thinks she's a vamp (which supports the feminist notion that 'patriarchy' views disobliging women as 'vamps'). He vows to 'replace' the missing money 'with her fine soft flesh' (another mixed-up metaphor, inspired by Shylock's 'pound of flesh'). His choking rage moves Marion to a crooked smile, which, lingering, seems faintly demonic. (In the script, Marion, hearing Cassidy's tirade, feels such 'revulsion' she closes her eyes. So the mean smirk was a second thought – by whom? Hitch, Stefano, Leigh, their mutual response?)

In all the imaginary conversations, the centre of attention is Marion herself (perhaps as compensation for Caroline's family calls?). They bring a second brief mention of her sister. Before she was merely a chaperone – a negative function – now, she takes a lively initiative. But her voice is never heard, and still her name is unmentioned: she's only 'Marion's sister'. Hitchcock may well have reasoned that her low profile now will make her eventual, very aggressive, appearance even stronger (on the same principle as not foreshadowing the murder). But also, perhaps, Marion's mind relegates her sister to a 'no-name extra' – in which mental 'absence' Freudians might see 'sibling rivalry'. If that over-interprets the film, it rather fits the script, which, later on in the story, has two pages about twisted love between the sisters.

DUMB SHOW WITH VOICES

Marion says not a word; all the speakers are unseen. The 'image-track' shows one scene, the soundtrack shows others. The silent film carries a radio play (though Marion's expressions, responding to the 'audio-drama', link the two 'media'). Another aesthetic touch: all office 'sound-scenes' pass through audio-apparatus (intercoms, telephones), and give one side of the conversation only. Brief phrases deftly convey who rang whom. Normally, sound and image make a scenic 'unity'; these conversations make a split-screen sequence (separate scenes run simultaneously).

OUTSIDE IN

We're outside and inside Marion. We hear her mind, we see her face. The voices in her mind are not her own, only other people's; only her face and her body, especially her hands, shifting their grip on the wheel, convey her inner feelings. The voices make her 'interior monologue' (but not a 'stream of consciousness'; they're too focused, too themed, which streams of consciousness are not). As the audio-scenes are in her imagination, and that's in a jumpy state, we can doubt their veracity. But their general tenor is so reasonable, plausible, probable, one can also accept them as 'realism', or its 'functional equivalent' (in realist terms, the reason for this strange construction would be tight dramatic structuring – they remind us of the office, but we don't lose sight of Marion).

Consider, for example, Marion's most 'improbable', most arbitrary, invention: Cassidy's Shylock fury. I found myself treating it as *his* reaction, and admiring its dramatic irony (he brags he can bear to lose this cash, but when he does, he goes ballistic, or rather, hysterical – a feminine 'loss of mind' plus macho aggression? But then again, who hasn't, briefly, vowed to kill, for much less serious affronts?). So these scenes invoke a possible reality, not 'fantasised' by her, but *intuited*. She's quite sharp and shrewd, as with Sam's bare feet, when she's not impulsioned. So maybe she's the *sub-narrator*, of a story-within-a-story. It's freely used in documentary: indeed, *David* (Paul Dickson, 1951) has a flashback by one narrator within a flashback by another. The plausibility of the scenes themselves establishes their 'reality' status.

IMAGINING THE REAL

The voices in Marion's head are vivid, clear and exact (because spoken by the actors). This may well be just film convention, for 'inner speech': that part of the flow of thought which comes into the conscious mind, from the Preconscious, in the forms of verbal language. But then again, the rendition of her thought may be more 'realistic'. Just as some people have a 'photographic memory', which presents to their consciousness a visual 'display', which they can watch with their 'mind's eye', others have a *'audio*-graphic memory' which exactly replays other people's voices. And some people have a 'photographic imagination'; their imagination can offer highly plausible extrapolations from the real. Many artists, some autists and some very ordinary, prosaic people possess this enviable faculty.[22] So, perhaps, Marion, especially in her excited state. Here, the stereotype 'opposition' of 'realism' and 'fantasy' breaks down completely; the *imagination* is *realistic*. Indeed, imagination is usually a *realistic* function; a fact unfortunately obscured by 'vulgar Freudian' fixations on Unconscious fantasy.

CINE-SYNTAX *PSYCHO*-STYLE: TAKE THREE TENSES

Insofar as the 'audio-scenes' are imaginary, they're happening now. Insofar as they're realistic, they're a succession of scenes next Monday. (Except for the first sound scene, between salesman and cop, which seems part of a 'running present'.) Insofar

as they're 'flash-forwards', they're in a 'future' tense; and, insofar as it's conjectural, perhaps they're in some 'subjunctive' voice. So they're in three tenses simultaneously:
present objective, future objective, future subjective. But then again, maybe images,
unlike verbs, and like nouns, have no tense at all.

THE PHENOMENOLOGY OF MOTORING

Marion, reflecting while driving, looms large in her story and, as Michael O'Pray
pointed out to me, long drives can induce a meditative state. 'There's a statistic, that
more men cry while they're sitting in a car, than anywhere else.' Especially before car
radios became standard, the car could afford 'time outs' from one's usual surroundings, distractions and friends. Long, unfamiliar roads, streaming past monotonously,
perhaps a little hypnotically, can induce a faintly altered state. The actions of driving
are performed by the Preconscious, by direct line from perception. Continuous
motion, half-attended to, is both a stimulant and a relaxant, and can blur space and
time. Cinema, of course, loves reproducing it, through varied idioms. Sometimes
montage edits chop long flowing movements into spiky cuts (spinning tyres, whizzing
trees, fluttering scarves). Sometimes, long 'travellings' (apt term) abstain from cutting,
to maintain a steady kinetic of 'rolling along' – as when landscapes stream past side-
windows: the solidly fixed scenery rushes backwards, the window-frames are graphically static but known to be moving: instead of separate shots colliding, one sustained
shot presents a 'contra-flowing' of in-shot elements. *Psycho* deploys a variety of
idioms. There is 'Marion in a static box', *but*, the rear window, centrally placed, beside
her face, *puts the road inside the car*. And there are Marion's night drives, which have
chop-chop cutting, even as modern lenses pull wide fields of view into tightened perspectives, vigorously asserted. Their 'flow-momentum' carries 'across' the cuts creating a 'double rhythm' – the road is a flowing sostenuto, the cuts come in staccato,
neither rhythm dominates the other; it's an equal counterpoint. Flowing and cutting
– it's a dialectical synthesis. Here Hitchcock mixes the old 'montage' dynamic with the
more recent 'roadscaping' style.[23]

The 'frontal fixity' shots are an extreme form of a stylistic tendency ruling *Psycho*:
shots so bold and simple they're aggressively upfront. The many, many shots of a
single person at a time range between 'close shots', 'bust shots' (head and shoulders)
and 'waist shots', with strong body shapes set forward in space against backgrounds,
and quietly emphasised by a fall of light. It was indeed a televisual technique. But TV
images these aren't; their texture is fuller, more solid, they're more salient in space,
the very *light* has more substance, and heads and bodies, set at different angles to

the frame, cut sharply against one another. The shots' overall similarity gives small differences greater emotional weight: a shift of shadow changes the 'weight' of the face,
sometimes the eyes are looking out, sometimes they're fixed wide in thought, the
slight dissymmetry of Leigh's eyes becomes anxiety and poignancy. In broad principle,
it's quite a conventional shot construction (often used as 'climax close-ups' of scenes,
or glamorously or sentimentally). One might speak of 'strong cuts', for they're not the
'hard cuts' of montage collisions. They're as strong as 'smooth cuts' can get, and the
consistent closeness of variously worried, deceitful, resistant faces to camera keeps
an unyielding pressure on us. I wondered where I'd seen that effect before, until,
watching *Mother* (1926) and *Earth* (1930), I realised how often Pudovkin and
Dovzhenko construct shots and whole sequences around 'frontal one-shots', with a
character's upper body, placed centrally in frame, parallel to the frame-edges, while
'face', 'bust' or 'trunk' shots are cut against each other. The slightly oppressive similarity of composition gives evocative power to quite small differences (a lighting change,
shifted bodily positions, eyes looking out or still with thought).

SHINING IN THE NOIR

The impressive storm has neither thunder nor lightning, only near-silence, rain and
headlights. Louder than the rain are the windscreen wipers; beams of headlights hit
Marion's eyes. The silvery-black rain makes various agitations – first an odd speckle,
then an all-over stipple, then water swaying over the glass. Oncoming headlights
appear on a low horizon, shoot forward and rake the windscreen, passing diagonally.
Light and water criss-cross in an agitated chiaroscuro. The scene builds up to a *quietness*, as, in that ever-active rear window, two following headlights arrange themselves,
one on each side of Marion's white face: graphically, three bright ovals, in tight formation, float towards us, in line-abreast formation, as if two bright angels from Hell,
two Lucifers, were escorting Marion home…. This 'motion painting' ranks with two
famous 'rain symphonies': Joris Ivens' formalist documentary, *Rain*,[24] and the 'overture'
of *The Last Laugh*, with rain gleaming in city lights and streaming off shiny blacks (oil-
skins, metal, ashphalt). Thus Hitchcock disguises expressionism as lyrical realism,
achieving a *tertium quid*.

DOWNHILL

Though *Psycho* is a psychological film, it's also meteorological and topographical.
Marion moves from a hot, bleached afternoon to this nocturnal flash flood, and
negotiates different landscapes – dawn hills, a rear-winding road. Now, Marion drifts

downwards, almost like a glider circling lower, her face pale in a weak dashboard light, her own beams as if 'pressed down' by chaos and old night – until the neon sign looms *on high*, its letters slithering in the rain. As her car moves between the level line of cabins, another continuity paradox disorientates us, subliminally. Hitchcock redeploys the 'reverse on car moment' to a different effect. In one shot, the camera, adjacent to Marion, and looking forward, as she is, surveys the line of cabins on screen right. In nearby shots, the camera, in front of Marion, looks back through the windscreen at her, as she looks, presumably at the cabins, sharply screen left. Continuity-wise, that's quite correct (the camera has turned around, reversing left and right) but here, it's highly disconcerting; it's as if she's looking the wrong way. The reason is that here, two 'action lines' compete: the car's direction is one, but her look is another (at right angles to the first). This sort of contradiction is why shots from moving vehicles can push the continuity rules to beyond one of their limits. It could have been hidden, as it usually is, one way or another, but here the size of the car, relative to the road, emphasises the contradiction – appropriately – so we're as disoriented as she is.

WE'RE ALL SCHIZOS TOGETHER

Voices in your head may (or may not) symptomise schizophrenia, and the vividness of these voices comes across as a 'mini-schizo' episode, like her 'impulsion', and her mental absences, which get more serious as she goes, from mangling metaphors, to zonking out, to forgetting how to shop, to leaving her stuff in the car, a minor narrative event, but a major event stylistically. In *Psycho*, everybody's schizo, to a minor extent (within normality) or seriously. The only exception is Lila, perhaps because she's fiercely loyal, moral and suspicious – is that ferocity *her* 'impulsion' (and a *realistic* one)? Sam is mini-schizo while oscillating indecisively and talking like a scrapbook of quotes from contradictory magazines. (Ah, the power of ideological plurality, to abolish the subject, and make him 'a thing of shreds and patches'.) Lowery's blank gaze at Marion is his mild, brief mental 'split'. Cassidy's view of his family life is wilful 'bad faith', and if Norman is a 'schizo-son' to one woman, his mother, maybe Cassidy is a 'schizo-father' to another, his daughter. (Partial symmetries are a Hitchcock speciality, and well he knew it. As he said of *Strangers on a Train*, 'Isn't it a wonderful design? You could study it for ever.')[25] *Psycho* itself is a schizo-text, with its weird ellipses and contrary retrospections. As for us spectators, we're completely schizo: we know 'it's only a film', but our screams bounce off the walls, though we stay in our seats.[26]

SITTING IN LIMBO

Were *Psycho* about 'desire', Marion's long drive would have stressed her destination
– Sam. How easy and natural would have been, for instance, his photo pasted on the
dashboard, her constant glances at it, the cop quizzically noting it, a four-second diner
shot where, in the middle of eating a sandwich, she pushes it aside and tries again to
phone ahead. How normal too, to make the point that, when she loses the right
road, she's only 15 minutes from Sam's small town (as will later transpire, very
quietly). The film shows little interest in her *progress towards*. She speeds along, glued
in her little box, thinking voices from a world she hopes she's left. Yet, on hearing
Cassidy's threats, she grins complacently; she's entirely unafraid – quite a change in
one so nervous. It's as if she's reached some limbo-zone of self-assurance, *beyond*
fear or desire. She's running on empty – of feeling for others. It's ominous and
promptly, perhaps in response, the storm descends.

MARION AND THE PHANTOM OF LIBERTY

If this is her 'touch of evil', is it also her touch of spiritual *freedom*? Freedom and evil
together. Here, I suspect, Hitchcock agrees with Robert Louis Stevenson's moral
fable, *Dr Jekyll and Mr Hyde* (1886) – a semi-Calvinistic tale, now usually misunder-
stood. What it's *not* about is 'good Dr Jekyll' versus 'evil Mr Hyde'; and the other thing
it isn't about is 'consciousness (ethical and rational)' versus 'libido'. For once the good
doctor tastes the fruits of evil, he can't wait to become Mr Hyde again, and he never
repents (unlike his colleague Faust); his only problem is making the change between
his happy self and his social identity, and that's for chemical reasons (and very possibly Stevenson, who relished Bohemian low-life, shared a, then legal, vice with Thomas
de Quincey and Sherlock Holmes). Jekyll's problem is, not conscience, except in passing, but the hypocrisy needed for respectability. Influenced, critics think, by Scots
Calvinism, Stevenson says happiness is *libidinal*, that is to say, *wicked*. So does Jean
Renoir, in his version of the tale, *Le Testament du Dr Cordelier* (1961). Renoir's weary
doctor, while he's Mr Hyde, feels 'light … light …', and practically *dances* along. This
anticipates the all-dancing, all-singing thugs in *A Clockwork Orange* (1971).
Conceivably, it's Marion's spiritual *emptiness*, if only for the moments of that smile,
that brings down the storm upon her head.

NARRATIVE PATTERNS AND MORALITY

If you're a plausible, you might say that cop and salesman between them delayed
Marion for the precise amount of time needed for the storm to confuse her onto

Norman's road, when she's almost reached safety: this storm lasts just long enough to propel her 'the wrong way'. However, all these events are so diverse and scattered, and time in film is so approximate and elastic, that narration would, I think, have had to upfront this point, in some way or other. So I rather focus on the smile/storm synchronisation which hints at uncertain connection. Normally, such vagueness suggests some low-grade poetic association, such as myth and melodrama use blunderbuss-fashion. Here, however, it's teasing, as good ambiguity is. It's cannily *un*canny.

THE PROBLEM OF EVIL

What Marion steals, she doesn't desire: money (she herself would have 'licked the stamps': the money is for Sam). What exactly is her impulse? Sexual desire? Or its 'opposite', desire for respectability? Or desire for Sam, as an individual? Hitchcock never separates these things. Which figures: her immoderate desire is for marriage. And marriage is all of the above: sexuality *and* respectability *and* the man for himself. The complete package, the full Monty. There's no sin there (and if there was, it mightn't merit punishment; it might merit forgiveness, with or without repentance). Maybe her sin is, that she followed an 'impulsion', without pause for thought (whether rational or intuitive, moral or prudential: the last two are different things, but both essential in a big decision). Maybe she's a victim of a culture which advocates 'life, liberty, and the pursuit of happiness', but not patience or morality; so, the only restraints are *conformism* (like the hollow lives of the office people and Sam and Norman); and the only resistance to 'impulsion' is from fears provided by the Superego (whose morality is libidinal and cruel: hence Marion's nervousness). One purpose of religion is to *soften* the Superego (even when it retains something of that primeval, unreasoning cruelty).

A Catholic moralist of Hitchcock's generation might argue that freedom from morality is alienation and breeds the excesses of *anomie*, one form of which is *obsession* (in Marion, 'impulsion'). To that extent, Marion's sin is wanting marriage and wanting it *now*. She wants happiness all round, quickly – just like 'buying with pills'. Many people, and not only those old-fangled Christians, but half the Old and New Lefts, feared that new, consumerist capitalism would destroy the honest, old 'work ethic', and favour demands for instant gratification. Marion's urgency, to buy a car at which she barely glances, persisting in the purchase when it becomes pointless, might emblematise an easy decline from consumerist hedonism into character weakness.

In Marion's moral drift – as in the Ancient Mariner's and the ballerina's – spiritual confusion has *unforeseeable* consequences. The 'original' choice was *not* deliberate, *not* rational, and its consequences were *unforeseeable*. That *should* be frightening – as Kierkegaard said, we're all *condemned* to work out our own salvation, in *fear and trembling*.

REASONS TO BE GOOD: 'THOU LORD SEEST ME'

The 'moral' of *Psycho* may be that Marion's 'impulsion' puts her on a course where everything is *even more dangerous* than it is already anyway. It's in that sense, and that sense *only*, that 'crime does not pay': it's not so much that it's 'definitively doomed', as that it attracts *even more* hostility from the world around than it gives out anyway. Being good is not idealistic but *prudent*. Some moralists, like Kant, would strongly disapprove: *prudence* is a *selfish* calculation, sadly devoid of love of others, or of good for its own sake; it's another form of wickedness, it's the wickedness on which the system runs. And humans, left to themselves, are naturally wicked (like Dr Jekyll). This isn't to say that they're *entirely* wicked but their altruism isn't very strong. As for 'enlightened self-interest' and 'honesty is the best policy', and well-meaning attempts to make altruism merely *rational*, modern logics (theory of games, probability theory, etc.) suggests that from the point of view of every individual, the best policy is not honesty but hypocrisy – society thinks you're honest, and treats you accordingly, but you bend or break the rules when you're sure you'll get away with it. This would explain why hypocrisy is always popular; in the way the Eleventh Commandment is: Thou shalt not be found out. But, if there's a God, which for Hitchcock 'as a Jesuit' is always possible, the odds against wickedness become longer still. This brings us to the famous dictum of Blaise Pascal (and so to Rohmer's *Maud*), whereby the logic of belief in God is like a bet. If you behave as if God existed, your reward is Heaven for all eternity; and if you're wrong, what have you lost? Only this short and miserable life – a life beset by blind chance (like this sudden storm). Kant would denounce it as a wickedly selfish calculation, and certainly the tensions between selfish and unselfish reasons to be good are clear enough to keep us all uneasy. On the other hand, it's strange how often seemingly *rational* moralists fixate on *sincerity*, almost for its own sake; for a *truly* rational morality would relegate to a very low priority so ethereal, so rarely ascertainable a property. Generally, therefore, moralising is not purist and more pragmatic: it accepts, perhaps regretfully, the *linkage* of morality with selfish interest. Hence homely advice like 'honesty is the best policy', 'cheats never prosper', 'what goes around comes around', etc. My suggestion is that, for Hitchcock, as for most spectators' 'common sense', Marion's 'sin' is not some immoral desire, but, in the first instance, 'imprudent praxis as an immorality in itself' (like 'behaving with culpable foolishness' or 'asking for it' or behaving like 'an accident waiting to happen') plus 'desire pushed beyond the inhibition which morality is'. Put like that, it sounds quite unlike traditional morality, but much *worldly* moralising works out like this. As my Victorian godmother, a Congregationalist, suffragette, Left Liberal and pacifist, who lived half her life just around the corner from Islington Studios, used to say: 'If you can't be good, be careful.'

◆

SCENES 88–90 MARION CRANE MEETS NORMAN BATES

Leaving her car, Marion dashes through the rain to the motel office on the porch, but finds no one there, or in the dark room behind it. Beyond the end of the porch, a path with rough steps leads up a steep slope to an old-fashioned house. Across a lighted upstairs window, the silhouette of an old lady moves slowly. The light goes out. After waiting a while, with nothing happening, Marion dashes back to her car and angrily sounds its horn. In the doorway of the house, a young man appears and runs bare-headed towards her; on reaching her, he opens an umbrella for her and apologises for not hearing her arrive.

KEY-CHANGE: FROM AMERICAN REALISM TO AMERICAN GOTHIC

Psycho so far has been modern and realistic. Now the Bates house marks a change of key, from realism to American Gothic. (But the idioms weren't incompatible; *American Gothic*, the painting by Grant Wood [1930], features in most histories of American realistic art, and was regional–realist in intention). When Truffaut implied that Hitchcock had resorted to a cornily creepy old house, the director replied that it was 'to some extent, quite accidental', since in northern California, 'that type of house is very common. They're called California Gothic or when particularly awful "California gingerbread". I simply wanted to be accurate.' However, the production

designer reckoned Hitchcock did intend a sort of 'ghostliness', as another red herring, to distract suspicion from Norman. One might wish Hitchcock had avoided any
hint of the old convention; however, real-life reactions to lonely houses on stormy
nights easily take on a 'Gothic' dimension. Indeed, the inspiration for a film called *The
Old Dark House* (James Whale, 1932) was a novel by the English realist writer J. B.
Priestley, in which he tried to treat the old themes realistically (but later confessed
that he failed). Hitchcock and Priestley were same-generation compatriots, and very
likely Hitchcock had a similar intention.

All this to-ing-and-fro-ing by Marion and Norman has negligible narrative significance. (If Norman is in his office at the start, nothing else need change.) The
main purpose of all this activity is 'atmosphere' (description, as distinct from narrative: if the storyline is horizontal, 'atmosphere' is vertical). It also introduces Mrs
Bates, sooner instead of later; it's a *plant*, a figure of narration, *not* a narrative event.
Its third function is psychological; it makes Marion angry with Norman's delay
(once again, she's impatient). His business with the umbrella shows self-forgetfulness
and gallantry towards women. This helps mollify her and prepares their friendship
(all the warmer for a first little quarrel). For some while now, Marion has been
guilty, always 'on trial'; now, she judges Norman's inadequacy (as, earlier, Sam's). To
put things another way, these little events owe as much to description as to story.

THE QUICKNESS OF THE EYE DECEIVES THE MIND

Marion's wait seems so long we can understand her indignation. Actually, it's about
55 seconds (from first leaving her car to receiving the umbrella). The strangely shifting differences between actual screen time, diegesis time (i.e. the time the screen
action would take in reality) and audience sense of either run far beyond our present scope (alas); but, in a nutshell, one may say that narrative movies rarely, if ever,
depict time accurately. Rather, they relegate it to a property of actions; and they
depict an action by only showing some brief slice of it, to imply the whole, yet spare
us the clutter of redundant details which would slow things down and, more important, wreck the concentration on relevance which drama since Aristotle has generally
preferred (not without good reason). What looks like movie 'realism' is really a tissue
of *implication* and suggestion – a succession of 'part-actions' smoothed together to
disguise what Stefan Sharff, in his magisterial analyses, calls 'deletions'.[27] The ratio of
screen time to diegesis time is wildly variable, even within the same scene. Here, a
few seconds of inaction, then Marion indicating impatience, suggests – how long? Five
minutes? Ten?

THE FINE ART OF CHEATING

Many mystery novels make a point of giving their audience a sporting chance to deduce the criminal's identity, before the text reveals it. *Psycho* being a mystery, many spectators would approach it with that active kind of participation in mind. Hitchcock was determined to play scrupulously fair with them, by providing 'necessary and sufficient' clues without misinformation (as distinct from red herrings, which the rules allow). In film, the indefinite elasticity of diegetic time can cause problems. Since the woman in the window moves, she's not Mrs Bates' mummy, she's Norman dressed up: does screen time leave him long enough to change his clothes and get down to the door? Second-time viewers may well have their doubts. However, a later scene shows that sometimes Norman dresses up by simply slipping a dress and wig over his ordinary clothes, and we see him shed them in a very few seconds. To rush down a flight of stairs takes a fit young man very little time, so Hitchcock could argue that here he has played fair. (Graver problems will appear further on.)

◆

SCENES 91–103 NORMAN INSPIRES MARION'S BETTER SELF

Marion's vexation is soothed by Norman's lively charm and his gentle humour about doing very little business since 'they moved away the highway'. She signs in as 'Marie Samuels' from LA (prompted by the newspaper). Norman's hand hovers between the keys to Cabins 3 and 1, before selecting the latter, as conveniently adjacent to the office. He settles her in solicitously and, realising she's too tired to drive to the nearest diner a few miles away at Fairvale, invites her to share sandwiches and milk in the kitchen in the house.

After looking around the cabin for a place to hide the money, Marion folds it in the newspaper, and is suddenly distracted by a voice from the house: Norman's old mother scolds him for inviting 'a strange woman' into her house, to eat his mother's food and satisfy his 'cheap erotic fantasies' about 'supper by candlelight'. Marion moves out onto the porch, as if to spare him embarrassment about their meal, but meets him bringing their milk and sandwiches on a tray. 'I wish you could apologise for other people', he says, bravely smiling. She steps aside for him to enter her cabin and, as he hesitates, smiles at his timidity. He suggests the office is nicer and warmer and, once there, that they settle in the parlour just behind it.

Its Victorian furnishings are heavy with stuffed birds. Norman's hobby is taxidermy, though he frankly admits it can't fill his lonely life in the service and shadow of his mentally ill mother, for whom he does everything, including the linen round and the cleaning. He loves and hates her, but when Marion refers to putting her 'some place', he angrily denounces those cold, depressing institutions. His open, sensitive confession and loyal self-sacrifice touch a chord in her and she indicates that their talk has saved her from a trap. He would like to talk longer but next morning she must leave early for the long drive (back to Phoenix). She lets slip her real name, before returning to her cabin.

MORE ON HANDBAG THEORY

Marion prowling about for a place to hide her money, her suitcase open on a bed, makes a lighter, quicker 'variation on the theme' of the earlier 'solo'. Its everyday, 'local' quality generates some anxiety. The script is clear that she deliberately leaves the newspaper out in plain view, an idea akin to Poe's *The Purloined Letter* (Lacan's favourite fable). However, 40 per cent of my student seminar, cajoled into voting, thought Marion *forgot* the paper, having been distracted by Mrs Bates' voice. This would fit the theme of mental lapses. Another lapse occurs when Marion lets slip her real name – just after reverting to her usual honest self.

ANOTHER INVISIBLE SCENE

Critical focus on Norman's voyeurism risks occluding Marion's moment of écoutism – she listens to Mrs Bates haranguing Norman. Not that it's morally equivalent to Norman peeping, for this is thrust upon her and, after a riveted pause, she turns away. Mrs Bates haranguing silent Norman makes another 'sound-only' scene, with uni-vocal dialogue; it's also another 'soliloquy', for Mrs Bates *is* Norman talking to himself/herself. Plausibility-wise, it's dubious – Marion hears every word, from about 50 yards away, across an intervening landscape, on a windy night (though the rain seems to have stopped), through a presumably closed window-pane (though Norman has just opened hers a chink). However, our 'willing suspension of disbelief' (vital concept, Coleridge, 1817)[28] depends, *not* on detailed realism, nor on illusion, but on our *consent* to a film for otherwise deserving our respect for its lyrical atmospheric, and because we want interesting things to happen. We won't quibble over minor points, even if we notice them. Tucked away, *within* the overall scene, low down on the left, is a beautiful little vignette of bare black trees against moonlit clouds. Here, production design finds an optimal balance between 'photographic realism' and 'magic realism'. It's a different style from the earlier photo-realistic shots of driving as dusk falls. Within its overall unity, *Psycho* has many 'mini-shifts' of idiom.

A CHARMING VILLAIN

From a certain angle, Norman is a variation on Hitchcock's favourite (and stock) figure – the charming, well-mannered villain with just enough humanity to elicit odd pangs of concern. In *Foreign Correspondent* (1940) there's Herbert Marshall (always the sensitive English gentleman), in *North by Northwest* there's James Mason (always darkly romantic), and in *Notorious* there's quizzical smoothie Claude Rains (who like Norman has a 'guardian mother'). But these earlier figures are melodramatic, living 'dream-palace' lives, with no roots outside entertainment conventions, and as dreamily abstract as their MacGuffins; whereas Norman's conversation with Marion is subtle, intimate, original. His plight echoes an 'everyday martyrdom', familiar to many spectators in their own real lives, or the lives of neighbours, or as dreaded possibilities: having to care for aged parents, or petulant victims of Alzheimer's … The *odd star out* Anthony Perkins often played sensitive or redeemably neurotic young men, in the wake of Montgomery Clift and James Dean (and their older cousin, Jerry Lewis). Handsome, vivacious, though brooding and volatile, and clearly a troubled spirit, his dark, sharp eyes and tall, gangling figure made an intriguing mixture of quick intelligence and calm rusticity. In *Fear Strikes Out*, *The Lonely Man*, and *The Tin Star* (all 1957) and *Desire under the Elms*, he plays the nervous 'sons' of daunting father figures (respectively, baseball hitter Karl Malden, Old West bandit Jack Palance, sheriff-turned-bounty-hunter Henry Fonda and harsh rural patriarch Burl Ives). His enormous appeal to bobby-soxers extended to more mature women in the audience: in *Desire under the Elms*, he was the lover of his father's new wife (Sophia Loren) and in *Goodbye Again* (1961), the lover of Ingrid Bergman. His quick switches between sensitive vivacity and an 'injured vulture' stare were part of his 'cocktail of possibilities': whatever his role as *written* might upfront, a dark light dancing in his eyes, and quirkily wry smile, kept hints of other possibilities alive, like a running subtext. He had every chance of long-term major stardom, with particular appeal to male teenagers and to women of all ages. From a certain angle, he's not so far from Cary Grant; but where Grant slid lightly and politely over everything, like a mildly irascible eel, Perkins put more depth, thoughtful or disturbing, into every role. Crucial to *Psycho* is his ambiguity – and its 'chemistry' with Leigh's businesslike directness.

NORMAN AS WOUNDED HERO

With hindsight, it's hard to believe that as first-time viewers we weren't instantly and thenceforth entirely certain that Norman is a killer. The very title promised us one and half an hour into the film it's odd's on Norman's the one, what with stuffed corpses all around his walls, his invisible mother, his spider-like chat-line (literally, 'come into my parlour') and low camera angles with lumbering chiaroscuros. However, dangerously neurotic maybe-heroes had long been all the rage; quite apart from troubled teenagers, and many noir crime protagonists (like Burt Lancaster in *Kiss the Blood off My Hands* [1948], indicative title), Robert Ryan in *Clash by Night* [1952], Humphrey Bogart in *In a Lonely Place* [1950], Kirk Douglas in

Detective Story [1951], even Ronald Colman in *A Double Life* [1947], Brando in some grown-up roles, and Robert Mitchum coming on all cynical and saturnine). Perkins' vulnerable likeability is decisively supplemented by an admirably written conversation which, set in balance against the sinister elements, overcomes them, and transforms them into pathos. His invitation to Marion to join him in a simple meal is nervously breathless, yet bravely enthusiastic. His self-forgetful chivalry with the umbrella, his un-macho attitude to domestic chores, including feminine ones like freshening linen, his loyal obedience to his 'Mom', his stoic admission that he hates as well as loves her (still a bit new-ish in the 1950s) when phrased in his reasonable, reflective way touch us as they touch Marion.[29] Peter Biskind points out that Norman, while sane, prefigures the feminists' new man. Or perhaps he expertly, sincerely depicts himself as a put-upon victim, and blames himself *just enough* to get even more sympathy, and cosset his contented miserabilism. He's also a stickler for Family Values ('A boy's best friend is his mother,' he says, before gently smiling at the sad joke against himself) and for the old American work ethic (although he's denied its 'American dream'). Once scolded by his Mom, he dare not enter Marion's cabin though, a few minutes earlier, he was in there discussing her mattress, and her dress closet, as innocently as a younger brother (though even then he couldn't say 'bathroom' in her presence – as she immediately discerns, though she thinks his neurosis harmless). His form of words, 'I wish you could apologise for other people', is a masterpiece of tact. It tells Marion he knows she knows about his shame, addresses *her* embarrassment about it, admits his own humiliation, but also passes lightly over it, and – finally – it *avoids* blaming his mother. Nor does he blame whoever built those new highways (the federal government, or 'capitalism', or 'modern materialism', or 'society'). So, after four scary, tricksy men, Marion finds, at last, a, serious, friendly and amenable one.

Although the dead birds are melodramatic and macabre, they're 'rehabilitated' by the context: the film so far, and the conversation. (As usual, 'context transforms text'.) Marion looks at the birds seriously, but they don't upset her, and eventually she affirms that 'a man should have a hobby'. Marion's attitude guides that of the audience. The parlour with 'still life' comes to lyricise Norman's disadvantageous environment, his 'death in life'. And, after all, taxidermy, although an old-fashioned activity, is a normal, sane and well-respected one; it's no more symptomatic of a particularly troubled Unconscious than being, say, an undertaker or a coroner. It might well indicate *mourning* followed by some *restitutive* activity – especially as Norman is sensible and practical about it (it's cheap, it can't replace real life, etc.). From this hobby, no analyst would diagnose necrophilia, killing what you love, compulsive castration of the flying phallus, etc. – any more than he'd say such things about comparable hobbies today (tattooing, body-piercing, etc.). But here the unreasonable expectation will prove exactly right. Our first instinct was correct; anything is dangerous.

A SUITABLE CASE FOR TREATMENT

Norman *lives* that stoic acceptance of unhappiness, to which she confusedly alluded, in her mixed-up metaphor, about instant unhappiness with pills. Perhaps, too, his *Stimmung* harks back to that dark, old-fashioned lake or river, like a gloomy life with a peaceful death. So honest is his confession about love and hate that Marion broaches the possibility of institutionalising his mother. The anger that dangerously hardens his eyes is well within normal, social rights. Even after her semi-apology, his resentment rumbles on: evidence of his emotional integrity. Though polite and civilised, it's neither hidden nor repressed. Once his anger is spent, he relaxes, and admits that, well, yes, he has sometimes thought the unthinkable. Seriously neurotic he no doubt is, but a psychotherapist's first prognosis would be rather hopeful. Who would expect, beneath this in-depth sadness, lucidity, frankness, another character altogether?

THE CONVERSATION

In PAC (parent–adult–child) terms, Marion is 'the parent', Norman is 'the child'. She spots, and drily smiles at, his nervous problems. A few words from her elicit his eager confessions. He confides his whole life. He senses she's in some trouble, but she keeps her secrets until, as if to close their conversation, she drops a hint that something he said helped her avoid some mistake. In this scene, *she's* the one who changes her mind, yet everything, even the camera, emphasises *his* troubles (a hint of unfinished business). It's almost *his* soliloquy, with her brief, serious, comments and judgments (and no false charm). He sprawls heavily in his chair, while she sits like a white bird delicately alighted, one bright, white arm folded across her body, the other held in mid-air. Though each shot of him looks heavy in itself (low angles, shadows, the textured birds above him), their continuity is edgy, unstable, thanks to little angle changes, and eye-line matches at ungainly angles. He extends one arm right across the screen, as if absent-mindedly, to caress a little bird. The conversation ends with Marion's back disappearing round the doorway corner: a curious little shot, as if she were turning her back on his yearning for more company. And what's wrong with that? What's he to her?

THE ACCEPTANCE WORLD

What exactly does Norman's good example *mean* to Marion? 'Exactly', about *Psycho*, is always a wrong word; it's a *lyrical* drama, not an *analytical* drama. Perhaps it means, 'to do the right thing is a "package deal"'. It's sticking to one's moral principles plus old-fashioned loyalties, such as parents taught, plus 'roots' plus contented sacrifice plus acceptance of one's limitations. All these things overlap, each needs the support of the other: ethics, like roots, are synthetic, not analytic. As often as not the package deal is unfair. But if you're a moderately moral person, you take the rough with the smooth, the bitter with the sweet. Marion renounces the great American impatience, which wants it all, now, as a human right, and wants it so self-centredly that not getting it on a plate justifies stealing it from people more selfish still. Hollywood films asserted acceptance more often than one might suppose, sometimes tear-jerkingly. This moment in *Psycho* may evoke *Splendor in the Grass* (1961), Elia Kazan's quietly unusual, and therefore half-forgotten, Hollywood movie. Its title comes, via William Inge, from Wordsworth's 'Ode to Duty' (1807): 'Though nothing can bring back the hour/ Of splendour in the grass, of glory in the flower;/ We will grieve not, rather find/ Strength in what remains behind …/ In the faith that looks through death/ In years that bring the philosophic mind …'

'NOBODY'S PERFECT'

—as Joe E. Lewis says in *Some Like It Hot* (also 1959, also about quasi-transvestite quirks). Norman's quirks and faults make a list as long as your arm, but they finger hidden chords in us. Who hasn't capitulated to resented parental influence? Been culpably passive in some situation? Pursued some time-killing hobby – stuffing birds, watching duff movies, staring at pickled sheep in art galleries, with eyes as glazed as the exhibits? For spellbound denizens of Gothic mansions, there may still be hope – think *Wuthering Heights* (1939), *Rebecca*, *Jane Eyre* (1943) – and, by way of plain-clothes Gothick, *Suspicion* and *Notorious*.

DRAMATIC RECIPROCITY AND POETIC JUSTICE

As Marion's talk of an early start implies, she can, just, get back to Phoenix before the banks open. But do we expect the story to now follow her back to Phoenix and see how she gets on there? I don't think we do.

Briefly perhaps, we have wondered if something romantic might develop between Marion and Norman. Not really a full-blown romance. In the first place, she's not attracted to him. The dry way she says ' man should have a hobby' puts him

in another box and her body language shows a delicate indifference – especially
where one hand lies elegantly drooped, the other hand held up in the air, lightly aloof.
Their eyes meet, with a strong sight-line between the shots, but she entirely controls
her own space. He talks about himself and interprets her in his own terms. (He com-
pares her to a bird, and though he wants to talk to her longer, there'd be more about
himself. His noticing she's in a trap is surely a shot in the dark, more recognising himself in her than wide-minded sensitivity to her. Still, the film has interested us in him
and established some sort of symmetry or affinity. And her affair with Sam may show
a weak spot for lame dogs who need help over a stile. Perkins' romantic aura means
he might, to her and our surprise, seem for a while, a contender for some romantic
nostalgia in her. Drama *is* surprise, after all, and a male ugly duckling is as possible as
a female one. (After all, mother-bound Marty was played by Ernest Borgnine whose
screen roles tended towards his Black Bart in *Johnny Guitar* [1954] – the fat, cow-
ardly, inept, treacherous villain.) Or remember James Mason in *The Seventh Veil*
(1945) – how mean, moody, misogynistic, cold-hearted, crippled and cat-stroking
[gay?] – yet, in the final twist, Ann Todd walks past three perfect, younger (and rich)
suitors, to choose the disheartened cripple.

Her business with Sam is still unfinished and Norman is interesting. More important is that Norman, by so artlessly giving of himself, has helped her, and so, in a way,
she owes him one – not, of course, by any moral-contractual code, but by some
informal, or poetic justice, like 'one good turn deserves another'. Poetic justice can
be a mighty presence in drama; where it routinely contests, and even overwhelms,
more sensible kinds of justice, such as The Law (in letter *or* in spirit). Poetic justice is
an (often benign) form of irony: it fits, yet it's slightly absurdist. Here, it's aided and
abetted by dramatic symmetry. Romance or not, the immediate prospect is a battle
royal, over Norman, between hag-mother and wilful young woman: an archetypal
conflict, but here with myriad twists (e.g. the lady loves another, needs money …).

What Hitchcock strikingly does *not* do is hint at a dramatic development that conventional structure might be thought to prescribe. And which could have been promising. Sam is only 15 minutes' drive away. The Bates Motel has a telephone and so does
Sam. Sam's involvement offers a correct and fertile symmetry. As two strong women
fight for one weak man, two weak men fight for one strong woman. But Hitchcock
doesn't even *feint* a *provisional* Norman–Marion friendship that *might* or *might not*
become romantic – presumably because romance between 'strangers in the night' would
be too *soft*. In the event, the battle between two women does actually occur – with
this, very *extreme*, twist: Mother's pre-emptive strike ends the battle before it starts.

ORNITHOLOGY

Though the dead birds are less threat than pathos, it's important that they're macabre and have *some* threat. For thus they 'plant' the killing, which, with no preparation at all, would seem, indeed be, gratuitous, arbitrary, contrived, out of key (and less impressive, as it would have to start from cold). The birds are quite unnecessary to the plot and have no narrative role whatsoever, but they act like a 'plant' (i.e. they prepare an event, or a mood, but without encouraging the audience to think forward, and without giving away too much).

According to the script, Norman thinks the birds are looking accusingly at him. (Makes sense.) A couple of critics think they're looking at Marion (which also makes sense). I tend to think that their fierce sharp eyes aren't looking at anyone, as they're dead. Are these different readings mutually exclusive? Or 'subjective variation within a functional consensus'? Or even, 'same difference': whoever they're looking at on the screen (in the text), in our minds they're looking at us? They're mostly nocturnal birds of prey, as if to say 'the night has a thousand eyes'. Atmospherically, they're more than eyes; with their dark feathers, they're like bundles of the night, set up around the room, some stiffly watchful, some pinned up as if in flight; they're things that kill. For Norman, we humans are like birds in traps, who scratch and claw at the air, and at one another; this sounds mournfully compassionate (though in a less sympathetic context, it could sound cruel: did Norman trap, and watch, those birds?).

Before wrapping the newspaper round the dollar bills, Marion splits the bills into two piles, with money-counting expertise. For a brief moment her hands hover over the piles, fingers like talons.

Though she first mentioned food, it was only as an afterthought, and now 'You eat like a bird', Norman points out, and fears the details of his father's death would spoil her appetite. (She doesn't ask.) One thing after another slows her appetite: earlier it was making love, now it's mostly fatigue. Anorexia is over-stating it, but 'frugal' comes to mind. She'll enjoy a hearty steak, *once she's respectably settled* with her little family.

PSYCHO SOCIOLOGY

Blue Highways America

Actually, he's made another verbal slip: he means his mother's new lover's death. 'They moved away the highway, says Norman, ruefully. Since the 1940s the new interstate highways had bypassed the older, more local, networks of roads, and the small rural towns they served. (Which may be why Sam's business too is mired in debts. Marion, another lower middle-class person, comes from a modern, rising, sector: Phoenix real estate.) The 'demoted' roads were now marked blue on the maps and a 1980s travel book entitled *Blue Highways* became a long-running best-seller. It rediscovered those overshadowed communities: quiet, conservative, religious, prosaic, sometimes retaining the old mournful spirit of *Winesburg, Ohio* (Sherwood Anderson, 1919), *Our Town* (Thornton Wilder, 1938, filmed 1940) and *Lake Wobegon Days* (Garrison Keillor, 1985). 'Woe-begone' ruralism is manifest in *Psycho*, through its 'American Gothic', its edge-of-town loneliness and, coming soon, Sam's dull, grey hardware store. Taxidermy, too, evokes old-fashioned 'natural history' and the stuffed specimens moved from old schoolrooms, homes and hunting lodges into little local museums. Norman's vocabulary has old-fashioned phrases, like 'my trusty umbrella' (a jocularity derived from 'my trusty sword', in the Victorian literary 'classics' which schoolrooms used until the 1960s). 'The fire has gone out', broods Norman, visualising his mother apathetic in an institution: does his phrase evoke a domestic hearth (and 'plant' an empty fireplace, still to come)? Mrs Bates' screech, upbraiding her son, has an old-fashioned rusticity, like spiteful Miss Gulch in *The Wizard of Oz* (L Frank Baum 1900).

Mother/Grandmother

As Hitch's collaborators objected, Mrs Bates, by croaky voice, build and bun hairstyle (apparent in silhouette), seems less a mother than a *grandmother* figure. But The Master turned a deaf ear, rightly perhaps. For 'Victorianism' is not *only* a *period* style; it's virtually *mythological*. Its cult of domesticity and its strict constraints make powerful metaphors for the infant's idea that 'mummydaddyfamilyhome' is one claustro-monolithic unity. In this voice-aware film, Mrs Bates' voice evokes some cackling hag. Isn't she, really, a child-devouring witch? That is to say, the 'matriarch' of nightmare, complete with some 'patriarchal' attributes? 'Grandmother Wolf', with Marion as Red Riding Hood?

Mother Knows Best

By the late 1950s Hollywood studios sometimes consulted psychoanalysts about film subjects, and from this angle the popular impact of *Psycho* would owe something at least to its extreme case of matriarchy (or rather pseudo-matriarchy, since the wicked mother is really the far more wicked son). 'Momism', the matriarchal/schoolmarmish tendencies in American culture, had long been widely discussed: in anthropology (Margaret Mead, *Keep Your Powder Dry/The American Character* [1942], Geoffrey Gorer, *The Americans* [1948], Eric Dingwall, *The American*

Woman [1952]), in Broadway hits (*The Silver Cord* [1926, filmed 1933], cited by Norman Bates in Bloch's novel), in jazz (the very title, 'Momma Don't Allow'), in movies (*An American Romance* [1943], *Rebel without a Cause*, *The Ladies' Man*, [1961]) and in Godard's *A Bout de souffle* [1960], where oracle J. P. Melville declares: 'The American woman dominates her man; the French woman, not yet.') Although, in movies, hard patriarchs outnumbered hard matriarchs, the latter are not uncommon, as in *Tycoon* (1930), *The Little Foxes* (1943), *Mildred Pierce*, *Johnny Guitar*, *The Shrike* (1955), *Suddenly Last Summer* (1959) and *Gypsy* (1962). 'Momism' has much to do, of course, with 'the feminine mystique', though their interaction cannot concern us here.

Freudo-Linguistics

Not all Mrs Bates' phrases are archaic. 'Cheap erotic fantasies' sounds to me less like 1930s moralising than like the 1950s: Norman has been reading Old Morality mag-azines denouncing the *Playboy*-type stuff that Sam has been reading, about 'married couples who swing'. 'You have the guts, boy?' sounds less like a mother, even a tough old prairie-wagon-type mother, than like Norman echoing school playground taunts (from before he became a recluse). Here are early clues that Mrs Bates' tirade is Noman haranguing himself. She too is a thing of shreds and patches, a crazy quilt of fantasy, memory and quotes from disorganised readings. Norman hesitates before saying 'falsity', where the standard phrase expects 'fallacy', which suggests a smatter-ing of Freudian theory, the likeliest place for coming across that embarrassing phoneme 'phallus'. (If most spectators miss the word implied, never mind, the hesi-tation won't get in their way.)

Norman's free associations also run on non-Freudian lines: his gentle pun on 'office' and 'officious' suggests nothing Unconscious (except perhaps 'orifice', which so far as I know hasn't been suggested). I take it as a gentle pun, from his Preconscious, musing on a 'motel/home' distinction. He's given to 'lettrist' slip-ups, where Marion tends to mashed-up metaphors. Her sign-on name, 'Marie Samuels', shows she's think-ing of Sam, though she changes her name to his first name, not his last. It's a 'switch' such as dreams devise, but it's *not* a Freudian slip, for her desire for marriage is upfront in her conscious mind, and like her sexuality, is not repressed. (Dreams draw just as heavily on preconscious and conscious desires and anxieties as on forbidden ones; as Charles Rycroft insists, in his admirable *The Innocence of Dreams* [1979].)

Equivocal perhaps is the long heavy stretch of Norman's right arm, across the screen to caress a little stuffed bird. It seems a bit absent-minded, and who can say if it's preconscious – like needing to stretch, or caressing, for comfort, a hobby-object

– or if it expresses some irruption from the Id? An involuntarily moving limb can be sinister: in the umpteen remakes of *The Hands of Orlac* (1924), it indicates Unconscious stirrings, but in *Dr Strangelove* (1963), the good Doktor knows exactly what it stands for. A critic (not me) thinks it significant that Norman's hands move between his little bird and just in front of his crotch.

The Hidden Persuaders

In the 1950s Freudian theories, of a sort, swept US popular culture (including marketing theory, of which more anon). By 1959, many analysts of 'sales appeal' would have linked 'Momism', as above, and its special fondness for breasts and for drinking milk, with Marion's white bra, her two firm packs of dollar bills and the curvy milk jug on Norman's tray (it's his civilised self playing Mother).

Triumphs of Modern Medicine

Norman's rage at asylums may or may not be neurotic; it's certainly realistic. By 1960, admittedly, modern drugs were mitigating the horrors of *The Snake Pit* (1949), *Suddenly Last Summer* and *Shock Corridor* (1965), but old habits died hard, and mental homes quite as grim as Norman fears appear in *Titicut Follies* (1968), *One Flew Over the Cuckoo's Nest* (1975) and, in England, *Family Life* (1971).

SCRIPTWRITING AS DOUBLE-ENTRY BOOK-KEEPING (1)

While writing screenplays with Buñuel, Jean-Louis Carrière kept two 'account books'. One listed what each character knows (or should, but doesn't), in each successive scene, about the story so far. The other lists what the audience knows. (The disparities loom large in Hitchcock's favourite case of surprise versus suspense: the bomb under the table. The difference lies, not in diegesis or narrative, but in what and when the audience knows about it; that is to say, in the narration of the event, how it's described.) To put it schematically, movies intertwine four 'levels' of experiences. One is 'the world of the story' (with its experiences, values and 'poetic'). Another is made up of the values with which the auteur invests it for purposes of his own – his 'slant' or 'angle' on it, as they say. A third is 'the film *tel quel*' (its forms and signs and their customary implications). A fourth is the set of ideas the audience brings to the film itself. *Psycho* is two stories running in parallel. One is what the first-time viewer sees; it's largely right, but wrong in some key essentials. He gets enough right to interpret the rest wrongly. Even if he guesses right – for example, it may indeed cross our minds that the promised psycho should be Norman, and so on, but we're not sufficiently sure for the bubble of suspense to be pricked. Diegesis-wise, it's only a 'bubble', born to be burst, but, in terms of spectator experience, it's massive, it's satisfyingly agonising, it's just as integral to the structure of the film as the final reading, when we know everything. One may almost say that structure and content exist to generate the bubble, not vice versa!

Many first-time viewers will be fairly sure that Marion's story must have a happy end (they may even think all Hollywood movies have, although they don't; but exceptions are easily forgotten). For the second-time viewer, major points and countless nuances have changed meaning. (The famous example is Norman excusing his Mother to Marion: 'She isn't herself today.')

PSYCHO THE SECOND TIME, AND THE DÉJÀ VU PROBLEM

In a way, hindsight changes everything. The second time around, the big shocks (suspense, twist, surprises) are now much weaker; however, new, finer meanings start to emerge: double meanings, dramatic ironies, subtle connections. They may be smaller, but sometimes they're deeper. Just as people say 'you can't cross the same river twice,' one might almost say 'you can't read the same text twice.' The text is the same, but you're not; you have changed into the person who has read this text already, and now can spot finer meanings and connections.

Texts have a certain consistency, however. The first-time shocks don't disappear altogether; they are re-experienced, through our involvement with what the characters are feeling. Our perspectives are shifted by hindsight, but sometimes this sharpens our involvement. Moreover, many things in life 'never cease to surprise us', as we often say about human behaviour.[30] And we all have favourite films, whose diegesis so interests us that we want, nay, need, to re-experience it.

The Old Hollywood wisdom about suspense thrillers was that they could only work the first time around, for as soon as you know what happens next, suspense must evaporate. That viewers came back to Psycho was part of the revelation, to younger minds in Hollywood, that audiences had changed, and that a 'repeater' audience existed, substantial enough to affect the box office.

With merely competent thrillers, the first viewing leads us up a garden path, until climactic revelations invalidate most of what went before. That doesn't leave much for a second viewing. It's about the pattern with Clouzot's Les Diaboliques, which influenced Hitchcock, and with films which he influenced, like Michael Anderson's The Naked Edge – and with Vertigo (unless you're in tune with its 'alienation romanticism'). But when second-time viewers re-scrutinise Psycho, Norman's looks, hesitations, nuances carry a *double* charge. The first-time meaning is sufficiently finessed and touches us where we live; the second viewing *adds* another layer, which doesn't invalidate the first but *interacts* with it. Now, the sensitive and the mad are subtly interwined; how much to each do the nuances of Norman's behaviour owe? It's not just Norman: Marion represses her sensible self; Sam lacks a decisive self … we're ever uncertain at the sanity/madness balance behind phrases, hesitations, silences … Another such film is Dreyer's *Vampyr* (1932).

Countless melodramas, in every genre, have revolved around big, heavy, obvious personality splits. Our old horror friends include werewolves, vampires, cat persons and Dr Jekyll. 'Women's films' have vouchsafed us 'the good twin and the bad twin' (*A Stolen Life* [1939, 1946] and *The Dark Mirror* [1946]). Casebook-based are *The Three Faces of Eve* (1957) and *Crack in the Mirror* (1960). But *Psycho*, the second time around, hooks into *The Divided Self* meets *Family Life*, and Laing's idea that 'We are born mad, we live a lie, and then we die.' True, Sam and Lila prove otherwise. The superiority of *Psycho*, over its apparent genre, lies not in its structure, but in its fine detail (what Leavis used to call 'texture').

DRAMATIC IRONY

—is often defined as dialogue whose deeper significance is unbeknownst to the speaker and/or the audience, when uttered, but emerges as the play goes on (or for second-time viewers). In *Psycho* it's obsessive. Sam in that hotel bedroom complained about 'sweating for people who aren't there': he meant his father and ex-wife, but Norman too does all the chores for a person who's not there. Norman, showing Marion her cabin, commends the mattress (chaste echo of that hotel bed?), the closet for her dresses (thus linking the black bra closet, and, later, Norman's dressing up) and the hotel stationery (a scrap of which will be the last clue to her presence here). One reason for motifs is that since they change meaning each time they're repeated, they easily carry ironies.

ORNITHOLOGY (ADVANCED)

Birds often flutter through Hitchcock's mind. In *Foreign Correspondent*, a democratic politician pins his faith on 'the little people who feed the birds'. In *Sabotage*, an anarchist runs a pet shop, and lives by selling birds in cages. A coded message ('The birds will sing at 4:15') equates birds bursting into song with a bomb exploding. Though it's Bloch who named Marion 'Crane', Hitchcock may have liked that, and thought to share it with his 'unknown friends'. In Bloch she lives in Texas; it's Hitchcock who puts her in 'Phoenix'. His next film will be *The Birds* (again, not his idea: it's Daphne du Maurier's but Hitch found it congenial).

WHAT THE MIRROR SAW

In the motel office a mirror between Marion and Norman 'redoubles' her profile, as with the dealer's mirror. The vaguely romantic ornateness of its frame celebrates her arrival (and will be less evident when other people are reflected in it). Where the ladies', room mirror sprawled all over the place, this one makes a strongly centred 'knot of shapes'. It's strategically placed: on the line of glances between Marion and Norman, and in the centre of the screen, like that very active rear window.

♦

SCENES 103–12 NORMAN PLAYS PEEPING TOM

Glancing into the office register, Norman notices Marion's alias and, now recognising a lie, smiles wryly. Then he finds himself listening, through the wall (motel walls were notoriously thin), to Marion moving around her cabin. His expression darkens. He lifts a picture off the wall, revealing a peephole, to which he applies his eye, and watches as Marion, in Cabin 1, removes her dark underwear and wraps herself in a ladylike housecoat. He marches off towards the house, as if finally resolved to revolt against his mother's tyranny. But on entering the hallway, his nerve fails, and, instead of ascending the stairs, he walks moodily, hands in pockets, down a long narrow passage to a kitchen at the end, and sits at the table dejectedly.

'THE RIGHT TRUE END OF LOVE'

Norman's 'acceptance' brought Marion to her moral senses; now Marion's body inspires Norman to break free. Fair exchange? Admittedly, Norman's obviously habitual voyeurism is a very black mark against him. All the same, a certain common sense, and Freudian theory, could agree that occasional voyeurism, in moderation, by a hag-ridden chap, could be a step nearer a normal love-life than stuffing dead birds is. And by the 1980s, gross-out comedies like *National Lampoon's Animal House* (1978, set in 1962) and *Porky's* (1982) will treat peeking as a risky but jolly rite-of-passage in teenage life. In *Psycho*, it's a silent cry for help – so although it's a sin, perhaps it's a force for good. The moral irony chimes in with Marion's bedroom romp as a tender trap for Sam. Even if it's a sin, it'll help him grow up and settle down. Norman's sin may help him grow up and break out. Alas, he can't go it alone (which fits Marion's pessimism about good resolutions).

Some spectators may wonder if she might catch him spying, and let's just suppose she did. Her reaction, quite likely irate, would reshuffle this pack. Spectators don't just *follow* plots; from time to time they intuitively anticipate where things might lead. 'What happened *next*?' is the constant question, of every child. Suspense and surprise and the 'twist' and the proverbial twist-on-a-twist are all plays on *anticipation*. The interpretation of a story may work mainly from what *has* happened; the *experience* of a story involves intuitions, *thinking ahead*, to possible *effects* and *reactions*; and even events that *don't* happen may be 'in the air'. Many stories *depend* on choices, and alternatives, and are haunted throughout by their *potentialities*. *Hamlet* isn't only about what happens; it's also about what *might* have happened, at each successive story point.

WAYS OF SEEING

Norman's line of sight penetrates a four-fold barrier.

1. The picture shows Bible patriarchs, deep in gloom, surveying a buxom young woman. For most moviegoers, it's just sad, mysterious *Stimmung*, with, via the biblical dress, religious overtones. A few spectators may recognise or guess at 'Susannah and the Elders' (not from the Christian Bible, but the Jewish Apocrypha). It was popular with painters, largely for irreligious reasons. Lustful patriarchs spy on a virtuous woman, then falsely accuse and blackmail her. The parallel with Norman is more poetic for being so oblique (*old* men, blackmail . . .).

2. Under the print is a very neat hole in the plaster, through which shines a ray of light.

3. But there's also a dark, jagged hole, like an ugly gash. It's either that hole from

a different angle, or another layer of wall. Either way, it's an action painting from the Id.

4. A shot or two later comes a big close-up of Norman's eye, bulging in profile. The four 'layers of the hole' make a classic 'montage of contrasts': pious and sombre; neat and luminous; inchoate; blackly focused. The light from Marion's cabin shines back into Norman's eye, and as he moves, a dot of bright light dances about his shadowy form. What attention to detail! But then as they say, 'the art is in the detail' (as 'the devil is in the detail'); and all this illustrates just what 'fine' in 'fine art' means.

STORY OF THE EYE

Norman's glimpse of Marion in black underwear is made optically strange by the telescopic lens. In 1959 telescopic lenses still imposed a mild degree of tunnel vision plus compression of depth plus a 'laminated planes' effect, with things looking flat and flimsy. Conspicuous behind Marion's dark figure are, not the dark-ish walls of her cabin, but bright white tiles – a visual surprise, and our first sight of the fatal bathroom. Cut to the eye close-up: dark, massy, delicate. Cut back to Marion, safely wrapped up in white. It's Hitchcock's practical joke on the lustful males in the audience. The shot of the seeing eye 'blots out' the forbidden sight! But, in most audiences then, women outnumbered men; what of the female gaze? Did women yearn to see Marion starkers? I think they'd be rather pleased at Hitchcock's respect for Marion's modesty.[31] Some critical preoccupations – with man the sexual predator, with Hitch as sexual cripple and therefore a dirty old man, and the notion that female spectators are forced by films to adopt a male gaze while watching their on-screen sisters – risk eclipsing Hitchcock's rare skill, box-office-wise at least, at developing his thrillers in ways which women found romantic. Very likely Selznick had helped, and Reville still helped him with this; it might well explain why he took her advice very seriously. For instance, *Notorious* (be it Art, as so many colleagues maintain, or only expert entertainment plus aesthetic refinement) invests a fallen, self-debasing alcoholic woman with such dignity that Mr and Mrs Middle America could identify with her. Hitchcock knew two or three things about women, including the sometimes delicate balance of sexual desire and self-esteem.

WHAT THE IMPRESSIONIST SAW

After the 'flimsiness' shot of Marion, Norman enters his mother's house, and beholds an *opposite* effect: solidity and depth. To our left is a long, tunnel-like passage to a kitchen. To our right are the first few rises of a stairway up: they're thickly carpeted with a strong pattern, and rise like a vertical wall. Here's another play on 'layered depth'. Both shots pertain to Hitchcock's lifelong interest in perceptual distortions triggered by emotional states. *Vertigo* had the simultaneous backward track and forward zoom, *Spellbound* had Hitchcock's variations on the Dali dream sequence. Through such experiments, optical or acoustic, showy or subtle, Hitchcock continued a 1920s avant-garde – the 'impressionist' cinema of Delluc, Dulac, Epstein, Gance. True, Hitch's effects are shorter, very tightly geared to a story moment and come with no aesthetic 'manifesto'. But some ambitious spirits were too quickly satisfied with notional, 'approximative' ideas, as if experiment mattered and sensitive execution didn't. Hitchcock, as a merely pragmatic aesthete, 'thought about [the *Vertigo* shot] for fifteen years', and claimed he spent 'fifty thousand dollars' to get the distortion precise, which rivals Flaubert's mania for 'le mot juste'.

SCENE 113 MARION FIGURES HER RETURN

At a desk in her cabin, Marion scribbles $700 minus $40,000. Her bank-book, lying open, shows only a few hundred dollars. Wearily, she tears the paper into scraps. About to drop them in the wastepaper basket, she pauses, rises, crosses to the bathroom, and drops the tell-tale pieces into the toilet bowl, which she flushes, before stepping into the bathtub, with its shower attachment at one end.

PARALLEL WORLDS

The last scene ended with Norman sitting, thinking, facing left; this scene starts with Marion in the same position. (Again, no establishing shot.) The shots are graphic parallels, and may even overlap in time. But their similarities coexist with differences. Norman's weariness is dejected; Marion's is stoic, resolute. He's in long shot, therefore surrounded, 'captured' by his mother's house; she's in medium close-up, so her face, and therefore her thoughts, dominate her surroundings. He starts resolute, then sinks into passivity; she rises to cross the room. Having calculated what she must repay, she *corrects* her absent-minded impulse, to leave the evidence in the waste-paper basket. This 'good resolution' seems not just another 'impulsion'. Suspense still prevails, but now it's about changed things: what else may happen to her, on her return?

CRIME AND RESTITUTION

Marion's calculations imply repayment (though the text never says so). The dreaded plausibles, and other rigourists, might reason her situation, roughly as follows, though most of us would rest content with some purely intuitive estimate of her overall prospects, mixed in, perhaps, with some aspect or other divined partly from this film so far, partly from film conventions, and partly from our knowledge of the world. Marion's talk of an early start implies that determined driving could get her back to Phoenix and the bank in time to deposit the $37,000 she still has, and quickly take out a loan for the $700 wasted on the car, to be repaid from her weekly wages. As Sam has been doing all those years. So in a way she'll share his fate – but, alas, apart from him. However, she may still improve his attitude – and as things will turn out, he improves of his own accord, a week too late. As much as we'd like her repentance to let her off scot free, her debt is a rather cruel 'poetic justice' for her half-enacted criminal intention (and maybe for once there's a moral: 'Always be prudent; criminal impulses do not pay' – if that's a moral, it's motivated by selfishness, not by ethical considerations). As for The Law, should the bank trip fail, the money is tax-evasive, so her victims can't prosecute (and Arbogast will confirm they won't). Lowery might fire her and refuse to give her a reference, but, then again, this is 1959–60 and bosses across America are crying out for secretaries. His gullible trust suggests she might get around him, with the odd white lie. (Come to think of it, the film is as vague as he is about *when* and *where* he saw her in the car.)

OBSCURE POINTS

Through a Wall Darkly

Behind Marion in her cabin is a mirror on a piece of furniture placed against a rather plain wall. In the mirror is a patch of wallpaper, whose heavy, tight pattern of darkish blooms (Victorian roses?) is subtly ominous and, being a bit old-fashioned, evokes the house. The second time around, it may occur to us that the wall of roses thus reflected is roughly where the screen, the camera and we the audience are. (If we've also read the script, we'll realise this shot presaged a very startling shot – 199, cut out of the film, in which the camera tracks very slowly in on one of those rosebuds to show that it camouflages Norman's peephole, of which it's a fifth layer – its other side, in fact.)

Mirror, MIrror, Off the Wall . . .

A mirror, in movies, as in life, has a strong uncertainty effect. It reverses left and right, it shows the other side of intervening things, it displaces (and sometimes doubles) things. Moreover, the image 'in' a mirror seems, optically, *further away than the mirror itself*. This particular mirror isn't *on* the wall, it's rather in front of it. So the sombre roses are simultaneously 'opposite' the mirror, 'in' it, 'beyond' it, and 'in front of it'. No wonder that wall-within-a-wall seems to *lurk*. It's one of several, quietly strange, 'patches in background walls' (the two office pictures, Marion's dress closet, the shower tiles – also opposite Norman's eye – his peephole sure gets around).

◆

SCENES 114–18 THE SHOWER

Marion relaxes in the shower. Then its plastic curtain is pulled aside by the silhouetted figure of a tall, old woman, in whose uplifted arm is a large knife. Marion, turning, sees it and screams; the knife's downward stroke enters her stomach. Briefly she holds off the striking arm, but as she weakens, further blows stab her body, and her blood mixes with the water from the shower. Her assailant turns and flees, leaving Marion dazedly clutching the curtain until, collapsing, she brings it down with her. She lies with her face beside the toilet pedestal, her eyes stare across the floor. From her face the camera tracks past the bed and past the folded newspaper and over to the window. Beyond, lights snap on up at the house, where Norman screams, 'Mother, oh God, what— ? Blood— ?'

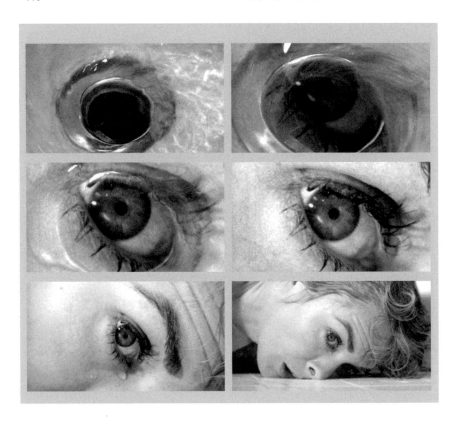

THE HALFWAY MURDERS

Shocked as spectators were by 'the star of the picture' dying halfway through, in fact it counts as Hitchcock's third exercise in the sudden death of a protagonist so innocent, worthy and identifiable-with as to enjoy audience presumption of immunity. In *Secret Agent* an English gentleman (Percy Marmont, veteran star and audience favourite) is mistaken for a rival agent and murdered by our heroes (albeit in uncanny ellipsis). In *Sabotage/A Woman Alone* the heroine's cheeky kid brother is killed by a bomb, placed in a reel of film by his stepfather, a cinema proprietor. (The eventual explosion in a cinema mischievously reflects the spectators' real position.) Both films were box-office disappointments and though Hitchcock offered various other reasons, it's reasonable to suspect that audience upset at 'poetic injustice' had much to do with that. Still, these victims were 'secondary major' characters, while *Psycho* kills its principal or *only* identification figure. Admittedly, the compulsory 'happy end' had peaked around 1939, since when the unfair death of a star–hero was a little less unusual: it occurred in box-office hits like *Duel in the Sun*, *No Sad Songs for Me* (1950), *Butterfield 8* and *The Wages of Fear* (the last is Clouzot again, working a bitterly absurdist twist). But such deaths were carefully prepared by moral-dramatic patterning: they follow some sin or tragic flaw, or they're morally affirmative or gloriously vitalist, or 'a good cry'. Here the death of Janet Leigh, normally a happy star, is carefully *not* prepared, and defies all standard dramatic protocol since Aristotle. It proclaims a state of chaos, especially rare in American entertainment then.

DEATH IN THE SHOWER

The shower scene blasphemes against a modern American religion: fresh hygiene, bodily health, sensuous happiness, ever-renewable innocence. Its 'mechanics' negotiate daunting limitations. Its *mise-en-scène*, confined to a tiny space, must conceal both the assailant's identity and three scattered areas of the naked victim's anatomy. Hitchcock's solution is extreme shot dissection – a montage flurry of actions and reactions, conveyed by close-ups and 'marginal' parts of the body. Mrs Bates becomes a scarcely glimpsed silhouette with a slashing knife, an 'old lady' bun of hair and a broad-shouldered vigour attributable, first time, to the proverbial super-strength of the insane. Being of only secondary interest, s/he disappears halfway through, leaving Marion to die *alone* – a key 'detail'. The murder of Marion is, visually, her solo, like an 'aria' or a soliloquy with no word spoken or sung. To paraphrase Faulkner, it's 'as I stood dying'.

To that extent, it's a study more in terror than in cruelty. It's both sadistic and masochistic (as 'opposite', or complementary, as those attitudes may be). Audience screams and remarks like 'I was a bathtub person from that film forward' suggest that sharing Marion's fear is the dominant reaction. Few 'normative' spectators, in those days, would identify with a shadowy, crabbed, mad old woman (the first time round), or this stunted, hag-ridden loser (the second time around). And even if *everybody* has a sadistic streak, which Marion's tortured nudity would arouse, it would *also* arouse the *resistances* applied to this sadism by the 'ordinary decent spectator' – who, although no saint, is a 'moderately moral' man or woman (or so democrats must pretend to believe).

However, old high culture media theories felt free to attribute extreme moral debility to moviegoers and latterly Freudo-Marxism has followed suit, effectively *equating* moviegoers with their libidinal Unconscious and infantile responses. Nonetheless, it's counter-arguable that moviegoers, like other art consumers, become, at least while absorbed in a film, *more* sensitive, *more* generous to other people than most reality situations allow; so that the arts in general are conducive to consideration for others.

This relatively cheerful estimate of typical spectators by no means rules out the possibility of wicked, and in this case sadistic, excitations. For cruelty to excite, identification with the screen assailant is *not* required; the victim's suffering is spectacle enough. The murderer's very *shadowiness* allows the sadistic viewer to substitute a fancy-dress (but not always disavowed) portion of himself. Hence traditional pornography so often depicts a beautiful woman assailed by shadowy or grotesque male figures – skeletons, monks, febrile debauchees – as in Sade, Buñuel and Pasolini. Moreover, those younger filmgoers who shocked Hitchcock by treating *Psycho* as a saturnine comedy belonged to a generation which, in fantasy situations, easily let its sadism, whether sexual or just *cruel*, rip. It was shedding some of the moral scruples of a 'liberal' generation – that of the 'social problem pictures' by men like Kramer, Zinnemann, Foreman and others, and adopting more radical views whereby anything goes in fantasy, which is either a victimless sin or no sin at all. My impression is that subsequent fans of slasher films read torture not as an appeal to their compassion, but as a *challenge* to their weakness, and as subversive resistance to the sentimental view that the routine relation between people is tender loving care. As that philosophical pessimist Hobbes pointed out, the basic relation between individuals is mutual fear plus mutual need, and as Sartre observed, 'Hell is other people'.

IS THIS A PHALLUS THAT I SEE BEFORE ME?

Much Freudian theory tends to pansexualist reductionism: whatever it is gets explained by some sexual component. Hence a popular idea that the 'real' meaning of Norman's knife is that it's a phallus. This too quickly assumes that if a sexual analogy with a detail is *possible*, it *must* be in play, it must contribute *most* of its meaning and emotion, and it *must* have determined its choice. For this approach, Hitchcock's knives are sitting ducks (though his other interest, throttling, sets a problem). Knives are emotive because they're dangerous in non-sexual, reality-related and entirely conscious ways. The 'vulgar Freudian' equation of long weapons generally (from snub-nosed automatics to ICBMs) with the phallus brusquely overlooks some intriguing differences: no knives desire a woman or give pleasure to the person in whom they're stuck, or start a new life. To that extent, the shower attack is *anti*-sexual. And even if we suppose that all the Normans in the audience get excited, is it sexual excitement, or action adrenalin, or excitations of cruelty and power? Marion's nakedness, albeit sexual, is *also* the *vulnerability* of nakedness – and spectator *tenderness* towards the maternal body, first object of love to both sexes. As bestial and vile as everybody's libidinal ('forbidden') drives may be, love and protectiveness are radical instincts also, and equally 'libidinal' (in that word's other sense, of life-force energy, including permitted, indeed encouraged, drives). Tenderness may actually be a powerful unconscious drive (though *not* 'libidinal' in the usual sense of 'morally bestial force'). That *Psycho* in its time had as little trouble with censors as it did rather supports Hitchcock's judgment as to the *negation* of natural sadism by *equally* natural instincts, some moral (e.g. objections to murder) and some (like sympathetic identification with Marion) part of the instinctual basis of community.

STRICTLY FOR THE BIRDS

As with knives, so with birds. Sometimes, no doubt, they denote, or connote, the phallus. And sometimes, being soft and feathery, they're female, as per 'bird' and 'chick'. Sometimes their beady eyes evoke a malignant gaze, or a sharp one ('hawk-eyed'), or a benign one ('a wise old owl'). Sometimes flight evokes sexual excitement, sometimes it stands for something else, as in *Birdy* (1984). Sometimes the flap-and-flutter of birds evokes hysteria (more evident in females than in males, though males too 'get in a flap'). Is Hitchcock's avian complex to do with *fear*? Or with tensions between psychic tendencies which the bird seems to *combine*: darting attack and softness, panic and escape, victimhood and hatred – as in *The Birds*. Is Daphne du Maurier's novel 'really' an exercise in phallophobia (which, incidentally, is a widespread attitude, for, in unconscious symbolisms, the phallus is a frightener of rivals, as well as a sexual instrument). Or is her novel a broader reflection on civil society versus nature?

'ORRIBLE MURDER: A BLOW BY BLOW ACCOUNT

As a narrative event, the killing in the shower needs only one line: 'Mrs Bates stabs Marion to death in the shower.' Hitchcock's *narration* spreads these nine simple words over 70 shots. The single event comprises six phases (or, since they're so lyrical, let's think of them as 'stanzas' in a poem).

1. Induction.
2. Marion, showering, relaxes.
3. Prelude to attack.
4. The struggle.
5. Marion dies alone.
6. Marion lies dead.

Each phase has what Eisenstein could call its 'dominant' – some principal mood, emotion or activity – and its 'turning point', or 'moment of truth'.

For 'spooky house' murders, convention prescribed chiaroscuro. But these high-key visuals make a 'symphony of whites': creamy grey (Marion's body) plus blonde (her hair) plus shiny dazzling whites (tiles) plus silver-pearl (the water) plus chromium. It's virtually shadowless – though the shower-head has fine black lines, and the fine black holes in the rose make a texture, as if of 'steely threat'.

First stanza. The camera follows Marion as she walks from her calculations, past the toilet bowl and into the bathtub, while also tilting down her body to show only her feet as her bathrobe slips down around them. Tilt-downs to a disrobing woman's feet were a stock device, sometimes suggestive, sometimes respectful: here, I think, it's both (as through the peephole earlier). Her walk has a certain 'momentum', a little 'thrust', as if annunciatory. In the tub, the plastic curtain obscures her body, its amorphous shadow continues moving leftwards. (The vague grey shape is not an outline, which would be overly sexual.)

Second stanza. Marion starts showering, her expression grave. Then she lifts her face to the shower-head, which showers upon her sensuous blessings, banishing her cares about tomorrow. She doesn't use a shower cap, and her wetted-down hair gives her head a cannonball roundness. (Quotation-lovers may think of Falconetti in Dreyer's *The Passion of Joan of Arc* [1928] and Jean Seberg in Godard's *Le Petit soldat* [1960.] She smiles exuberantly, soaps herself vigorously. For the first time in this film, she's at peace (but with active energy). There's a hint of 'ritual self-cleansing', of a pagan, guiltless kind maybe. 'Unabashed pleasure' strikes me as the dominant mood. Moral rigourists may have reservations about the way physical pleasure and 'taking no heed for the morrow' roll in. There's almost a 'silent duet' between Marion's face and the water spray. But a close-up of the shower-head, as a hard geometrical shape, like a blank impersonal face Up There, makes it inhuman, relentless.

Most spectators remember this phase as just a shot or three, mostly Marion front-on to camera. But more goes on, to do with subliminal spatial change. Her left-ward walk establishes a particular orientation. But in almost the next shot, the curtain is sideways on to her, screen right. And in subsequent shots, the spray hits her face from different directions. To be sure, one turns around in a shower. But here I think the spatial inference is that the camera has 'crossed the action line' (proverbially a continuity no-no, because visually confusing, unless special precautions are taken). It's not too confusing here, as the shower locates her precisely. But from *both* continuity *and* montage theory it would follow that these spatial shiftarounds give the 'static' space a subliminal unquietness. To Eisenstein's list of types of montage collision (by movement, tone, shape, line, etc.), Hitchcock adds 'collision of spatial orientation'.

Third stanza. Marion's face is relegated to the lower-righthand edge of the screen; the rest of the screen is the white, plastic curtain, visually 'empty' save for a haze of light, and its slightly sharper source just above her head. In one respect it's a conventional move: the camera pre-introduces the area in which some development will occur. Unsettling, however, is the sudden cut to a 'nothing' nebulosity in an 'unbalanced' composition. For a moment or two, it's an 'Antonioni shot': a woman's face in a cold, blank space. Then a shadowy agitation attracts the camera, its quick pan-tilt lets Marion's face 'fall off' the lower right corner, the curtain jerks aside, a big tall figure blocks out the light (with, directly behind her, a patch of that flower-blotched wallpaper). The violins start.

Fourth stanza. Marion turns and screams, in a segue of three, progressively nearer shots of her face: close-up (full-face), big close-up, (eyes-to-mouth), very big close-up (mouth only). A major visual 'theme' begins: the knife's slanting down-strokes contrast with Marion's mostly lateral movements. Her face threshes from side to side; her long left arm stretches out to grip her assailant's wrist. Her other arm is defensive across her breast. As her defence fails she turns to flee, but is trapped against the wall, leaving her back defenceless (the turnaround motif?) Conspicuous close-up details include shots of her abdomen and side, so close that they're a bit featureless, like slabs of meat and (an early switch to vertical) her feet trampling in panic, as blood mixed with water flows between them. (Though entirely natural and logical, Marion's turnaround, and her outflung arm, echoes other such movements, such as Norman's outstretched arm and her own U-turn around the hotel bed. Maybe they qualify as motifs – appropriate, in an art of movement and of body language.)

It's both lyrical and *narrative*. The very first stroke seriously injures her: the knife slices down past her face and shoulders and disappears below the frame. A sound like slapped meat says the blow has struck home, 'down there'. (To be pedantic, knife strokes are silent, so perhaps the sound is poetic licence, but then again, if it went in to the hilt, and the side of the fist made contact …) In the 1950s, stabs to stomach or belly being readily fatal, this early blow establishes a serious, doom-laden suspense, very different from the suspense of, say, *North by Northwest*, which, although 'nail-biting', is exuberant, hopeful and as amusing as it is hysterical.

Hitchcock claimed that no stroke of the knife is seen drawing blood and in some prints this may be so: but in one at least, the sharp-eyed can see a little blood swell out around the apparently entering blade. The 'moment of truth' – the moment when her death seems certain – is heralded by an 'apex' shot: a quick, low angle of the knife lifted high in the air, making a thin shape against an expanse of ceiling. After this 'skeletal emptiness on high', Marion's flesh fills the screen, as her side and waist turn and she vainly presses the front of her body against the tiles behind her.

Fifth stanza. Marion, dazed, stretches one arm forward into space – a blankly mechanical act? A confused appeal? But no one's there – even her killer has gone. Is she too confused to know how alone she is? Her hand encounters the shower curtain and, falling, she pulls it down with her. In low-angle close-up, the curtain hooks snap and jerk up, like bells – do they 'claw the air'? Then the camera, flat down near floor level, looks at the toilet pedestal as Marion's face falls into frame and lies with one cheek pressed on the floor, staring at the camera. The camera looks up at the shower-rose above, pouring water down upon it. It smacks of Marion's POV (thanks to the juxtaposed eye, and the above/below effect), but it can't be (she's looking out, not up). It's *our* POV – (audience subjectivity, not character subjectivity – the water seems to hit the camera-eye itself (though the shower-rose had been fixed to spray all round it, or the first drop would have blotted out the shot). The camera pans with water, and threads of blood (more thin and light than melodrama would require) flowing between Marion's feet, and swirling around the plughole, onto which the camera closes, so that it dominates the screen.[32]

Sixth and final stanza. Cross-fade from the black hole to Marion's wide-open eye. A lone drop of water trickles from her eye, but then flows in a strange direction (for her face is on its side). As if to 'mirror' the swirling water, the camera rotates the staring eye. Then, from Marion's face it moves back past the toilet pedestal, into the cabin and past her robe upon the bed, moves up to and continues past the newspaper (with its hidden contents), and tilts higher still to the 'window-scape', where Norman's cries get the story moving again.

The script indicates, in circumspect terms, a shot not used. Marion lies 'half-in, half-out of the bathtub, her head tumbled over, touching the floor'. Not spelled out is what immediately strikes you when Gus Van Sant filmed this shot for his 1999 remake: Marion's body is folded over the rim of the bath, with her bottom hoicked up, presented to the high-angle camera. A pathetic but obscene and nasty shot, unacceptable then.

ALICE DOWN THE BLACK HOLE

Marion's glazed eyes, as she gropes for the curtain, cap the 'mental confusion' theme. They also cue an eternal human curiosity about people's dying thoughts and, especially for Catholic spectators, concern for the state of a soul at the moment of death. Most Christians today would suppose she's 'saved', for she just decided to 'do the right thing' and because, in Christian principle, 'Between the stirrup and the ground/ He mercy sought, and mercy found.'[33] But only one thing is sure – that in this world, all consolation is denied her. And perhaps there is no God, only a dark tunnel – 'down the plughole' (in Old Cockney idiom).[34] The cross-fade says nothing exact, but metaphors hover about it: the frozen eye against the blinded eye, the very eye of night, the midnight mirror from which no light returns – or even, as a Freudian might suspect, it's that fantasy figure, the anal mouth and eye. Her 'speaking look' to the rotating camera is her last 'silent soliloquy', though when the dead try to speak to us, we can't quite make out the words. Is her stare indignant protest? Pathetic appeal? As for Christian hopes of an afterlife, or moral rationalism, or stoicism – same difference, all values are futile... it's as merciless as *The Seventh Seal* (1957).

An actual moment of death is suggested – although uncertain – when Marion's fall brings down the curtain (a Hitchcock pun perhaps). Or, indeed *rings* down the curtain, for in low-angle close-up the curtain hooks jangle and dance in mid-air like crazy bells. I'm reminded of a mysterious detail in *The Man Who Knew Too Much* which prompted Peter Bogdanovich to ask, 'What is the purpose of the unravelling sweater towards the start?' Replied The Master, 'It's the thread of life that gets broken', adding, 'One could still get pretentious in those days.' Why 'pretentious'? Perhaps because the rich domestic detail doesn't point us towards the metaphor. The two 'planes of meaning' rather disregard one other, which impedes the leap from sign to meaning. Moreover, the signifier ('thread') is part and parcel of a complex description (a rich, domestic scene), and *this* signified obstructs the other signified ('life ending'). The unravelling thread and its second meaning ('life snapping') can't escape the scene and attain the realm of more abstract meaning. A pity, because the semantic project was an interesting one (packing together womanly solicitude, the fragility of life and a 'force of summation' such as proverbial metaphors possess). In contrast, Marion's dying tell us what the snapped-off curtain and the hooks going arse-over-tip are about; no detour via metaphor is required; the *kinetic* (as in 'kinema') acts directly on the nerves, like a concrete *event*.

THE SHOWER MURDER AS DYNAMIC FORM

The shower scene is a *tour de force* of montage editing, of an unusual kind. It's not what Hollywood called a 'montage sequence', a weave of cross-fades and optical effects. It's mostly bold cuts, more like montage Eisenstein-style.[35] Marion's scream in three, successively bigger close-ups, all from the same angle, is a 'classic' Russian montage trope. (Russian montage prized the visual 'collisions' between ever-closer shots;

the usual Hollywood equivalent was a short, swift track-in, which is smoother and less distracting.) Though the shower-scene has a certain 'Russian' quality (in its swiftly changing rhythms, and its sense of a cutting *system*), it's visually softer, on the whole, for three main reasons.

1. Hitchcock, like Hollywood generally, 'cuts on strong movements', which usually softens cuts,[36] whereas the Russians got harder cuts by using a higher proportion of more 'static' compositions (i.e. compositions whose static elements are stronger, relative to moving ones).

2. Even when Hitchcock's shots stress bold, hard shapes (the shower-head, Marion's head with slicked-down hair), the 'grey-to-silver' tonality softens the visual images.

3. At these cutting speeds, plus furious action, the shots can't quite 'fix' in the mind and 'collision' becomes a sort of 'staccato flow'. Though fast and furious, the shower sequence is much softer than Eisenstein's cream separator sequence. The Hitchcock shower is a 'liquidiser' sequence, the Eisenstein is all chops and churns.

As a flow of 'fleeting impressions', Marion's death is half akin to the 'impressionism' of French avant-gardes in the 1920s, most especially, the axe murder in Kirsanoff's *Menilmontant* (1925), but also to certain aspects of the snowball fight in Gance's *Napoléon* (1928). Of its flurries of images, very few are character POVs. For example, the shot of Marion's abdomen being stabbed is far too close and low to be Norman's POV; what it conveys is impact (not, perhaps, pain – yet) in the part of the body shown. This is true of so many shots, and Mrs Bates is so rarely seen, that even when an occasional shot *might* be from her POV, her experience is eclipsed, over-whelmed, by that of the person whom we do, vividly, see. It's another case of spec-tator preoccupation with, not *the act of seeing*, by an invisible person, but by the character whom the camera shows us. In much the same way, an *objective* close-up of an expressive face can vividly convey its *subjective* experience, where a *subjective* shot from its POV would *hide* the face, occlude its experience and divert the spec-tators' thought to what fills the screen. (This golden rule has many complications, and POVs can have a powerful effect when combined with reaction shots; but that's down to the combination; and Hollywood has excellent reasons for its limited use of POVs alone. All that's another essay; meanwhile it's worth off-setting the preva-lent idea that POVs are a royal road to identification and themselves explain Hitchcock's effects. It's arguable that POVs suit certain confrontations but have less relevance to inner experience (and physical melodrama is a condition of his use of them). The shower sequence emphasises one person's fast-changing experience over dramatic interaction.

CHAOS COME AGAIN

As a 'character-centred' sequence, it's more 'individualistic' than Eisenstein's montages, which, generally centring on crowds, are 'collectivist'. Both perspectives are equally 'modernist', the tendencies of which included an exacerbated individualism. Marion's 'impressionistic panic' is one woman's stream-of-consciousness-in-these-fleeting-seconds – but it's also how *any* human mind might perceive such an event. It's not so far from the Futurist sense of 'perception running at brutally high speed, disrupting individual structure'. 'The Stabs of the Knife Interpenetrate The Woman' might be its Futurist title – it pursues the idea of reality *as* disruptive energy, tearing body-mind structure to shreds. Marion's body-identity is shattered by a man whose body-identity is shattered already. Here's a *double* 'abolition of the human subject' – considered as atrocity (not surveyed complacently, as a collectivist desideratum).

MURDER BY MONTAGE

Marion's death is 'ecstatic', in Eisenstein's sense, where 'ecstasy' means some extreme mental state of horror and pathos. It's an 'individualistic' cousin to his 'atrocity montages': frenzied butchery in *Strike* (1924), panic on the Odessa Steps in *The Battleship Potemkin* (1925) and, in *October* (1927), crazy ladies jabbing their parasols into a male Bolshevik's bared stomach. The morbid aspects of these scenes don't invalidate their moral purpose. Both directors demonstrate, on our pulses, how 'pleasure' is not just *overwhelmed* but *cancelled* by horror we see.

NARRATIVE MONTAGE

Some left-wing formalists like to contrast a 'modernist montage cinema' with a 'bourgeois narrative cinema'. But the shower montage is a 'bourgeois' narrative, and indeed a classical five act drama (an 'organic drama of pathos', as Eisenstein described his *Potemkin* film, to contradict modernist extremists). It comprises

1. A peaceful, apparently stable state of affairs.
2. An 'attack'.
3. A climax.
4. The 'falling action', and
5. A new 'equilibrium' – death – as 'closure'.

Though this 'closure' leads – seamlessly, within the same shot – to 'de-closure' – Norman's voice restarts the story. A major anomaly: the 'antagonist', Mrs Bates, appears only briefly. However, there's a secondary antagonist – the shower itself. Prosaically, of course, it does nothing at all. Poetically, it's active, as, in poems and novels, settings often are (Egdon Heath in *The Return of the Native* is a virtual character; and so are the dead presidents in *North by Northwest*). The shower-head gets big close-ups, like a hard, strong face and (thanks to context) its attitude changes, like a character's, from benign to cruelly indifferent. At the start, it blesses Marion with its 'healing rain', and she turns her face gratefully up to it, like a sunflower to the sun; as she soaps her face and neck, her hands come together, almost like a prayer (serendipitously I'm sure). But then the hard, round shape of the shower-rose is steely, enigmatic, indifferent to her happy adoration. In the sideways-on 'premonition' shot, it's a jutting-out shape, 'oppositional' to her. During the killing, it's hardly seen, but its water keeps on pouring down (to Leigh's discomfort). It glares down on Marion's dead body; its unseeing indifference may remind Hitchcock-watchers of other, aloof faces, up above, like an uncaring deity: in *Blackmail*, a pagan god in the British Museum, in *Saboteur* the Statue of Liberty, in *North by Northwest,* the dead presidents, and the Master of Suspense himself, in countless jokey publicity poses. The shower-rose, Marion's glazed eye and the bath drain make three round Os, mirrors of one another. Meanwhile, the shower itself becomes hostile, Marion can't escape, only press herself against white tiles ….

A PERVERSE RESPONSE: TEENAGE SADISM AND YOB CAMP

Very early in the film's release, Hitchcock heard with alarm of audiences treating *Psycho* as comedy. In default of further details, I suspect this 'perverse' response links with a new, gleefully wicked attitude among younger audiences. Pauline Kael too was shocked to hear teenagers gleefully chanting during a horror movie, 'Somebody's going to get it …The young were displaying a new *Schadenfreude*, lacking in the traditional family audience. (That did have a certain moral elasticity – exactly *how* elastic we'll never know, for the Hays Code made sure its limits were never tested.) It vastly enjoyed such 'comedies of murder' as, for example, *Arsenic and Old Lace* (1944) and *Kind Hearts and Coronets* (1949), and some late Cagney gangsters went some way into joyous sadism. But the balance of morality and mischief could be risky: in *Monsieur Verdoux* (1947) Chaplin got it badly wrong, in *The Trouble with Harry* (1956) Hitchcock got it not quite right.

My surmise is that the new youthful sadism, apparent and/or real, had a plurality of causes, requiring a committee of sociologists. *Rebel without a Cause* struggled to express some of them, and the psychoanalyst on whose case histories Nicholas Ray's yarn is based had serious predictive intent. And, as prophecies go, it has stood up rather well. Perhaps it's worth adding that joy in screen violence could reflect the unprecedented security of everyday life in the affluent West, plus a certain reaction against the obsolescence of many moral ideas, plus it's a yob counterpart to camp ('nothing is serious, everything is permitted'). As for sexual repression causing violence, it's a very pretty theory for which there's negligible evidence; especially if sexual repression also causes practically everything, civilisation included.

Quasi-sadistic teenagers, on discovering *Psycho*, would be second-time viewers that same week; recommend it to their pals and, mischievously disregarding Hitchcock's pleas, tip them off as to *some* of what would happen. Whereupon *Psycho*'s 'lyrical realism in the key of dread' would give way to sadomaso hilarity: Norman's shyness becomes slyness and 'Mother's not herself today' illustrates, not a loyal son's tact, but the new taste for sick jokes, which had not long emerged, in oral culture, with no mass media trigger. Soon, Saturday-night student audiences would roar with approval at the hyper-violence of Peckinpah and his ilk. Their hearty sadism, at the best educated levels, may lie behind Hitchcock's remark to Truffaut, that the long killing sequence in *Torn Curtain* (1966) arose because 'I thought it was time to show that it was very difficult, very painful, and it takes a very long time, to kill a man.' Moral reasons, as much as concern for Oscar-level prestige, may underlie Hitchcock's never attempting another film in the *Psycho* vein.

Years later, Perkins liked telling people that Hitchcock planned *Psycho* as a comedy, but, then again, he himself disturbed its NFT showing by loudly laughing all the way through it. It may well be true that while working on the film Hitchcock sometimes talked with collaborators in jokey terms; but a film's creator is in a rather special position; creating a work of art, thinking like its imagined audience, working day after day, puts him in an *ironic* position, and in need of comic relief (especially if, like Hitchcock, he had a strong sense of humour). Jokes ease the tension. Had The Master of Suspense really planned a comedy, his misjudgment would rival *Springtime for Hitler* in *The Producers* (1968).

DOWN THE PAN

After Marion's good resolution, the shot of the toilet bowl was a shock for 1950s America. It resumes sordid realism where von Stroheim left off, and may well be the first toilet bowl to appear on a Hollywood screen (porcelain adds another chilly white). Hitch compounds the offence by adding both white scraps of paper floating on the water and the flushing sound.

In some 1960 British release prints the screen's lower quarter was covered with a black band from edge to edge. Few spectators noticed, or, if they noticed, were 'alienated' by the film's abruptly changed 'format'. (And did the black band act as a presage?) Perceptive colleagues inform me[37] that some prints briefly and dimly expose Marion's nipples, though in a position (just above the bottom edge) where most spectators, concentrating on her face, would only see them *eventually*. Maybe Hitchcock planned another stealthy shock, but then thought better of it.

A HITCH IN TIME

The camera's drift-cum-flow-cum-rise from Marion's dead face keeps the film moving visually, though nothing on screen stirs, and the story has stopped dead. Movement-over-immobility is usual enough for the human eye, but from a movie camera it has a 'double rhythm' effect; the camera, which is outside the diegesis, is inserting movement over it. The flow of visual change occupies our mind and elasticates our sense of time; clock time becomes less obtrusive, the time of mental activity takes over. As Bergson might say, we shift from objective time to poetic duration. This indefiniteness gives Norman time enough to get back to the house, change his clothes and change his mind, which literal screen time would not. Earlier, the shot of Marion seated at a desk neatly separates diegetic from concrete time. It starts with her sitting there *already*, her very posture suggesting 'a while'. Deleted, therefore, was her decision to work all this out now, tired as she is, finding the right papers, and so on.

FORMS

On Camera Calligraphics

Entering, the camera *asserts* Marion (tracking in her wake, respecting her modesty, as her robe falls about her feet). It follows the Hollywood rule of thumb, that forceful camera movement should have a certain 'motivation' from the scene. A tilt-down to the feet as a woman disrobes was a stock device, sometimes more suggestive than respectful, sometimes, as here I think, more respectful than suggestive. Exiting, the camera asserts Marion's *absence* – her *lack*, if you like – empty face, empty robe, empty bed (three shots of mourning), useless money (fierce moral irony), sinister space. The closing movement is entirely arbitrary; it starts with no motivation, and no destination is pre-implied. Its trajectory – starting low, rising past furniture to 'penetrate' a window – reverse echoes the entry into the Phoenix hotel window.

Elegance and Dread

The opening shot enters this scene by following Marion's feet in from the bedroom, and then watching her shadow move along the tub to the shower itself (whereupon the camera puts itself inside the shower).[38] To leave this scene it starts from Marion's dead face, down on the floor (where her feet were), and follows the path which she would have walked, back into her bedroom, to her robe, and then deviates, towards the newspaper and the window-scape. Here's another cinematic elegance – opening/closing 'symmetry with variation'.

Script versus Film

The script presents what people call 'the shower scene' as six shots (114–18). The first is headed normally – 'Int. Mary's Hotel Room – Night', the others are headed unusually – 'Mary in Shower', 'Mary – ECU' (meaning extreme close-up?), 'The Slashing', 'Reverse Angle' (Mrs Bates' face and departure), and 'The Dead Body'. Shot includes the sentence: 'An impression of a knife slashing, as if tearing at the very screen, ripping the film.' Whether the perceptual shift, from scene to screen, becomes apparent, I rather doubt, but the idea must interest enthusiasts of pure/concrete/abstract cinema. It's made possible by the scene's whites and silvers (flesh, tiles, skin), and Bergman, in *Persona* (1966), will use a similar tonal tendency to relate, in near-concrete fashion, a lonely boy with mechanisms of cinema – in another story of schizophrenia, its voices and silences, its mental absences, its sudden violence. Great minds meet? *Zeitgeist* strikes again? Both, no doubt. Said the *Monthly Film Bulletin* reviewer: 'Bergman talking to himself again.'

This scene has no establishing shot. Instead its opening shot began in the previous scene (Marion leaving her bedroom), so that, as well as the 'scene' containing 'shots', the one shot contains two scenes. As for the closing shot, it starts as a close-up in the bathroom, crosses the bedroom and concludes as a long shot of the Bates house out on the hill – thus comprising two interior scenes and an exterior. Norman's voice from within the house establishes a fourth, 'audio' scene (for visual-space and sound-space are very different things).

It's a moot point whether the landscape is *in* the window (and so *within* the bedroom, like a picture on its wall) or *beyond* it (and so a different scene). Moreover, the shower set, the bedroom set, and the Bates house, were built far apart, and three separate shots were carefully designed to look like one long one.

The closing shot in particular challenges the practice of describing shots as 'close-up', 'high-angle', etc. as it moves through several positions and the spaces between.

Thus the shots are indefinable, in the terms of film 'grammar' or 'syntax', yet audiences understand them as easily as the standardised positions. Refractory, too, the reversed relation between 'shots' and 'scenes'. In *Psycho* many shots, including, of course, the spectacular opening shot, fit no linguistic paradigms.

All this suggests that the forms of film derive, not from some 'code' of standard, arbitrary, 'conventionalised units', such as rules the grammar and syntax of verbal languages, but from the freer flowing processes of visual (and acoustic) perception, which have their own structures, radically separate from those of language, in the human brain. Hence the *irreducibility* of the visual (and musical) arts to words, and vice versa.

Less controversially, one may note that Hitchcock places within one camera movement what Russian montage would more likely show in several shots. Pudovkin's typical alternative to the closing movement would be a little montage of static shots: close-up Marion, close-up her robe, close-up the newspaper, close-up the window (which might work rather well, though differently). To put it another way, the closing shot deploys what Eisenstein called 'montage within the shot'. It's been much less widely discussed than its subsequently wide use deserves. Eisenstein used the moving camera quite sparingly, though he spotted 'the moving viewpoint' in some Renaissance painting.

All this needs another essay. Meanwhile, cine-grammarians will be amused to note how the supposedly 'basic units' of film 'language' – scene, shot, close-up, etc. – collapse, when closely examined, into a sort of spatial soup, or rather, continuum.

FOR PEDANTS ONLY

While we're being rigorously logical, we might as well note that the 'shower scene' is a non-definable space. It's a space for *action*, not a *defined* space. To speak of 'the shower scene' is fair enough, as a rough description, meaning 'the scene with the shower in it', or, 'the scene where Marion is murdered in the shower'. But the shower is not a separate *film* scene; it's at one end of a tub in the bathroom, Mrs Bates *herself* is never *in* the shower (though her hand and knife go in and out), visible behind her is the wallpaper on the wall between bedroom and office, and half of Marion's body falls *outside* the shower.

NARRATIVE STRUCTURE VERSUS DESCRIPTIVE TEXTURE

The shower murder is one event, but it's two story points. For first-time viewers, Mrs Bates kills Marion; for second-time viewers, Mrs Norman Bates kills Marion. (Paradoxically, the story-points, *tel quel*, are mutually exclusive.) Our ten-line synopsis, above, of this scene, could easily be reduced to just one flat sentence, 'Mrs Bates stabs Marion to death in the shower'; and a filmic style as flat as that sentence is all that would be needed, if stories were structured by 'narrative events' and if 'narrative' shaped the forms of narrative movies. But what shapes Hitchcock's style here is not a structure inherent in the narrative, but the description of details specific to this particular event – right down to the kinetics of curtain hooks (or the tuft of Marion's hair splayed against the tiles as her dazed head slides down). Indeed, Hitchcock's forms respond, not to *narrative* as such, nor to some general *structure* inherent in *stories like this*, but to the *narration* of the event – that is to say, the *description* of an event. From this angle, description is the element that makes *Psycho* superior to most narratives of its kind, and distinguishes quasi-classics from their feeble clones. Another phrase for 'description' might be 'semantic density', but all that's another story (in another sense of 'story', meaning 'argument').

♦

SCENES 119–33 NORMAN REMOVES THE EVIDENCE

Rushing from the house to Marion's cabin, Norman sees the body and freezes in horror. Numbly closing the window, he sits on the bed to think what's best to do. Closing the door, which he left open, he recrosses the room to switch off the light, then exits cautiously onto the porch and disappears into the office; its neon sign goes out and he reappears in the moonlight, with mop and bucket. He braces himself to re-enter the brightly lit bathroom, stops the shower, extricates the shower curtain from under Marion's body, spreads it out on the cabin floor and hauls the body onto it. Returning to the bathroom, he rinses the blood off his hands in the washbasin. Vigorously wielding the mop and whisking a towel off a rail he wipes the blood from bathtub, floor and walls. Going back through the bedroom, he slips into the driving seat of Marion's car, repositions it and opens the boot wide. Returning to the bathroom, he wraps the curtain over the body, carries it out in his arms and fits it into the car boot. Returning to the bedroom, he retrieves the cabin key from the floor and gathers Marion's clothes, shoes, slippers, and other remnants, which he stuffs into her case. Taking mop and bucket in his other hand he steps onto the porch, just in time to be caught in the headlights of a passing car, and drop the mop in alarm. After tucking Marion's case in beside her body, he takes a last look round the room, spots the newspaper, overlooked until now, and tosses that in the boot too. Returning to the driving seat, he drives the car a little distance, emerges, and pushes it into a swamp. He's briefly disturbed by the sound of an engine – an approaching car? A low-flying plane? It's another false alarm and, complacently now, he watches the car sink, and pops a piece of candy into his mouth. The car stops sinking, and his mouth stops chewing; but as its descent resumes, so does his mastication.

AN ACCUMULATION OF EMOTIONS

As Hitchcock well knows, all movies, all texts, are geared to the mind of a beholder, in whose eye, all beauty, all meaning and all horror lie. After all, no movie, no text *tel quel*, contains any ideas or any experience whatsoever; its very signifiers are abstract forms, semantically null and void, if no mind brings meaning to them. Minds hold meanings; texts can only provoke them.

By this point in a film, every scene involves not only itself but also *the whole film so far*. It carries an accumulation of meanings, ideas and emotions, which, though *now* invisible on the screen, continue powerful in audience thought. Though powerful, they're not constant and are gradually fading, although at different speeds, depending on what follows and whether they're revived by some allusion, often indirect ones, like 'echo-motifs', or our knowledge that the money is folded into the newspaper, a fact established earlier, in big close-ups, along with Marion's briskly counting hands. This 'accumulation' of previous scenes and signs can have no sign, since it's a *relation* and an *interaction* between many, many signs.

After the surprise slaughter, the 1960 spectator needed a good few minutes to recover. Most Hollywood films alternated climax and relaxation (the successive climaxes lifting the relaxations to gradually higher plateaux of suspense until the *grand* climax). Sometimes, comic relief provides the relaxation, but that would be out of order here: so soon after the murder shock, it might well provoke disgust. A routine move would be, 'Meanwhile, back at Lowery's office ...'. Hitchcock allows *minimal* relaxation and stays with the body, simply changing 'key', from hysteric scherzo in shrill whites, to sombre, heavy, creepy. In one respect the scene is a 'relaxation' – in another, it drops the spectator from the frying pan into the fire.

IN WHICH THE SPECTATOR GOES FROM BAD TO WORSE

Marion's theft was a sad little caper, and, after identifying with her (critically and with much misgiving), for 30 minutes or so, we're violently deprived of her narrative

POV.[39] Norman is now the only identification on upfront offer, and it's a far more guilty, hopeless and morally disturbing one. It gets ever more disturbing as Norman seems to change from a pitiable victim in an impossible predicament, to cool, candy-chewing complacency. Hitchcock draws us deep into moral perversity, through three successive 'markers'.

1. Hitchcock's *Marnie* principle – our sympathy with people trying to resolve difficult problems, as in all those 'crime caper' films (some comic, some tragic, some nasty, some moralistic, some charmingly naughty). This conflicts with our feelings about Marion – we still identify with her (and we can indeed identify with the dead, and demand justice for them, demand revenge, libidinally).
2. Norman not noticing $38k and tossing it into the swamp inspires some of us to an entirely amoral dismay. 'What a waste! I could have done with that money!'
3. As Hitchcock coolly observes, most spectators share Norman's relief when Marion's car resumes its sinking into the swamp. Our relief coincides with Norman's maximum nastiness (candy and complacency) – a lesser director might well have had the car go down before the candy came out and tilted the balance of sympathy against Norman. It's a fine calculation.

MORAL SUSPENSE AS DRAMATIC SUSPENSE

Norman's actions are both immoral and moral. If his initial cry, 'Mother! Blood!', is melodramatic, it signals a clash of basic instincts, which are basic *moral* instincts – horror at murder versus filial devotion – the latter desperately protective. The ill-used son, returning good for evil, tries to save his mother from the consequences of her madness. (It's an unusual dramatic situation, and maybe a subversive one. 'Family first' is an anarcho-rightist position.) He *fathers* his infantile mother, becomes a criminal for her – an accomplice after the fact. Greater love hath no man, than to lay down his conscience for his mother's sake. In his position, which among us would not be tempted to put his mother before The Law, especially once the damage has been done and damage limitation might make sense? We're in the realm of Greek tragedy – with a three-cornered conflict, between, first, that well-nigh universal horror at senseless murder, and, second, that primeval, pre/a/moral tie, blood-obligation (per-haps Oedipal, probably instinctive), and, third, the moral claims of the modern state. How to balance our Marion-centred perspective against Norman's mother-centred perspective? These conflicts are not, I think, just the conscious mind (moral, rational, reasonable, responsible) versus unconscious libido. They're splits *within* the Unconscious itself. The Freudian Unconscious is not just 'raging sexual desire', it's also fear, and it has its own moral conscience, the Superego[40] – which, as part of the Unconscious, has barbaric punishments for even trivial sins[41]...A triple threat to our moral integrity (and identity) activates our 'existential insecurity'. It's as if we have two choices – to repress our immorality, and be 'schizo' in that dimension, or to not repress it, to be paralysed by the undecidable conflict, and to be 'schizo' that way.

In a sense, the very conflict incriminates *us*, along with Norman, and Hitchcock, having tendencies to moral rigourism, may well have reckoned it did. But also, the conflict works on contradictions between our moral codes. And movies, like art, offer us a special situation. For in a movie, even when everything is real*istic*, nothing is real; we have neither power nor responsibility; our mind can freely split between incompatible identifications. The film is set apart from real, outside consequences. Drawing on what tends to happen to others (realism), it allows us to think through how we might feel *if*... – to *speculate* (which, as etymology may remind us, links with *spectacle*, with *looking at*, and with *image-ination*).

THE BANALITY OF EVIL

This turbulence, a 'semiotic invisible', *saturates* the new shots, as they arise. They can dwell on familiar domestic activity: mopping, rinsing, wiping, tidying up, clearing things out, dragging and lifting. Is this the longest housework sequence in movies? It's certainly the quintessence of Hitchcock's poetic vision: an extreme situation, emblematising 'the horror! the horror!', saturates a familiar, mediocre, everyday activity. The champion of the prosaic made transcendental by invisible forces, without diminution of its materialism, is Robert Bresson – towards whose realm Hitch tiptoed in *The Wrong Man*. Admittedly, Bresson's spiritual antennae were attuned to the divine, where Hitchcock's turn more readily to the diabolical. But then again, Bresson's spiritual progress led him downhill, to (in 1977) – *Le Diable probablement* (the very phrase implies a preceding question: 'Do you believe in God?' and the first part of an answer, 'No, but—'). Marion's body is scarcely glimpsed: sometimes a fragment (her hands on the bathroom floor, sharp-etched in a hard glare), or blurred and vague (her body-form in milky plastic). The sequence is enhanced by quiet music (musical sounds are strange signifiers – they act like signs yet have no definable signifieds). Between 'ripples' of music silences register *as* silences – like 'the sound of silence' – that is to say, they're semiotic voids which are cinematic positives. Also 'charged' with undefinable meaning are iconic sounds – the steady hissing of the shower (indifference?), a car swooshing by (the sound of unknowing) and a droning aircraft. The last two play on off-screen space, an invisible dimension, whether visual or acoustic. And visual space is one thing, acoustic space is quite another.[42]

Though poignantly descriptive, the sequence is also *narrative*. Norman's state of mind evolves, from shock through dogged briskness, to a saturnine smile. It starts with a strong decision – to pull himself together, to resist emotion and perform the necessary action. The final smile, plus the candy, is, perhaps, an early clue as to who-dunnit; it's Hitchcock 'playing fair' with the detective-minded viewer. (Though I'd think most spectators miss it, being both shocked and morally confused.) The narrative details catch the 'ebb and flow' of much emotional change, which is more dialectical than linear. Mastering his shock, Norman makes his first practical action, closing the window, but, overcome anew by a sort of aftershock, has to sit down: his twitching cheek starts a mini-shudder in his body, and he gulps as if still nauseous. (Come to think of it, closing the window is a dubiously logical priority: is he shutting out the house, site of his 'terrible mother'?)

To be sure, the sequence shows Norman's feelings only superficially, compared with, say, Simenon, let alone Dostoyevsky (film culture is often hyperbolic, as if to be *worthwhile* was towering greatness). Hitchcock's *primary* interest is, not Norman's 'inner' psychology, but Norman's *practical* thinking and actions and their strange relation to the 'heart of darkness' that runs through all things. In the mod-erately moral person, murdering someone is *thinkable* (the many comedies of murder, by all sorts of people, including maiden aunts), and so, to a certain point, is fun and games with the body (as in *The Trouble with Harry* and, in *She Done Him Wrong* [1933], Mae West sitting the corpse of the villainess in a chair and combing her hair whenever The Law looks in). At Marion's death, Norman shows shock, but not pity; he gives her body not one regretful glance, just performs his task with alienated objectivity. His combination of voyeuristic and taxidermical proclivities might, at a push, reasonably prompt a whiff of necrophilia, but now that he has the opportunity nothing like that develops.[43] Perkins keeps us conscious of Norman *thinking*. Not obviously 'acting thinking' – stopping to ponder, grimacing 'Aha!', etc. – but by the deadpan of thoughtful concentration. The rhythm is that of a practical task, performed with dedication. Hauling Marion's body from the bathroom, he shifts his grip from her armpits, to her forearms, to her wrists. Emerging from the cabin, he holds his hands out loose, then wipes one hand off on his shirt, while the other curls round a scarred wooden pillar. Before entering the bathroom to clean it up, he braces himself, with mop and bucket pulling down his dejected shoulders – Emil Jannings, who was famous for acting with his back, couldn't have done it better, or with as much restraint (and Hitch's camera races round to set Norman at the angle to the door that emphasises 'an onerous duty of entry'). Perkins is acting thought, with his back, in long shot. (Now *that's* body language.) Acting-wise, it's silent cinema (but with sound-era finesse). In which regard, Perkins merits co-auteur status with The Master. Like the candy idea, these nuances are *his*. The script specified the actions, and The Master, very likely, established their trajectories and rhythms, but the *quality of feeling* would vary with every actor. I don't mean that Hitch 'had no idea', or was blandly heartless; rather, he knows to leave space for the actor's *persona* and nuances. Perkins' haunted eyes and gangling spire of a body mix 'American Gothic' with a quality of solemn thought, and one can believe that here is a rustic-neurotic sense of woe-begone duty. He could hold his own against Hollywood's 'hickory faces' – Henry Fonda, Raymond Massey, Walter Huston – though more weakly anxious, mischievous, wicked. Fonda's stare, reserved but penetrating, suggests a slow, reflective but deadly accurate moral intelligence; Perkins' look is darker, weaker, unsurer, more *modern*.

The sequence is structured not, as one might expect, around Marion's body, but around Norman's actions, including his 'forward planning'. (For example, he doesn't first deal with the body, then carry it out to the car, then open the car boot; instead, he wraps the body, then leaves the cabin to open the car boot, then goes back into the cabin to pick up the body.) A lesser director, going by the book, would strive to simplify Norman's activity for speed and avoidance of repetition. Hitchcock has Norman go in and out of the cabin five times (the variation is *within* the repetition). Instead of putting everything in the boot at once, Norman makes four trips (once to open the boot, once to lower the body into it, once to put the case in too, once to unconcernedly toss the newspaper in). The succession of uncompleted actions generates a sort of sub-suspense. Moreover, interruptions and resumptions split the actions and settings into smaller units which multiply occasions for contrast and 'refresh' one another.

These 9½ minutes, without a word, modulate through ten phases, or 'movements', each conceived like a 'motion painting'.

1. Norman Flies Downhill

Norman's cry rings out from the house on the hill, against the moonlight, and the luminous but creepy-crawly clouds (overtones of 'cosmic protest'?) Then he's a panicky silhouette *within* the house before flinging himself into the blackness of the steps, where he's fleetingly half-glimpsed before his reappearance large and close to camera, in a 'forced perspective' effect, such as Hitchcock loved (sometimes critics deplored their 'failure' of realism; I think Hitchcock geared them to audience excitement, and perhaps they qualify as 'magic realism'). This phase climaxes as his frantic figure bursts across the room (suddenly several sizes larger still).

Eisenstein thought of shots as having 'dominants' (dominant features or ideas) and the idea is applicable to these 'phases' of the sequence. Dominants here include: chiaroscuro hill-scape, agitated figure, its 'jump-crescendo' approach.

The camera's slow drift suggests the passing of a longer time than the shot itself, and is further extended by a convention film shares with theatre. Just as off-stage time can run faster than on-stage time, so that characters sent off on an errand can perform it remarkably quickly, so off-screen time runs faster than on-screen time, whenever convenient.

2. Norman's Reaction to the Body

After the downward rush, a 'freeze' figure shot. After the distant cry, a silent cry (hand over mouth). After the landscape, a tight space (enhanced by his shoulder knocking a picture off the wall, his closing a door, then a window), in which Norman moves to and fro, with numbed calm, through brief pauses (doorway freeze, at window, a moment's thought on bed, etc.). His movements start as if driven (passive), then become deliberate (active).

3. Norman's Retreat

Earlier Marion 'circled' rooms around money; now her body is the scene's 'magnetic pole', hardly seen by us, around which Norman orbits. Instead of 'closing in', he moves right out, onto the porch, and moves cautiously along it, pausing to look to the road (psychologically off-screen space 'enters' the scene). The porch is dark grey in the moonlight (a new shade of pale), except for a neon sign in the window of the office, into which he now disappears completely, leaving a briefly empty screen. The neon sign goes dark (redoubled 'emptiness'). He reappears with bucket and mop – items so mundane as to raise a laugh from the young, newly sado-ghoulish, spectators.

4. The Corpse in the Next Room

Crossing the dark cabin, Norman enters the glaring bathroom. The camera stays in the cabin; his movements are 'boxed' in the bright doorway. His movements start light, get heavier; he stops the shower, rather delicately, then he moves the curtain, then he moves the body onto it. … As he goes between the rooms, bending over things, he's variously sharply defined in a hard white light, a hulking great silhouette in front of it and murkily grey in a dark grey room. Dragging Marion's body between the rooms, he comes at the camera backwards, like a slouching animal. (A dominant of the scene is the 'balance' of humpy slouch and stooping diligence.)

The lighting contrives to combine 'high key' and 'low key' – 'high key' is the white and silver bathroom beyond; 'low key' are the cabin's darker greys. Norman's skin and clothes, halfway between the two, are a chalky, dirty grey (faces in half-light recur thoughout the film).

5. Norman Cleaning the Bathroom

This phase is a quick succession of brief, quick, varied actions, with mop, bucket and towel. Norman's diverse activities, bending, stooping, crouching, drive the action through drastic 'deletions' (e.g. two sweeps with the cloth suggest 'thoroughly cleaning the entire floor'), and the succession of 'part-actions' cues a 'firework display' of deletions, hard cuts and 'montage editing'. Norman's strenuous actions are pursued by a fast, agile camera, apparently on a 360°-mount on a short, stubby boom on a dolly, allowing it to track, pan and tilt simultaneously. The overall rhythm is a sort of flowing *agitato*, with staccato cuts, 'clips' of forceful body movements and gliding camera, all working in parallel. It's a very 'modern' sequence, matching, by slightly different methods, *nouvelle vague* vivacity. The camera's agility becomes calligraphic, and rivals most hand-held work (given this prepared location and action and a few rehearsals). The cuts aren't literally jump-cuts, but vie with that boldness and raise the basic question of how a jump-cut should be defined, for almost all cuts are jump-cuts in space or time or both at once. (The enormous exception to this rule is Hitchcock's *Rope*, whose cuts between ten-minute takes are visually negated by each shot starting precisely when and where the preceding shot left off. They're cuts in the camera, but not on the screen.) Here is 'nervous visual music' – like the credits – though, unlike the credits, it's realistic, heavy, physical. The 'shocker' is the white towel: after the floor has been wiped, it has turned black – that is to say, red. (The colour having to be *deduced* is slyer, nastier, *dirtier* than a 'shock of red' would be.)

6. Norman Repositions the Car

Norman goes through cabin and porch and into the driving seat; potentially awkward movements (opening and closing doors, getting in and out of the car) become a smooth legato (breaking with the bathroom work rhythm). It's another passage of 'momentum sustained through pauses'. Then the screen is 'blocked' by the bulk of the car, glimmering in the moonlight. With Norman at the wheel, we expect it to move away, but it no sooner starts than it stops again, at a changed angle to the porch – Norman having executed two points of a three-point turn. It's a heavy, 'choked off' movement. Climax: a high-angle shot of the opened boot displays its dark vacant maw. (Squared lining paper 'echoes' preceding rectangularities – bathroom tiles, some white tartan curtains, the credits design).

7. Ghost-pale Burden

Back in the murky cabin, Norman bends over the body (*not* remorsefully, not senti-mentally, not nostalgically, not lustfully – just – blankly careful). He lifts it up in his arms (*not* tenderly, not even callously), and carries it across the porch. The dark, patchy shine of plastic, and the taut veil 'helmeting' the face, makes a shroud, but also evokes a wedding dress (carried over a threshold – the wrong way). Stooping, he deposits the form in the boot. (The 'not-feeling' is a 'dominant' – though easily overlooked; the body as *blur, weight, mass* is another.)

8. Marion's Paraphernalia

The tempo quickens again, as Norman, now hurried, restless, 'orbits' the room again, often back to camera. He snatches up small items, scoops an arm round Marion's clothes, stuffs them into her case, grabs from the top of a chest of drawers some-thing small and thrusts it into his lower lefthand jacket pocket, picks up case, mop and bucket, and steps onto the porch. After this fast momentum, another 'freeze', and then studied movement resumes.

9. From Gliding to Sinking

Norman's entry into the car is followed by a close, swift camera movement (an 'entry' quite different from the more distant, static shot of 6). But then, the car's visual bulk 'blocks' the screen; it's a 'heavy' shape, though in the pallid moonlight its tonality is 'light'. It completes its three-point turn and then U-turns away behind the cabins. Its heavily gliding momentum narrowly survives two static close-ups of the number-plate. They're matched almost like the cuts in *Rope*, but the change of light on the car itself hints at what the widened-out shot confirms, that the car is in a rather dif-ferent night-scape (and that the two number-plate shots have bracketed a 'deletion' so conspicuous it might almost qualify as an ellipsis).

10. Off to the Swamp

Norman slips out and laboriously pushes the car forward, from the side. As it creeps forward, the shadows of branches flow sideways over roof and boot. Norman watching the car's stop-start descent is done in alternating shots (close-up of 'vertical' head against long shot of lateral car).

Most of these sequences are variegated, quick 'inserts', a big close-up of the odd, selected objects: the fallen picture, the towel whisked off a rail, the mop jiggled in a bucket, the overlooked newspaper.

The phases average around 60 seconds' screen time each. Yet each feels like experience lifted clear out of time – it's to do with 'duration', not the clock.

TELLING DETAILS: THE POETRY IS IN THE FINE PRINT

As a ten-minute 'mood', this sequence seems monolithic, but it's constantly 'refreshed' by the series of 'little surprises', of 'spot ideas', such as lovers of art appreciate. Of Coppola's *The Cotton Club* (1984), English film director Gavin Millar observed, 'What a wonderful film! A new idea in every shot!' Meaning, some new, imaginatively eloquent 'touch'. Of this sequence in *Psycho*, much the same is true. 'There's a new *attraction* in every shot', Eisenstein might have said. In his theoretical essays, he gave 'attraction' three senses:

1. Its original sense, for him, was the music-hall 'attraction' or 'turn' – the act which commands one's attention before the next, distinctively different, one.
2. At first, the equivalent, in film, of the 'turn' seemed to be the shot.
3. But then, as he delved into the complexity of the shot, he realised its composition was *itself* a montage of elements, of details, each of which might attract the eye and hold the interest for a moment.

One might call such elements 'attractions' – if they attract the eye, touch the mind, hit a nerve or strike a chord. Following this logic, such 'attractions' would range from major story points, to what old-fashioned aesthetics calls 'little touches' (of description, of style, whatever).[44] Sometimes they come in series, like variations on a 'motif'; often they're 'once-only' touches; 'spot ideas', they might be called, but such 'one-offs' may be very powerful, very memorable. The medium itself can concentrate our attention, and our 'emotionalisation', by a gripping film, can imbue little, superficial details with a certain 'poetic', as the film's own 'atmospheric' meets, and mixes with, a phenomenology of details. It's irrespective of 'deep symbolism', or 'deep meaning', or unconscious meaning; it's more to do with the mental concentration.

Three conspicuous examples (given close-ups):

1. In high-angle close-up, the blackened towel drops in the bucket and the mop-head plumps down on top of it, with brisk finality.
2. The mop-head in the bathtub is a creepy-crawly thing, and the bucket is a black pit.
3. In the hand-basin, Norman's hands wash each other, then flick outwards to cleanse the basin, then turn back in on each other.

Thus context, close-up and phenomenology, working together, 'magnify' the sinister potential of things.

THE MAZE OF MOTIFS

Marion's disappearance from the film climaxes several motifs.

Psycho and Topography

Psycho is often topographic (two landscape paintings, shadow-furrowed hills, road-scape windings, Marion's downward glide between two highways, Norman's down-hill rush between two buildings). Marion's 'burial service' begins with a man rushing down a hill and ends with a car sinking in sludge. *Downhill* (1927), an earlier Hitchcock title, about a *social* decline and fall, might explain The Master's interest in falls from heights, as in *Blackmail*, *Saboteur*, *Vertigo*, *North by Northwest*).

It Never Rains but it Pours

Marion's 'pilgrimage' passes a desert, a lake, a brutal rainstorm, a blissful shower, a flow of blood and water, a swamp. (The script, though not the film, pursues the theme, of which more anon.)

Smilers with a Knife

Norman's sly smile ends this sequence, as Marion's sly smile ended another.

Nature Studies

The little painting of a bird (Audubon?) shows loving observation, which a botanical print nearby extends to nature generally. The bird, though only a picture, seems so vividly alive, that its sudden fall is a 'little violence' – almost a shot bird falling. Very different from Norman's big, darkly looming birds, and his scant knowledge of their lives. No realism – only fetishism. They're more than 'realistic', they're *actual* birds – but they're dead, and so they're not birds at all. And – birds being on Hitchcock's mind, can we say Norman *flies* down the hill, and stoops *like a vulture* over Marion's corpse? (But the metaphor distracts from the real strength of the sequence, its *physical* solidity, its *phenomenology*.)

A Case in Point

Norman roughly packing Marion's case makes a third 'case-centred' sequence.

A Foot Note

Marion mocked Sam's bare feet; Norman considerately noticed her wet shoes; she tossed her slippers into her case, near lingerie, her bare feet led her into the fatal bath, where they frantically tread her own blood. Now Norman's filthy ragged mop-head approaches her flat, empty slippers and he holds her shoes in one hand, splayed out like horns. (The meaning is emptiness, absence and pathos, not sexual fetishism.)

Peeping Tom's Blind Spot

The camera shows us the newspaper which Norman has overlooked. When, almost accidentally, he spots it, he fails to look inside it. (Here, *seeing* intersects with *mental lapse*.)

In the script, Norman, on first seeing Marion's butchered body, covers his eyes with his hands; in the film, he covers his mouth. Both gestures emphasise the eyes – one by covering them, the other by underlining them! Every close-up of eyes, whether or not it emphasises their look, reveals the feeling behind them – they're more looked-at than looking.

After this first shock, Norman the peeping Tom hardly *looks* at her corpse, except practically, as an object to wrap up.

He buries Marion four times over – in a curtain, in a boot, in a car, in a swamp – there's a total negation of nudity.

The Night Has a Thousand Eyes

The car flares by, the plane drones over; Norman's looks into off-screen space obeying, not voyeuristic desire, but fear, i.e. the survival/power instinct. (But neither car nor plane could see anything suspicious.) Two or three films around this time featured brief attention to a passing aeroplane, notably *Eyes without a Face* (1959) and *Lunch on the Grass* (1960). (Around this time, planes newly impinged on minds: helicopters proliferated, air travel had mushroomed; the sky was newly an overhead highway, planes distracted you, yet had no meaning.) They blended a micro-*temps mort* (a 'nothing doing' moment, a *nouvelle vague* interest) with emptiness (Antonioni).

Hitchcock adds suspense and relief. Or maybe more. There's something cosmic about the sky at night, especially in those wide, American spaces, where the patch of sky above seems strangely close. For 'traditional Christian' spectators, a significant part of Hitchcock's target audience, the sky could still suggest 'Heaven', and the empty blackness can mean: No sign from God. (In *La Dolce vità*, a statue of Jesus flies over Rome – hanging from a helicopter – another play on the relative positions of aircraft and God.)

Light Relief

Looking for Marion's things, Norman opens and shuts a mirror-fronted bathroom cabinet It's not, I think, about mirrors *tel quel*, but about the flash of light, as a 'variegation' of the scene.

Drifting

Marion 'drifted' from one mood to its sinister opposite, through a cross-fade; Norman 'drifts' from one mood to its sinister opposite, while working diligently away, his face in full view all the time.

SPOT POINTS (SELECTED)

1. The curtain exploits the tactility of some 1950s plastics: clumsy yet cloying, dimly translucent but opaque. It's pulled forth from below the body, then spread flat in half-light towards the camera, then folded over a presence just below the frame, then lifted up, at changing angles to the camera. Its clumsy *stretch* makes Marion's body into crude forms.

2. Bright in the bathroom's hard light, Marion's hands lie palm up on the floor, as if caught in mid-movement (and where we'd expect her feet); a few shots later, as Norman drags her out, her hands are dark silhouettes, hanging thinly down.

3. A quiet shot of Marion's immobile car encourages us to note a lightning-slash speed-stripe on its side. We're shown it only now. Why? Because from here the car will crawl, creep, trundle, start-stop, sink into the earth.

4. Norman cleaning up dirties the world spiritually.

5. The sequence concludes with a fast-fade from black swamp to black. Fast-fade is a standard figure, but black-upon-black has a sort of 'doubled finality'. (It's the first fade to black since Marion's abruptly slowing/sleeping.)

6. As the white car shifts onto the swamp, it's the bright 'figure' against the 'ground'. But as the shadows of the branches slide over it, attracting our eye,

they become the 'figure' and the car becomes the 'ground'. They move in a surprising way: as the car edges forward, they're like a net sliding backwards, and because the boot is a rounded form, they also slide sideways, with a slight rotation. Shadows suggesting furrows across the swamp may remind us of the long shadows across the dawn hills.

OPTIONAL OVERTONES
Though Hitchcock plays his audience 'like an organ', thus creating a (temporary) consensus among spectators, those spectators (and *a fortiori*, thoughtful critics) are *also* separate individuals, with different interests and ideas. That consensus therefore co-exists with a dissensus, varying, often extensively and profoundly, between different audiences and different individuals. The following points may not strike everyone, and conceivably I'm a minority of one, but even readers who decide to dismiss them may find them interesting to reflect upon.

Candy Man
Norman plucks his candy from his lefthand jacket pocket – into which he thrust something small and indistinct that he found in Marion's cabin. Presumably, Marion had left it there – and he put it aside 'for afterwards' – as a little relaxation or reward. But, he pops it in his mouth before his task is finished (hence his stop-start chewing). So, he couldn't wait long enough for his little pleasure. A point in common with Marion? – though its moral context is quite different, of course.

Touch Wood, Touch Flesh
Standing on the porch, Norman's right hand curls around a wooden pillar, while his left palm wipes his shirt. The touchings linger long enough for sensuously inclined spectators (especially women?) to note the physical sensations (even, perhaps, their difference/similarity?). For less tactile spectators, the hand on shirt gesture may still suggest nervous relaxation, like steadying and comforting oneself – or, heart/breast as the site of decent emotion – or, self-reassurance about his physical solidity (like the pillar). This gesture chimes in with a broadly similar gesture (discussed by several critics) in Powell's *Peeping Tom*, where another serial killer of young women touches his own lapel as if quietly confirming his own body. Odd that Hitchcock and Powell, both solitary souls in different ways, shared this idea, at about the same time. (Second-time viewers can suppose Norman's gesture is a transvestite reflex.)

Transmogrifications

A colleague comments: 'The white car "symbolises", "becomes" Marion's white body, its boot and tailfins evoke her buttocks.' This seems very likely, given the widespread understanding of anatomical overtones in car design, spread by bestsellers like *The Hidden Persuaders* (1957), by Vance Packard and *The Strategy of Desire* (1960) by Dr Dichter, the consultant who 'sold' his applications of Freudian theory to a broad swathe of American industry. (Capitalism assimilated Freudian theory well before academic Marxism supposed it was 'subversive'. By the mid-1950s, several Hollywood studios were consulting psychoanalysts about films and stars.) The car/body 'echo' finds two encouragements from the text itself: 'ANL' and deleted shot 118, with its hoicked-up buttocks.

Lord of the Flies

Marion's dead face settled upside down below the toilet bowl; now her car, her surrogate body, sinks into black ooze. To cite a popular idiom, she's in deep shit. Here Hitchcock evokes what Aldous Huxley called 'The Excremental Vision' – human decency is swallowed by 'the horror, the horror'. This nightmare is shared by diverse pessimists: St Augustine ('We are born between urine and faeces'), Dean Swift ('But Celia, Celia, Celia, shits …'), Céline, William Golding (*Lord of the Flies*) and, maybe, Clouzot and Greenaway.

'What people do to good things'

Hitchcock outlined to Truffaut his abiding idea of a film about '24 hours in the life of a city'. His outline oscillates between two storylines: the cycle of the day and the cycle of digestion. 'It starts out at five a.m. with a fly crawling on the nose of a tramp lying in the doorway. Then, the early stirring of life in the city and an anthology on food: its arrival in the city, its distribution, the selling, buying by people, the cooking, the various ways in which it's consumed. What happens to it in various hotels, how it's fixed up and absorbed. And, gradually, the end of the film would show the sewers and the garbage being dumped into the ocean. So there's a cycle beginning with the glossy fresh vegetable and ending with the mess that's poured into the sewers. Thematically, the cycle would show what people do to good things. Your theme might almost be the rottenness of humanity …'.

FREUDIANA

Psychoanalytical theory, like the Rorschach Test, allows an infinite variety of interpretations, especially when the patient, being only text, has no mind at all, either conscious or unconscious, and so can't answer back. A text, after all, is a passive receptacle, an embalmment of past thoughts, but not thought itself; and the beholder is free to project into the text itself, and the gaps and spaces between the words and between the lines, whatever he thinks appropriate.

Phallomania?

For whatever reason, amateur psychoanalysts of film tend to spy phalluses all over the place. All this risks overlooking the female anatomy, and the oral theme from which 'English school' psychoanalysis might focus to link Marion's bra, her frugality with food, Norman's milk jug, his candy (substitute for the disappearing woman?). Candy beside a swamp: it's an oral/anal juxtaposition (and might even yield the equation: Norman equals swamp equals shit – an equation with substantial vernacular back-up, as in 'You little shit' or the slang 'bog' for toilet). Like a baby, he's oral/anal but not genital: he's anything *but* the adult phallus. Is Mrs Bates' knife a phallic symbol (as is just about possible, in her sick mind), or is it a 'lack-of-phallus symbol'? The two things are rather different and, indeed, binary opposites, yet the term 'phallic symbol' very easily confuses them (as it confuses 'representation' with 'replacement'). At least as likely, the knife-in-the-flesh is a *tearing mouth*. Which, like everything else in the Unconscious, has contradictory aspects (such a mouth could be Hannibal Lecter's or Monica Lewinsky's). Either way, it might link with Marion's not eating. When too much is 'explained' as phallic – rockets, knives, words, breasts – the term becomes a synonym for *any* sort of 'power', yet scants the complex, diverse and sensitive skills which power so often requires, and without taking into account whatever functions and roles female sexuality is prestructured to perform.

Down There

Has 'downhill' a sexual equivalence? Like flying/falling? The film's first sexual 'attraction' is Sam's be-trousered crotch and Marion's body, flat on its low level. Then emphasis shifts to breasts: hers covered, but very 'present'; his bare (to please female specta-tors, 'beefcake' being a Hollywood routine). In the shower, the action points down around her groin (the knife in her lower belly). As she turns about, her sex and her anus would 'change place' – much as, a moment later, her eye changes place with the plughole. Disgusting confusion. In the 1960s, several psychoanalytic radicals (Marcuse, Norman O. Brown, Deleuze) denounced the tyranny of the genital and hailed a new era of 'polymorphous perversity', the realm of infantile delights which a post-bourgeois (post-modern?) culture would enjoy. From Hitchcock, who once gave a handcuffed man an overdose of laxative, one would expect a keener ambivalence.[45]

A Symbolic without Desire

It's conceivable, though not probable, that somewhere in Hitchcock's deep dark mind, the mop in the bucket is a 'degraded' sex act (the prick in the pussy), that the hairy-spidery mop-head is a muff or bush (like the women's scalps on the cross at the end of Buñuel's *L'Age d'or* [1930]), and that spectators' unconscious minds get subliminal sexcitations (thanks to heavy help from context). A film can have Freudian symbols coming out of its ears (trains going into tunnels, burning cactuses, a mule's ears pricking up) but, if other interests are weak, they arouse not one jot of emotion, sexual, subliminal or other.

The Eyes Have it

Norman's horrified reaction comes, very likely, from his normal, moral side. Hiding the eyes, as in the script would have better fitted obvious Freudian ideas (the Oedipus complex/self-blinding/'primal scene' theory). But here, hiding the eyes might have looked too childish, whereas hiding the mouth leaves the eyes, and their eloquence, in view. The stifled cry invokes self-control (*adult* psychology). After all, horror at a slashed corpse isn't infantile or 'Freudian' – it's adult, realistic, appropriate. Norman's passionate look is fearful, vulnerable, aghast – hardly 'active' or 'phallic'. But neither is it 'passive' or 'vaginal'. Indeed, active/passive, phallic/vaginal, like so many binary oppositions, are a very poor guide to real-life structures (especially mental and semantic ones). Norman's horrified look is *response*; that is to say, passive *and* active – in other words, receptive, responsive, reactive.

◆

SCENES 134–5 (DELETED FROM FILM)

Norman hoses away the tracks of Marion's tyres, ascends the stairs towards his mother's room, finds heaped on the floor outside it a blood-stained dress and a pair of old lady's shoes, and carries them downstairs towards the basement. From the chimney, a curl of smoke arises.

SCRIPT VERSUS FILM (2)

The script's Scene 134 is captioned 'Close-Up Norman', but that's hardly the normal term for a shot which travels from the motel porch to the house, goes up its stairs and onto the landing, and then back down the stairs to a further staircase down there. As well as showing us, in some detail, other things (like the pile of clothes) along the way, the scene description specifies an 'Extremely High Angle' in which 'we look down on Norman as he bends to pick up the stained dress and shoes'. Later in the film, at the first of the famous plan views of the landing (Scene 173), the scene description specifies that the angle on Arbogast ascending should exactly match that of '#43' (evidently a misprint for 134).

Though the shot was unused, the very idea is so 'structural' as to reward discussion. Shot 134 would have been the first of three plan views of the landing (the others being Arbogast's death at 173 and Norman carrying Mrs Bates down to the fruit cellar at 188 – Hitchcock said the reason for this angle at 173 was to conceal Norman's face; at 188 it also hides Mrs Bates' mummification). Though simpler methods of concealment were at hand, the bold, disorienting, cinematic trope was appropriate for the climactic moment, and its recap at 188, though it's *not* climactic, follows quite naturally. Less obvious is the rationale for its deployment here, where Mrs Bates never appears, and there's nothing to conceal; and the action is quite minor, a sort of 'trailing away' into mysterious depths. However, use of this angle where there's nothing to conceal would help 'camouflage' its subsequent function being to conceal something very specific.

As Hitchcock liked virtuoso effects, for sheer love of film, my suspicion is that 134 starts as a close-up, but then becomes a much wider follow-shot, on a marathon 'travelling', whose various distances from Norman might out-Ophuls Ophuls, until finally it 'takes off completely', and flies above him, like a bird (!), to give us a 'bird's eye view' of the landing.

Be that as it may, a certain disorientation here would have several other functions, some *immediate*, others, *eventual*.

1. 1950s craft practice tended to 'plant' – to prepare, to pre-hint at – striking points, to make them more 'natural' when they did burst forth.[46]
2. Preparation, even when not really necessary, was felt to be elegant, like the 'subtle symmetries' which can have a 'cumulative' effect. By, in the end, deleting the 'plant', Hitchcock presaged the 'modern' tolerance, or indeed preference, for less prepared, less tidy structures.
3. At 134 as at 188 no striking action distracts us from the top shot's 'pure strangeness'. It's centred at the top of the stairs (a realm resonant in dreams), but then leads out in off-screen directions (behind the closed door is a 'naked mother', the stairs descend to a basement).
4. The mother's clothes, absence and closed door suggest Norman's and, more importantly, *our* exclusion from a 'mother's bedroom' realm.

5. This ghoulish version of 'doing the laundry' is a little sample of 'life with Mother' (Norman is treated like a servant).

6. Mrs Bates' clothes are present, but Mrs Bates is absent – a hint to plausibles with sharp detective minds?

7. The 'old lady' shoes, on top of the clothes, contrast with Marion's (which we've been shown in close-up) and help separate them, in our mind, from Norman and from Mrs Bates. 6 and 7 are contradictory – 6 hints at something odd, 7 confuses the hint. And that ambiguity is standard practice, and part of the brain-teasing fun in detective mysteries.

8. The bloody laundry 'echoes' Norman's linen-changing; the hose 'echoes' the rainstorm, the shower, and so on., but nice and peacefully (the scene description mentions Norman's relaxed and innocent air).

The 'jump' from Norman going down mysterious stairs *towards* some vague 'down there', to an overcast skyscape, is another ellipsis and contrast (the missing terms being 'basement' and 'furnace') and, of course, a contrast.

It's hard to tell if Hitchcock cut (or didn't shoot) the sequence, perhaps in response to some question of running time and *regretted* its loss, or whether he *liked* the faster, rawer effect. It's often assumed that aesthetic choices are somehow 'necessary', thus phrases like 'this scene is necessary to the plot', or 'nothing an artist does could have been done differently'. But 'necessity', in narrative, and in aesthetics generally, is an over-used concept; many things *could* have been done *differently* but *equally well*. (This helps explain why artists handle the same syndrome of ideas over and over again, differently each time. It has no definitive form, or, if only one, it's too complex for just one art work; the mind can *always* conceive 'just one more' recombination of possibilities.) The 'rules' of art, unlike those of language, are largely non-prescriptive: they don't tell you what you must do, or that *if* you do *a*, you *must* do *b*. They give you good advice as to what you *can* do. To that extent, they're not 'rules' at all, they're moves, or strategies. They're like the 'rules' of discourse which exist to help you deploy a wide range of different alternatives. The essential function of language is *not* to tell you what to say, but to let your message do that, especially whenever what we seek is information about the signified (and not about language). This is 95 per cent of the time (except, of course, when we're studying linguistics or language-related philosophy).

◆

SCENES 136–8 SAM, LILA AND ARBOGAST MEET IN FAIRVALE

In the back room of his hardware store, Sam writes a letter beginning 'Dearest right-as-always Marion', and proposing marriage. Lila, her sister (Vera Miles), walks into the store, in war-like mood, having assumed that Marion is here, and that Sam is somehow to blame for her crime. Their perplexity is compounded by Arbogast (Martin Balsam), a private investigator, hired to retrieve the $40,000, but not to prosecute Marion. Aggressively suspicious of the suspect's boyfriend, and of her sister, whether acting together or separately, he warily softens to Lila, but remains suspicious of Sam, and, convinced that Marion must be somewhere near him, leaves the shop to start making enquiries round town, leaving Sam and Lila to come to terms.

A CHANGE OF STORY

Marion's story was a crime story (told from the criminal's angle). Now, *Psycho* becomes a detective mystery. Far from being too pat, the near-simultaneous arrival of Lila and Arbogast is logical (Lila came because she knew about Sam; Arbogast shadowed her, on the same plane, maybe). The 'double arrival', replacing two separate arrivals and re-explanations, bustles things along, hurls two new characters into action (and redevelops a third). In its three-way criss-cross of accusations and counters, everybody shifts position (Arbogast from suspecting Lila to suspecting them both to warily believing Lila and meaning to nail Sam; Lila and Sam are nudged towards a still fissile alliance; Sam's honourable letter vindicates him, and he's promptly accused by two people in succession). The enormous irony is, of course, that in this scene Marion gets everything she wanted – not only does Sam propose but it turns out she won't be prosecuted. Life's little ironies …

A CHANGE OF GENRE

As a detective mystery, *Psycho* ignores all the stereotypes of the genres and demonstrates its, often forgotten, flexibility.

1. The audience knows more than the detectives, as in *The Fourth Wall* (A. A. Milne, 1928), which starts with a murder in full view of the audience, and develops suspense, not from our wondering, along with the detective, who-dunnit, but from watching his deductions getting 'warmer' or 'colder' and maybe inculpating the innocent. (Here, we think we know more than we do; we only *thought* we saw Mrs Bates do it.)

2. There's no 'mastermind', or somehow 'superior' detective; Arbogast, Lila and Sam are rather ordinary people, with different attitudes and involvements (Arbogast only cares about the cash, Lila is fiercely loyal; they both accuse and insult poor, muddled Sam).

3. One detective suspects the other two. Will they compete, co-operate, turn on one another?

4. Our detectives have virtually no clues and though Arbogast is our main hope, he's chasing the wrong crime, the wrong man and the wrong place (he thinks Marion is near Sam and in Fairvale).

5. We *desperately* want this crime to be avenged (where the 'classical' mystery is more cool and detached, working to lighter, more abstract ideas of order and justice).

6. This fast-talking scene contrasts with the many long silences, soliloquies and one-to-ones, and promises some hectic cerebration.

THREE CHARACTERS, THREE POVS

All three characters attract spectator sympathy, but in different ways. Sam and Lila become our protagonists, while Arbogast is both a protagonist (like them he's looking for Lila, though he goes his own way) and an antagonist (he suspects them both, to different degrees).

1. Poor Sam

He surrenders to Marion, with four-square humility. His reward is a bombardment of accusations, from two different angles. His head keeps swivelling between them, arms drooping helplessly. Passive, victimised, he nonetheless maintains a latent force (as we note, for future reference). He asks Arbogast, 'Who are you, friend?', giving the old-fashioned, slightly 'country' term of politeness to strangers the proper balance of placidity and sub-growl.

2. Fierce Lila

In Transactional Analysis terms, Lila is accusing 'parent' to bewildered Sam, and pro-tective 'parent' to her impulsive sister. 'Music Makers' Music Store' suggested a silly, cheery blonde, but she's responsible, respectable, anxious, aggressive. Her retort to daunting Arbogast is a full-face glare and 'I don't know you!' But she's a realist: when Sam (wrong again) asks her to confirm her sister's irreproachable character, she lowers her eyes (as if she knows Marion is overly impulsive – as the script will later confirm). Her silent embarrassment here tells us she's very moral; but she's not legal-istic: she raced here to *protect* her sister *from* The Law. At first she's angry at Sam, as if he might well have led her morally weaker sister into crime (as maybe he did, though not as Lila supposes). She stands for family loyalty – like Norman. Vera Miles is admirably vehement, though subordinated to the pattern of the film; in any case, she's a 'character star', not a glamour-puss. Many critics think that, since she's a lady-like blonde, she must be Hitchcock's failed effort to construct another glamour-puss like Grace Kelly until, full of sour grapes, he dressed her primly and photographed her drably (unlike Janet Leigh). But throughout this second part of *Psycho*, *everything* is drabber and darker than in the first (there's a partial change of style, as well as a drastic change of narrative POV and genre). It's as if, with Marion's death, all joy, all sensual shine, has gone from this world – which makes poetic sense. (Gavin, too, is drabbed down – no more beefcake.) Had Hitchcock wanted another Kelly, would he ever have *started* with Miles, who's an *anti*-Grace Kelly, with her *quiet* beauty, small mouth (very un-American), 'tight' presence, defensive reserve (as distinct from showy aloofness) and fiery edge. She's a woman with a private purpose, or cause, through a (WASP/Germanic?) sense of self-effacing duty. In *The Wrong Man* already, she played a dowdy, discontented, clinically depressed woman far more realistically than the *glamour* neurotics of 1940s' noir like *Suspicion* (1941), *Notorious Under Capricorn* (1949). Hitchcock's Lila goes with the 1950s' flow to realism, as per Chayefsky and 'anti-glamour' heroines like Shirley Booth in *Come Back, Little Sheba* (1952) and Anna Magnani in *The Rose Tattoo* (1955). Often, of course, realism is relative, and I wonder if Miles is meant to be *read* as plain, as beautiful stars sometimes were, like, for example, Jane Wyman in *The Blue Veil* (1951), and in Hitch's own *Stage Fright* (1950), Dorothy MacGuire in *The Enchanted Cottage* (1945) and Betsy Blair in *Marty*. (The convention was much ridiculed by critics, but had its *raisons d'être*, of which the most important was the pleasures of female spectators – beauty metaphored their *potential*, their *soul*, their *ideal ego*, and softened the 'reality-pathos' of the plot – see the proverbial moment in soaps when the hero removes the heroine's glasses and exclaims, 'Why, Miss X, you're – beautiful!', as if no one had noticed, is wish-fulfilment of this kind.) Lila's elegant, flowing coat expresses a woman's good taste *for women*, not for sexual response in the human male, and the wave in her hair is too tight, too disciplined, to mean what 'blonde' means sometimes. Lila is an assertive (but not selfishly assertive) woman acting as her sister's keeper.

3. Arbogast Attacks

Arbogast, the accuser, is a touch scary, like his name. He shrewdly awaits his moment to butt in, and takes over the conversation. By insultingly suspecting both of Marion's friends, he helps nudge them towards their alliance. Unlike Lila, he's very relaxed and leans back at ease as he keeps up the attack (to Sam he says, not 'Marion stole', but 'Your girlfriend stole'). When, softening to her, he tries to mollify her, she bristles at the attempt. He's solidly cynical but warily sensitive to Lila ('with a bit of checking, I could believe you'). He's a rather realistic private eye: not the romantic, Chandler–Marlowe kind, the knight-errant in a white trenchcoat, a beacon in the maze of moral mean. He's a mellower version of the two insurance men – one corruptible, the other pitilessly incorruptible – in *Double Indemnity*, where James M. Cain, Chandler, Wilder, Stanwyck, MacMurray and Edward G. Robinson all combine to construct that quite rare thing, a truly *dark* film noir.

Arbogast's brutally simple philosophy, at least in his professional activity, boils down to 'It's the money, stupid' and 'self-interest rules'. It's deeply upsetting to most moral idealists, who compound their own hypocrisy by going along with the hypocrisy of others. Though morality is probably instinctive, it's also a conspiracy, a structure of half-truths, that is to say half-lies, essential for social life. Sometimes, therefore, cynicism is liberating (though *total* cynicism, nihilism, might be something else). Arbogast is half-right, half-wrong. Money did make Marion run and it stopped Sam marrying her (until too late). But, each wanted the money, not for itself, but because the other seemed to need it. Is that cynical or altruistic? Unselfish or indirectly selfish? Such opposites work together (they're dialectical, not binary). Marion, alas, became too 'impulsioned' to bargain 'properly' – 'properly' meaning, 'as you owe it to yourself to do', involving a quality of moral obligation which is not just selfishness, since a moral loop has been inserted; similarly self-respect is not mere narcissism. But, even in altruism, Money Rules OK. Is that cynical? Yes – but also no, for money, being power, is also obligation, prudence, duty.

SPECTATOR ENGAGEMENT: THRUSTS, SHIFTS, SPLITS

Arbogast's cynicism brings hope (of trenchant action, with no more detours, uncertainties and complicated sentiments), freedom from one fear (his clients daren't pursue Marion, quite a twist after Cassidy's mean fury, and Marion's long panic) and *new* fears in this disaster-prone film (of cynically rational noir, already going wrong). Through this admirably written scene, our identification shifts and splits. Sam wins new sympathy, especially from female spectators, for proposing to Marion, and then for being the passive, humiliated one. (Men perfectly understand all that, and can respect Sam's latent force in defeat.) A healthy respect for Lila, as 'avenging angel' and 'conscience figure', is more conspicuous than identification, but that's not lacking; she's clearly moving into lead position (as Miles' star status further guarantees). As she tears into innocent Sam, we can identify with both of them at once (to different degrees, according to our gender); initial conflict leading to romance is a well-known situation. According to Hollywood theory, we're much less likely to identify with Arbogast (he's less prepossessing, less propitious for the standard wish-fulfilments), but he attracts respect plus the ambivalent fascination attending 'character stars' (like Edward G. Robinson in *Double Indemnity*). He starts by threatening our new friends, but he too seeks Marion, so he's both an antagonist and a co-protagonist, and this ambivalence adds intricacy when he mellows to Lila but not to Sam.

WHAT MAY HAPPEN NEXT?

We may think we know how things will turn out (a Sam–Lila romance, no doubt). All the same, we half-expect, nay, we demand surprises along the way and this situation crackles with alternative possibilities. Each character seems broadly consistent, but their consistency is 'open' not 'closed': it leaves room for inner contradictions, changes, twists – that is to say, *in*consistencies and unpredictabilities. Few good narratives are '*chains* of events' in which each event *entails* the next in some 'quasi-logical' way. On the contrary: narrative *suspense* and *surprise* both imply that *alternative possibility* looms large in spectator experience of the story.[47] (We remember Hitchcock films for their *suspense*, not for their *happy end*, and in many noir or heavy melo/dramas, happy ends don't negate or devalue the long periods of gloom.) These first manoeuvrings between our three new protagonists allow countless possibilities of further development, all equally 'logical' (Sheriff Chambers will spell out one, and others are easily thought of, e.g., for starters, might Arbogast, with good intentions, frame Sam, or prove as corrupt as he's cynical, and agree with Norman to split the $40,000, or, Sam and Lila might fatally disagree about Bates). Drama is less a chain of events than a succession of surprises which *turns out* to *suggest* a *certain degree* of pragmatic coherence. Any implications of inevitability, freedom, determinism, unknowability etc. owe less to some 'logic' of narrative than to whether a *lyrical mood* suggests 'heavy converging pressures' or 'light inconsequentiality' or other such patterns, which are 'probabilistico-normative' generalisations.

BYSTANDERS

Two minor characters, almost parts of the setting, make a counterpoint. A gloomy battleaxe-type old lady fears that a brand of insecticide 'guaranteed to exterminate every insect in the world' may be not entirely painless: 'I say, insect or man, death should always be painless … or if it isn't painless, quick.' (As Marion's was? Small mercy, then!) Her ruminations were quite likely inspired by DDT, which through the 1950s still seemed a wonder insecticide (though 'insect or man?' is accidentally prophetic). Chemistry versus pain reprises Caroline's anti-unhappiness pill. The old lady's remark means well, but her gloomy face casts a spell on it, and 'insect or man, I always say' gives a morbid sweep to her thought. And gardening becomes genocide, the mass murder of as many species as man feels inclined to slaughter. Is this imposing, earnest lady a sister, under the skin, of Mrs Bates? (Mrs Bates, we will learn, won't hurt a fly … She has a dead garden, of wallpaper roses … as Norman has an aviary of dead birds.) Disturbing, too, is the implication that pain is worse than death. Christians of Hitchcock's generation, reared in medically cruder times, were sensitive to the problem, that though life is a gift, from God or from nature, all life involves pain, and to fear pain more than death may amount to a deep death-wish. That very fear is spelled and acted out, from a non-Christian, humanist angle, in the 'suicide is painless' plot of *M.A.S.H.*, Altman's sarcastic smash hit of 1974. It's discussed again in that religious bestseller, *The Problem of Pain*

(1940), by C. S. Lewis, whose abiding appeal to Protestant America explains his celebration in *Shadowlands* (1993).

Sam's shop assistant combines a fresh, friendly, healthy face and pleasant name (Bob, and, adds the script, 'Summerfield'), with a tenacious curiosity. He's not a voyeur exactly, for that's a clinical condition, but he does swerve into eavesdropping, which is sad in a vigorous-looking young man; perhaps he's trapped in this dreary town, even more than Sam. He's a twist on movie stereotypes. Small-town nosey parkers had always abounded in movies, but usually they looked the part before they spoke a word, and nine times out of ten they were vinegary, gossipy spinsters. (Sexual loneliness in small-town America, with consequent disorders, rears its ugly head in several stage and film hits, notably *Our Town* [1943], *Oklahoma!* [1955], and *Picnic*.)

PATTERNS IN A TUNNEL

Sam's hardware store brings a new kind of space: a long tunnel running straight back from the screen. The light in it is a drab, stagnant, chalky grey. Long rows of pots and tins on shelves give the walls an oppressive texture. (That they're mostly pots of paint is an extra deprivation – of suggested colour.) Conspicuous from the start are knives arrayed in patterns on the walls, on high and pointing downwards (like Mrs Bates' knife in the shower). The prongs of stacked rakes fan out exactly behind Lila's head, and, catching a stray beam of light, make a nasty, dismal halo – threatening victim status. The back end of the tunnel is visually 'choked' by Sam's back and office furniture and by our having to read a page of his writing. The other end is more cheerful; there's a sunny street, and the approaching Lila walks quickly by, though the window through which we see all this is a very narrow one. Arbogast's entry is different again: abruptly, a stranger's hard, silent face 'chokes' the screen (another sphinx?). The dreary internal space is variegated, but oppressively, by a fast track-back through sales racks (visually busy planes), and the insecticidal customer, sweeping out, provokes another heavy track. The main conversations work *across* the tunnel, that is to say, 'against' the dominant shape of the space. Many changes of camera position give each line of dialogue its own little 'space', or underline a change of posture (Arbogast leans back on a counter, Sam's arms make a helpless gesture, Lila's eyes and words stab forth). It's lyrical realism; like 'realistic' novels, it works 'the poetics of the prosaic'.

Formalists will note that Arbogast walks right through the camera. As he steps assertively forward, Hitch cuts from a close-up of his light grey face to a reverse-angle close-up of the dark back of his head, with Sam and Lila in deep focus beyond.

TIME'S EVER-FLOWING STREAMS

Marion's 'happy end', coming too late, gears in with the film's time-consciousness: from the opening date/time title (flashy and unnecessary), through lunchtime love, talk of hanging around and awaiting a plane, a late return to the office, the boss is later still, banks close at weekends, Marion drives till exhausted, imagines next Monday, plans an early start back: the action flows past a 'clock ticking' in our minds (and jumps sudden gaps).

   Psycho's time structure is two long, fast, urgent 'time-runs'. Marion's story runs from Friday lunchtime to Saturday night/Sunday morning, when she's buried. Sam's and Lila's story will run from the following Saturday lunchtime to Sunday night. The time gap is about a week, during which many narrative events, unshown or unmentioned, must have occurred (Lowery and Cassidy discover the crime, maybe much as Marion pre-imagined, they call and brief Arbogast, who decides his lead is Lila. She looks around Marion's flat, finds evidence of Sam (his letters, the script will tell us) and conceals from others his possible involvement).

FOR THEORISTS ONLY: ALL STORYLINES ARE INCOMPLETE

These 'omitted' scenes remind us that *Psycho*'s narrative, although classically well-constructed, is far from 'linear': it's a sequence of *jumps*, across (sometimes enormous) omissions. And since each character has his *own* storyline, the story of *Psycho* is not *one* 'line', but a spaghetti junction of lives converging, criss-crossing, and maybe diverging. Stories, like films, are like icebergs: from the tips you see, you can only guess at the unshown shapes. Hence critical and spectatorial 'guesstimations' differ widely. But the dissensus coexists with consensus, both being significant.

FOR FORMALISTS ONLY: A HITCH IN TIME

After Marion's burial, which is closure of the film's 'Act One', convention dictates a slow fade to black. There is a fade to black, but it's short and fast. The reasons may be these.

1. Though Hitchcock feels he should mark the gap, he wants to keep the story momentum going.
2. The swamp swallowing the car is like a 'fade to black' itself.
3. The proximate letter slows the visual pace, while imposing a 'mental shift' – from *seeing* to *reading* – which keeps the spectator's mind working fast.
4. How long after Marion's death does this scene take place? Hitch could have reprised his starting device (a running subtitle) but he does things more

obscurely. The letter is headed 'Saturday', which may briefly confuse, since the last clear talk of time was Friday afternoon, and, if we count back, Marion dies on Saturday night/Sunday morning. Subsequent clues suggest Lila gets to Sam a week later, and in a later scene Arbogast semi-confirms: 'about a week'. I suspect Hitchcock wanted another brief 'uncertainty', like Marion's cross-fade change, and her crossing the state line. The *speed of fade* and the *time length* of the black reminds us that movies aren't moving *pictures* only: structurally, they're *time-based graphics* (like a black screen), some of which aren't pictures at all.

FINER POINTS: 'LET'S SPELL OUT SOME SUBTEXT'

1. It's a love letter, but the calligraphy is quite black and heavy (as befits our mood of mourning): the one loud sound is the prickly scratching of pen on paper. Simple, headed notepaper, in a humble abode, echoes Norman's modest jest about the motel stationery's headed paper,[48] in *his* dull cabins. Slow readers won't get past the letter's starting line, so it implies the rest: 'Dearest right-as-always Marion'. Very fast readers will get to the last line on the page: it's 'If you haven't come to your senses, and still want to' – so the whole point of the letter ('marry me') remains unstated for them too. Hitch likes these little 'gaps', for sustaining 'slight uncertainty'. The gentle irony, in Sam's last line, implies that Marion must be mad to want to marry him. He means it kindly but, on the one hand, she *did* go mad about him, fatally, and, on the other hand, it's *he* who has come to his senses. All this echoes his slightly fanciful side, but now it's reconciled with steadiness.

2. Arbogast concedes to Sam that Marion may not be 'back there with the nuts and bolts'. He means 'on these premises right now'. Some critics posit dramatic irony: Marion bolted; the Bateses are 'nuts' and she *is* buried near them.

3. Arbogast's penultimate line is: 'We're always quickest to doubt people who have a record for being honest.' It's his roundabout way of excusing himself to Lila, for suspecting her. It's oddly awkward, almost self-contradictory ('We always suspect those whom we never suspect'). It's another garble, like Marion paying with pills. His very next line is direct linguistically ('I think she's here, Miss Crane. Where there's a boyfriend …'), but dramatically oblique (he's talking to Lila, across Sam, about Sam – an expertly pitched insult).

STRUCTURALIST SPECULATIONS

In *Films and Feelings* I proposed what I think it's fair to call the 'genetic structuralist' idea (deriving from Jean Piaget and Lucien Goldmann) that all the characters in a story are 'repermutations' or 'variations' of one another (by contrast, variation and modulated similarity). That's clear enough, as between Marion and Lila, and Norman and Mrs Bates, and, as mentioned earlier, fellow-critics have linked Norman with Sam (as dark, handsome, confused lovers). Along similar lines, Arbogast is a 'selective combination' from Cassidy, the cop and the car dealer. Like Cassidy, he's a money/power character (but, his cynicism isn't syruped over by pseudo-fatherly gush). As a detective, he evokes The Law, like the cop. (Arbogast aggressively suspects everybody, but to Marion he brings forgiveness. The cop was not suspicious enough, though his uniform threatened punishment.) Arbogast represents a twistily commercial world, like the dealer (but he seems more urban than rustic, and he enters a 'straight' space, not a maze). It's also been said that, in any 'rich' work of art, every character and setting metaphors an aspect of the artist, and the work *as a whole* figures forth his character-structure (or one of them). It's a logically elegant idea, worth a whirl or two here. A Jungian might see Marion as Hitchcock's *anima* – his idealised, feminine side – as Joan of Arc was to Dreyer. Lila might correspond to what he needed in his wife, Alma Reville (Hitch married his boss). Cassidy is Hitchcock's coarse, tricksy, manipulating, sad side (as Stetson theory suggested, though along a different slant), Lowery his worryguts side, the Bates' ménage his (and our) Oedipal side (in one of the many unstable combinations on the boil in our libidinal kitchens). The insect lady as a serial killer is a 'normal' version of Mrs Bates, and her insecticidal concerns gear in with Freud's comment that insects in dreams often represent children. A horrid thought, based on broad physical resemblance (like Sam/Norman) occurs to me: is she 'halfway between' Mrs Bates and what Lila or Marion, grown old and spiritually lonely, might become? (In a way, she's a 'witch', opposite of Marion, 'martyr of love' – a combination preoccupying Dreyer and quite different from Madonna/whore, though perhaps it's a Protestant counterpart of it.) A moot point, of course, but a prime use of theory is to propose thoughts otherwise unthought.[49]

SCENES 139–49 ARBOGAST LOOKS
ROUND FAIRVALE
On the doorsteps of progressively lower-class houses and hostels, Arbogast enquires after Marion, always drawing a blank.

GUMSHOEING

The script makes much of Arbogast's (white) car on the highway; he twice *drives past* the Bates Motel, on his way to other places, before finally driving up to it. One such 'driving' shot takes in Norman sitting quietly on his porch (and echoes, perhaps, the cop's 'wrong way' looks?). Instead, the film's 'doorstep' scenes develop more diverse social and human interest. Maybe Hitchcock decided we'd seen enough driving now and resolved instead to presage, in silent long shots, the next key scene: a detailed, thickly verbal conversation on a threshold. The 'downwards' social progression is a 'wrong way' touch: Norman is very respectable.

FOR CINE-GRAMMARIANS ONLY: FORM TENSIONS

Silent under music, this series of scenes, linked by cross-fades, takes us from, presumably, Arbogast leaving Sam and Lila at the store, to some time after dark. Structurally, it borders on the Hollywood 'montage sequence' – a series of short scenes, usually depicting bits of indefinite actions in different places, all linked by opticals, and continuing music. However, the pace is too slow for the separate scenes to quite 'liquidise' into a 'flow', as they do in the 'obvious' montage sequence, though there is a sense of 'scenes linked by opticals'.

◆

SCENES 150–4 ARBOGAST FINDS NORMAN BATES

Sitting on his porch, Norman greets Arbogast with an offer of candy and, mistaking him for a customer, leads him into the office, where Arbogast explains that he's looking for a missing person. Norman embarks on his affable routine about rarely having guests, but Arbogast, briskly opening the register, sees the signature, 'Marie Samuels', spots the word play (Marion/Sam) and tactfully cajoles Norman into remembering that, yes, he did have a visitor, who probably was the girl in the picture, that her hair was wet, that she ate a sandwich ... Stepping up the pressure, Arbogast talks of getting a warrant to search the cabins, but Norman laughs amiably, and invites him to accompany him now on his linen-changing round. Following Norman, Arbogast notices that he walks straight past Cabin 1; Arbogast takes a step the other way, and sees, in the house, a woman's figure sitting in a lighted window. Norman explains it's his unwell mother. Arbogast, sure he's on to something, starts needling Norman, and suggests that maybe Marion bribed him to conceal her or perhaps fooled him into protecting her romantically. Norman retorts that a girl might fool him, but couldn't fool his mother. Arbogast guesses that the women met, and asks to talk to Mrs Bates, as 'sick old women are sharp'. Norman won't let her be disturbed and Arbogast drives off.

MAKING CONVERSATION

This affable chat is really a cross-examination and intensifies the detective mystery interest. The battle of wits, in words, between two differently cunning men, both coming on friendly, has a certain intellectual interest, like the cross-examinations in trial scenes, and the battles of cunning which are the main attraction of such films as *Sleuth* (Mankiewicz, 1972), *Death Trap* (Lumet, 1982) and *The Spanish Prisoner* (Mamet, 1997). This time, Arbogast is the protagonist, carrying our 'rooting interest', and attracting our admiration, though not a 'full' identification. Norman, although our antagonist, attracts more identification than Arbogast. An unusual and intriguing crossover. (But not unprecedented: in *The Young Lions* [Dmytryk, 1958] Brando played another such identified-with antagonist, what people used to call 'a good Nazi', meaning a good German deceived by a bad cause.)

Towards Norman, first-time viewers can still have mixed feelings: obnoxious as his new complacency is, it 'goes with the territory', so to speak, for it flows from loyalty to his mother. As deceitful in this conversation as he is, it's in a vulnerable way, as a victim of Arbogast's aggression, so he benefits from the 'Marnie effect' (audience sympathy for a hard-pressed criminal in difficulty). He's very sensitive, in a way quite fresh among villains, and it elicits what Hollywood called 'audience recognition' – the audience recognising, on screen, its own, intimate experience – in this case, of exasperating conversations. Our behaviour is friendly, modest, unpretentious, we helpfully try to remember, we find we're being interrogated, insultingly accused of being complicit in crime and (even more demeaning) being duped. Our family relationships are queried until, finally, our humiliation turns to righteous indignation. We show our anger, yet politely, controlledly: our action is firm and civilised. Norman's situation may be 'melodramatic' ('extreme'), but his 'surface sensitivity' finds echoes aplenty in us. Enriching our moral turbulence about him, it conflicts with our *opposite* admiration of Arbogast's cunning harshness, and our desire to see justice done. The dramatic dialogue becomes a conflict inside our own psyches. We introject the state of conflict, at least for the duration of the scene. One line, at least, gives us a clue. 'She might have fooled me, but she didn't fool my mother!' In other words, he *agrees* with his mother, that Marion was deceptive. (Which she was, but he doesn't know that; he's agreeing with his mother's rant.)

WATCHING THE DETECTIVES

In his very first scene, with Sam and Lila, Arbogast stepped right through the camera and dwarfed Sam and Lila beyond. This second 'conversation piece' starts before anyone says a word. Norman standing on the porch, and Arbogast rising from his car, enhances their difference in height. Burly Arbogast seems dwarfish. Never mind; how will he attack? Here too, he's rather different from before: now he's affable, rueful, he shares his problem with a sigh. Is it standard operating procedure for unpromising situations? Has his long, useless day on doorsteps tired him out? It reminds us how little he knows, compared with what we want him to find out. Never mind, he's a formidable character. Soon he warms to his task, pounces on Norman's little slips, keeps burrowing. His eyes have an eager, innocuous gleam (must be false tact – that's good), while using every trick in the interrogator's book: suddenly throwing in a key question, sussing out an emotional weak spot, and continuing to needle it, while seeming to apologise ('I didn't mean that as a slur on your manhood'). He switches back and forth between a gimlet eye for trivial inconsistencies, working them like the thin end of a wedge, and throwing out the sudden hunch. He switches *kinds* of detective thinking: rigorous, practical logic instantly applied to detail; associative recognition (of Norman's openness) prompting a guess (Marion fooled him); the juggling of alternative hypotheses. Thinking on his feet, he pitches two scenarios at Norman. In one, Marion makes Norman her accomplice; in the other, she fools him. We know they're both wrong, but they're both plausible and the sudden possibilities 'enrich' the film.

His line of questioning, far from being 'linear', chops and changes, keeping us surprised. Like everyone else in this film, Arbogast swerves between half-right (inspiring hope – but also fear of Arbogast running into the unpredictable Mrs Bates) and half-wrong (generating frustration/despair). As a form of suspense, it's more intricate by far than 'hope against fear': for this hope *brings* fear, which *differs* from the *other* fear, as adrenalinised action differs from baffled impotence.

But Arbogast misses the scenario that matters most, the story we saw. Leaving, he talks of getting a warrant, but even Norman knows it's just bluff, for form's sake: that a guest has left a hotel is no grounds for searching it! So this conversation, too, ends on an anti-climactic 'escape' by the guilty party. Earlier, we wanted Marion to escape, though with misgivings, and though 'worry-after-relief' soon prevailed. Not here! A flicker of hope (uncertainty) remains. Arbogast goes off as if defeated and yet he found out so much, so he can't be. (The next scene will restore 'relief-after-worry'.)

ARTFUL DODGES OF THE DOORSTEP TRADES

The eager gleam in Arbogast's eye, his joy in discovery, his tactful dissection of Norman's slips all enliven us, like jiu-jitsu, or kung fu, in words. He smacks of the commercial world and perhaps his butting-in evokes the 'foot in the door'-type salesman. He knows every trick in the thousands of books about salesmanship. He elicits sympathy from his 'prospect' (or suspect), acts weary but hopeful, switches deftly between disarming reassurance and light threat, shoots the sudden direct question. In movies at least, he's the first *cunningly deferential* detective, as later elaborated by Columbo (Peter Falk), from 1971. In PAC terms, Norman's the child, Arbogast is the father, though he sometimes *plays* the child – eyes bright, open, hopeful, asking for help. He pushes Norman to protest that he 'can only take so much' (echoing Sam's words – another 'similarity within difference'). All of which mixes the suspense with human warmth, with everyday experiences of the audience. Though the situation is 'melodramatic' (extreme), the 'detail texture' preludes later, realistic films about doorstep-trade wiles, notably *Salesman* (Maysles, 1969), *The Tin Men* (Demme, 1987) and *Glengarry Glenn Ross* (Mamet and Foley, 1992).

NORMAN NORMAL

The opening shot of Norman, in a rocking chair on the porch, quietly reading a magazine, evokes a traditional America. The candy would be a fondly critical touch – for which Norman Rockwell had a gift. Norman's chat is quite a shock: frankness turns out to be his standard patter (like the car dealer's opening gambit). With Norman, however, it is more sincere. His equivocal state – 'the good son' or complacent accomplice – teases first-time spectators, still in their shower-shocked state: second-time spectators, less shocked, have an additional uncertainty as to *how aware* Norman is, moment by moment, of lying. Murderers' states of mind, the shifting frontiers of madness and lucidity, are an abiding fascination. They're nursed, in *Psycho*, by the last two scenes, which, far from *resolving* and closing our curiosity, re-open and *aggravate* it.

Norman's opening defence is all-round denial (he's had no guests, he can't recognise Marion). It's a plausible strategy and often the correct one, but he's *too* perfunctory so Arbogast catches him out. His second line is to pretend he's forgotten and to pretend an effort to remember, but actually recollect as little as possible. (*Pretending* to forget is neatly ironic: his life is built around a *real* amnesia.) He's too confident: to show sincere goodwill, he volunteers trivial details (the sandwich, Mother) on which Arbogast pounces. Norman is betrayed, not by his Unconscious, but by his conscious, civilised façade. 'Arbogast versus Norman' could serve as an instructional film, on the importance of keeping Mum. In 1944 Hitchcock had made two instructionals on that very topic: *Bon Voyage* and *Aventure Malgache*, commissioned by England's wartime Ministry of Information, warned Allied agents in Nazi-occupied France how to guard their tongues. Following a common strategy, they showed people making a series of mistakes. (Same 'moral' as *Psycho*: friendliness is dangerous, if you've got a guilty secret, and who hasn't?)

SHOWING THINKING

With very fine feeling, Perkins finds a common tone for the freaky and the normal. Norman's pretence of having quite forgotten Marion, and then of gradually remembering her, have a light emptiness, his eyes moving gently, as if his mental images of her might be just off to the left, or to the right, or floating in the air. At the normal end of his behaviour is his reasonable, dignified, polite anger. At the freaky end is a short, high-pitched titter. (Sticklers for realism may object that some of Norman's reactions *shriek* guilt at the audience, but aren't noticed by Arbogast only 18 inches away. This reverts to a performance arts' convention, that characters show strongly, for the audience, attitudes 'invisible' to the other characters, as established by their [non-]reaction. It's a convention, but not an arbitrary one, having an obvious function.) Norman, like his accuser, invents scenarios: is Arbogast a customer looking to buy a motel …?

But his mind is slightly out of synch. He interrupts the conversation to switch on the neon sign, forgotten again. Coaxed by Arbogast into thinking back, he flounders amidst part-truths, pretending to have forgotten and pretending to be trying to remember. He says he's making a 'mental picturization' – archaic phrase, like something out of 1930s popular psychology (and even more rustic than old *Reader's Digest* stuff, as gently mocked in *Rear Window*). 'Mental picturization' suggests, not just 'mental image', but the *mental process* of forming an image and auto-correcting it as one goes along. She was 'sitting back there, no, she was standing up, with some sandwich in her hand, and she said … Odd, how quickly he moves from a total blank, to Marion *poised in mid-action:* his memory is not just photographic, it's cinematic. Most people produce a static list of features: Norman describes a *shot running in time* after giving a *running commentary* on what's going on in his mind. Very intimate, very deceptive – he's a past master of amnesia/imaginings. He remembers what we noticed (in the very pretty shot of Marion holding a sandwich delicately) but his switch from 'sitting' to 'standing' is a switch from truth to falsity. He picks out her 'wet hair', remembered by us in two different conditions in the shower: first, damped down on her forehead by the rain, then, tufting up as she slides down the tiles (as happened in the shower, after he ran off).

Hitchcock's previous moral perverts – in *Rope* the Nietzschean aesthetes, in *Strangers on a Train* the father-hater and mother-figure-strangler – had, at times, an insidious reality to their thought, as compared to his 'suave gentleman villains'. Norman is more realistic still – in terms, not of motivational psychology, or 'deep psychology' (Freud with everything), but of something more delicate, difficult and close to our hearts: the flow of 'superficial' feelings, the *stream* of emotional consciousness, the volatile finesse of which eludes (and subverts) all the big pat terms. Closing the scene, Norman's mean smile, as Arbogast's lights sweep across him, repeats the swampside slyness gesture, as if to re-emphasise the suspense polarity.

Arbogast versus Norman is a 'battle of wits', and of rationality, with its plausible hypotheses, its detail, hastily improvised and sceptically scrutinised, its introspective memory, its masked anxieties and its thickly verbal form. Thus it continues to upfront *fraught thought*, in a different mode from Marion's, which was almost silent (and reticent), a numb undertow expressed in action (and speech imagined as if heard). Thus *Psycho* harks back to the 'classic' detective mysteries, with their emphasis on *thinking* (all those masterminds, with their 'little grey cells', and their eccentricities like little mental imbalances). In pulp thrillers, deductive interest was eclipsed by thick-ear thrills and by chaos-defying logic: their nearest approach to *thought* was a lyrical confusion, plus shell-shock, sap-shock, amnesia, etc. *Psycho* blends the two genres: like the 'classic' mystery, it upfronts cerebration, but Arbogast is clever-cunning, not clever-superior. Its amateur detectives grope blindly through the night; lost in a delirium of half-right, half-wrong interpretations while Norman, who knows more than anybody, even the spectator, is blind to his own past.

A PLAUSIBLE OBJECTION

Were this yarn less gripping, a plausible might complain that a real-life Arbogast would surely hit on a third hypothesis, closer to the truth and more conducive to effective action: namely, that Norman chanced on Marion's $40,000, and killed her for it. If we come to think of it, we hardly care, as what's going on is so interesting. This neatly contradicts his chatter about always suspecting those above suspicion; he misses an obvious suspect.

Arbogast's 'hypotheses' about Norman are film noir scenarios. From out of the night, haloed in the rain, a lady in distress appears: really a vamp-on-the-run, she either corrupts or fools our lonely, hitherto honest hero. However, Arbogast works not from Hollywood cliché, but from what Norman has been saying, which in 1959 was entirely novel. (By 1959, noir-type vamps were old hat, even among adolescent highbrows: though with Norman dated ideas fit well.)

A CONVERSATION PIECE

As mentioned at the begining, Balsam and Perkins hit such a cracking pace, with such nervous electricity, that at the end of the take the film crew broke into applause. But then, runs the story, the breakneck speed left too little spare for cutting as Hitchcock wanted. A likely problem is that swift dialogue run-ons would give audiences insufficient thinking time (a reason for Welles' very clever dialogue, given overlapping speed, arousing audience resistance). Hitchcock wanted split-second pauses, to keep audience thought in synch. The eventual edit, unusually, given just two men close together, has very few two-shots: each man appears in his 'own' shot and this would help the 'thought-punctuation'. (The account suggests that Hitchcock designed the scene as one continuous two-shot, which, though unusual, is possible.)

HOW STATIC DIALOGUE BECOMES PURE CINEMA

Hitchcock's nine-page dialogue is 'cinematised' in several ways. Scenes 150–2 involve six scenes: 1, 5, 7, the porch between office and road; 2, 4, inside the office they include two 'inserts' from other scenes (3 being the porch neon sign lighting up, and 6, the house glimpsed from the porch). Much of the time, the men talk while on the move, but the main scene is a very static dialogue exchange between two men facing each other across a desk, neither changing their position. However, it's rich in 'little' movements, such as body language – which *look* big, thanks to Hitchcock's cinematic style, and a stream of cuts.

TENNIS-MATCH CONTINUITY

The office scene settles into a very routine structure: alternating shots, all from one side, of two men facing each other. It's how a spectator, seated on one side of a tennis match, looks to his left and right alternately. Unlike the continuous two-shot, this 'lateral alternation' emphasises each face in turn (while briefly eclipsing the other). Thus it offers the spectator an 'alternation of identifications' between antagonistic thoughts and feelings (in the continuous two-shot, each would always 'qualify' or contest the other – a different, though viable, participation, as Bazin implied when championing 'deep focus' against montage). If the alternating shots are very 'symmetrical', and the editing rhythm very regular, the 'ping-pong' effect can become monotonous. But here Hitchcock maintains strong variations, of one sort or another, between successive shots, and (no less important), between the 'alternated' shots of each subject. The two 'big heads' yield strong graphic 'collisions' (not so far from montage 'collisions', though softened by their predictability). Others combine smaller changes, of actor and camera position (giving different angles, vertical and/or lateral angles, different sizes of medium to close shot, views of the face (profile, half-face, three-quarter face, etc.), changes of lighting (which alter the shape of the face, its mood, its attack), different backgrounds. Many shots are 'cheated', for expressive purpose. Thus the editing bristles with 'disparities', nicely judged to combine aggressive interaction with the *separateness* of these two minds: Norman is 'defensive', in his mental world, while Arbogast 'attacks across the cuts'.

Each shot must fit what it shows *and* the continuity pattern. Hitchcock sets Arbogast's short, chunky shape and its upward attack against Norman's tall but defensive stance and the thinking conspicuous in his eyes. Arbogast's bright look is outgoing, Norman's dark eyes are concave. Their relative height dictates the camera angles (low on Norman, high on Arbogast). This was easy to override, had Hitchcock so wished, and going with it is a stylistic choice – which subverts the alleged rule that low camera angles make faces dominate and high ones make them seem dominated. And 'dominate', a vague word, covers too many things. 'Low' Arbogast dominates, insofar as he sets the agenda, steers the conversation, keeps attacking and continuously upsets, embarrasses and humiliates Norman. But Norman dominates insofar as he parries successfully and has an awesome secret. The low, low angles on Norman evoke Arbogast's 'low' point of view, and the high angles on Arbogast Norman's 'high' one: thus POV competes with 'dominance' (even when the lateral angles are *not* POV, as when the camera looks up at Norman from his left, though Arbogast is on his right).

Conventional in outline, this quietly virtuoso sequence demonstrates the infinite variety available within what may *seem* a simple pattern ('lateral alternation'). Two examples must suffice. First: Norman, in mid-conversation, switches on the neon sign – throwing Arbogast's face into dark shadow. Otherwise, the light on his face changes regardless of his surroundings. Sometimes it's film noir lighting for villains with obscure potentialities (one-half of a near full face in deep shadow, the other a light-dark 'web'). Sometimes clear light on his face gives him an eager, unguarded look. Sometimes light emphasises his sharp sensual mouth, or gives his eyes a dark, slippery shine. Second: a spectacular effect is rightly famous – Norman, taking a closer look at the register, bends forward over the camera, which takes a closer look at the underside of his moving jaw, which makes a dark triangle above us, evoking (I would say) the beak of a diving bird of prey, or (colleagues prefer) the down-arcing knife of Mrs Bates. Either way, it's 'pure cinema': only the odd viewpoint makes it macabre. Arbogast, from his POV, would see only Norman bowing his head (which might suggest docility). Nothing in 'tennis-match' syntax determines such a shot, and the sequence merits study for its 'montage' diversity within a 'continuity' routine. Structurally and syntactically, the sequence is ploddingly conventional, but every detail is highly individual. To put it another way, the great wealth of meaning lies, not in the *higher level* structures, as 'ideological structuralism' claims, but on the choices remaining at *lower levels*.

EXCEPTIONAL FUSSINESS OF THE MASTER

Hitchcock had built *Strangers on a Train* on various kinds of 'criss-cross' (railroad tracks, two tennis rackets on a lighter, a ball on a tennis court, a reciprocation of murders). A 'criss-cross' is a spatial paradox: two lines 'reverse' their relative position. This sequence harps on a kind of 'paradox': let's call it 'the ahead-and-behind reverse'.

1. Arbogast, following Norman to Cabin 1, sees, just ahead of him, Norman not entering it; just as Norman turns round and looks back at Arbogast, who turns around and sees, behind him, Mrs Bates, and then turns around to discuss her with Norman. (Spatially, it's two 'turnabouts', with Arbogast between Norman's two identities. Thus Norman 'brackets' Arbogast, like the police car bracketing Marion.)

2. As Arbogast drives off, Norman's gaze, to off-screen front and left, tells us the departing car is in that direction, but then the light from its headlamps shines on-screen behind him and to his left. (Thus signs of Arbogast's car 'bracket' Norman; and, it's 'split' (we *know* it's to our right, but it *shows up* on our left.)

3. Beside the office desk the mirror reflecting Arbogast reminds us it once reflected Marion. Then, it emphasised her face; now, it emphasises his back. A brief shot of his face and another brief shot filled by 'his' four hands fragment him further. (How restless, how fussy, when, narrative-wise, one unchanged set-up would have been much cheaper.) Is there some link, between these three motifs?

Hitchcock clearly shows us Arbogast notice Norman hesitate before the first cabin door he comes to, and then pass on. But it's shown briefly, silently and promptly eclipsed by a big distraction. As if to hide from Norman that he's seen him do it, Arbogast quickly turns *the other way* and sees Mrs Bates. My suspicion is that many spectators will quickly forget Norman's action, or not spot its significance. The pay-off comes in the next scene, where Arbogast tells Lila, 'I even know which cabin she was in. It was Number One.'

WORDS THAT MELT IN THE MOUTH

The Language of Thought

Norman describes his mother's condition by mumbling something like 'inimible' (some Freudian slippage between 'invalid' and 'mummy'). It's not in the script, and may be Perkins' inspiration (or a lucky fluff – and a Freudian one, if tales of *his* fearsome Mom are true.)[50]

The Food Chain

A sandwich not eaten (delicate); candy (childlike); gizzard (bestial). Arbogast: 'If it doesn't jell, it isn't aspic, and this ain't jelling.' The first part sounds like a modern proverb, which the switch to 'ain't' makes vulgar. Here's 'city American' cynicism? About gourmet pretention? Given Arbogast's 'vulgar' style, might this encode some background vignette, about chefs in a hotel kitchen? (A contrast to 'hot as fresh milk'.) In *Frenzy*, mouths (food/tongue/finger-bones amidst potatoes) top a thematic agenda.

Mirror Whispers

Arbogast, like Marion, signs in beside that eye-attracting mirror. Having stressed her profile, it now reflects his back. But, after Marion, that mirror 'doubling' suggests: 'Sign in here for death.'

SCRIPT VERSUS FILM (3)

The candy is not in the script, of course, being Perkins' idea. In the script, Norman darns an old sock (another foot note) which I rather prefer, as a *different* aspect of Norman's life, *another* link with everyday lives. (I take the overtone as more 'lonely bachelor', than 'man doing woman's work' as a presage to transvestism. Though clearly opinions may differ – especially as, nowadays, sex/gender crossovers abound in entertainment and few bachelors darn socks – they buy new pairs instead.) In the film, however, candy 'punctuates' the scene, signalling, successively, Norman's contentment, a friendly offer of it to Arbogast, the jaw shot (like a bird's gizzard), as he senses danger, and, finally, contentment again. The script says of 153–4 only 'Omit'.

◆

SCENES 155–7 ARBOGAST REPORTS BACK TO LILA

Arbogast, in a roadside telephone cabin, tells Lila Marion stayed at the Bates Motel, in Cabin 1, regrets the boy won't let him talk with the sick old mother and says that as he's not altogether satisfied he'll go back there and look around and then come on to Fairvale, within the hour.

Spoilsport plausibles may complain that if Arbogast were all that smart he'd have wondered, 'If Marion just came and went, what is Norman hiding? Very serious guilt is going on here.'

SOLO FLIGHT

Here's yet another 'solo' scene and one-sided phone conversation. It starts as a quick cross-fade from Norman smirking to a long shot of Arbogast's back, as he walks from his car in the foreground to a distant telephone box. It's an establishing shot, but a fast-moving structure. Thereupon, Hitchcock spins things out. Arbogast enters the booth, then he dials seven successive digits, then he greets Sam, then he asks Sam if he can speak to Lila and then he fulfils this scene's narrative function ('before dying, he puts Lila on Marion's trail'). He then goes on for seven more speeches, mostly repeating what we've just seen. His lines are separated by little silences, as he listens to Lila's words, which we can't hear.

A LITTLE KNOWLEDGE …

A formulaic producer, preoccupied by pace and action thrills, and prejudiced against static dialogue, could cut nine-tenths of this. It works, I think, as a 'tempo of delays', in a constantly slow, lyrical film, and as another deterioration into uncertainty. Arbogast starts brilliantly right ('I even know which cabin she was in. It was Number One') and this resolves, by contradiction, the 'uncertain retreat' ending the last scene. But from then on, it's all downhill: he thinks Marion's departure was perfectly normal, the boy doesn't know much, Mrs Bates might be 'sharp' (!). His very *decision* to re-investigate is close to *in*decisive: 'Well, maybe that's because I don't feel entirely sat-isfied … I was, but I think I'll go back to the motel first.' Imminent confrontation restarts both hope and fear: can his earthy cynicism cope with madness? Alarm bells ring, not on the screen, but in our minds. The scene's 'kick' comes, not from the film *itself*, but from the difference between what *we* know and what he doesn't. It's in the text-spectator interface.

MELODRAMA OF THE ABSURD

Hitchcock calls Arbogast 'complacent', almost implying that 'complacency' is the little sin for which he's severely punished. And punished *unjustly*, who can doubt? He makes a mistake, that's all. As severe (or pessimistic) as Hitchcock may be, the idea of 'punishment' doesn't mean his fate was in some way deserved. There's *cruel and unjust* punishment (which wildly exceeds the victim's smidgeon of guilt), there's 'pun-ishment' by tyrannies and there's 'punishment' meaning just 'consequence'. Brand X feminists, convinced that Hitchcock 'punishes' women, seem not to notice how often men like Arbogast are 'punished' even more. If 'complacency' refers to not suspect-ing that Mrs Bates might be a slasher with a knife, such 'complacency' is entirely rational; fear of such a thing would be paranoid. It's like Tippi Hedren's 'complacency' about our feathered friends in *The Birds*. For Hitchcock, complacency and paranoia are Scylla and Charybdis: if the one doesn't get you, the other will, and if you weasel your way between them, that is more luck than judgment. But who could live his life in fear and trembling, whenever sparrows gather just out of sight? Back at the store, Arbogast accused the innocent, shrewdly, rationally, and wrongly. Now he's not suspicious, even more shrewdly and rationally, and it'll cost him his life. (Implication: it's better to be *slightly* paranoid than trust anybody. Of two errors, it's the safer.)

FINER POINTS AND MINOR GRACES

1. Arbogast is mellowing. Taking the trouble to call Lila, when he'll see her in an hour, is *very* considerate. His penultimate line is especially sensitive: 'And Lila, you'll be happy to know what I think. I think our friend Sam Loomis didn't even know Marion was here.' Has he half-sussed that Lila might be drawn to Sam, a likely story development?

2. Sam answers the phone, but Arbogast reserves the infomation for Lila. There's a logical reason (she, not Sam, is Marion's next of kin), but scenes like this owe less to background logic than to upfront character, and he speaks to Lila as the stronger character. Like Arbogast, she's an avenger, a pursuer (though in other ways they're opposites).

3. The script spins things out even longer: Arbogast dials Sam, who gives him another number for Lila, and he dials that too. This may have been a censorship precaution, by suggesting Lila doesn't stay under Sam's roof all night. But it wasn't necessary: she's too pure, too preoccupied.

FROM OBSERVATION TO DEDUCTION

'I even know which cabin she was in. It was Number One.' It's another 'odd reference back', but left a bit oblique. Hitchcock doesn't remind us *how* he knew ('because I saw Norman hesitate outside Cabin 1 before not going in'). Many spectators didn't notice then or forgot until now, and the half-obscured source of his knowledge makes it all the more triumphant (and maintains the mystery atmosphere). There's a 'semi-disjunction', of which a subtler version may strike some second-time spectators. Norman's non-entry into the cabin, a sort of 'negative action' in an action flow, in a *visual* and *silent* presentation. Now it's recalled in the form of a verbally stated deduction – obliquely, in different *media*. (The original action was apprehended as we apprehend 'reality' – *embedded in the phenomenal world*. But now, words state a

significance *abstracted* from the action. Is this another case of ellipsis 'shifting' a preceding scene?)

It's a minor case, no doubt, but artistic craftsmen often delight in little details.
Whether or not they're 'subliminal', they don't stand out like 'points', but they contribute to a 'texture', the weave of 'little roughnesses', akin to 'atmosphere', mood,
feeling, intuitive apprehensions (much as 'little', intrinsically meaningless, musical
notes are *also* dynamic and fraught – the *Psycho* music is a case in point). A musi-
cianly spectator could pinpoint its precise harmonic progressions, though the rest
of us would experience them only 'intuitively', as the stream of sounds charge our
viscera.

We're talking 'micro-points' here and no 'micro-point' can explain a 'big emotion'.
But streams of 'little excitations' can give them support and add a 'counterpoint' of
subtler experiences, some 'content'-related, some 'purely' aesthetic. Many a 'mere'
craftsman is *more* sensitive to subtle meaning than artists who, while having 'something to say', say it clumsily, or can't analyse the forms they intuitively deploy, or stay
within a narrow range of meaning.

◆

SCENES 158–74 ARBOGAST FINDS MRS BATES

*Still on his linen-round, Norman disappears into an end cabin, just as Arbogast
parks his car, a little distance from the office, and walks over to it. Finding it
deserted, he looks through into the parlour, investigates an open safe and makes a
random shuffle through some papers. Back on the porch, he notices Mrs Bates is
not at her usual window, and proceeds on foot to the house. Finding its front door
unlocked, he enters, removing his hat respectfully, and ventures up the stairs.
Unseen by him, an upstairs door opens slightly. Before he gets to the landing, the
mad figure of Mrs Bates rushes from an upstairs bedroom, strikes out with the
knife, sends him skidding backwards down the steps, and leaps upon him, stabbing
him repeatedly.*

THE SPACE OF SUSPENSE

Films routinely cheat on space and time, but Arbogast's long on-screen walk is Hitchcock padding them out to lengthen the suspense. Thus the prelude to Arbogast's death *reverses* the prelude to Marion's: that played on utter surprise; this plays on apprehension. It's structured, not on *these* forms alone, but on *recollection* of the previous ones, suggesting *possibilities* – which also have no form. Though Hitchcock cut the major 'plant', Scene 134, the stairs Norman couldn't face, and the window where Mrs Bates twice has been seen, sufficiently mark out 'the zone of maximum danger', for which Arbogast, unsuspectingly, is heading. Our mounting apprehension is counterpointed by (lesser) dangers from other directions. Mrs Bates' appearance in Marion's shower established a wide 'realm of possible fear'. Her complicit son is out there somewhere. Off-screen space, although invisible, is integrally part of this scene, which combines its *focus* of fear with 'background radiation' from *all* directions. Suspense exacerbates geography.

THE TEMPO OF SUSPENSE

'Suspense' comes in many kinds: 'low-key ominous' or 'climactic nail-biting', 'pursuit adrenalin' or 'haunted house creep with any-moment jump-out foreboding', and so on – it's high time for PhD theses on this deceptively simple term. This sequence has a steadily 'rising curve': it starts with Norman safely going the wrong way in long shot, shifts to office claustrophobia with quick, tight movements, reverts to landscape (this time the vertical hill, with the busy rhythm of the garden steps) and steeply increases as Arbogast climbs the stairs, until Mrs Bates rushing out and Arbogast tumbling down changes the tempo again. The suspense is partly contextual (it follows a shock precedent), partly situational (as outlined in the section on 'space'), partly *stylistic* (it's only as suspenseful as it is because of Hitchcock's style). Specific 'thresholds' include: Arbogast's view of the house (implying he means to go there); his appearance in front of the hallway's blank, somehow deathlike white curtains; and the upstairs door opening a chink. Behavioural psychologists, like the very influential H. J. Eysenck, might ask us to rate these passages on some scale of suspense, with 10 as shrieking, 9 as heart-stopping, 8 as nail-biting, 6 as ominous, 5 as diffuse and 4 or below as nil suspense.

THE SURPRISE OF SUSPENSE

After all this preparation, right down to the chink of the door, Mrs Bates' attack surprises us, as well as her victim! Suspense being *predictive*, we get what we half-expected, but it's still a shock and the manner is a surprise. Since suspense predicts *sensed (not defined) alternatives*, whatever we get is a surprise, relative to the other! We knew *roughly* what might happen, and the general *modus operandi* (fast attack with lifted knife), but we couldn't foresee such eloquent details as the disorienting configuration of the overhead shot, the mad old lady's unusual angle of attack (at 90° to Arbogast), the backward fall. Hitchcock was proud of a big montage effect: the cut from the overhead view to the 'big head' of Arbogast aghast. He compared the visual contrast to a musical one, a switch from violins to brass. So the long shot is 'soft' and intricate, like strings, while the close-up 'blares' – an intriguing synaesthetic, for the *smaller* shot is the louder one! Herrmann's soundtrack works in counterpoint, switching *not* to screaming brass but to skittering strings.

THE AFTERGLOW OF SUSPENSE

In itself, the death of Arbogast is less impactful than Marion's, but it comes on top of it and renews our disorientation and dismay. Moreover, the death of this powerful character defies the widespread tendency, in Hollywood movies then, to forewarn us of eventual failure by sympathetic losers by showing a slight, not weakness exactly, but – softness? – of character. (A simple example: in Hawks' *The Big Sleep* (1941), Humphrey Bogart *cannot* die, but Elisha Cook Jr has 'brave but doomed' written all over him.) From now on, anxiety is pandemic.

STYLE SHIFTS

Outside in the night, Norman's and Arbogast's 'walkabouts' are marked by their silhouettes against lit windows. (A reprise of Mrs Bates' and Norman's *interior* silhouettes?) Arbogast's short zig-zag walk in office and parlour gets steep low or high
angles. The dead birds, highly evocative to us, mean nothing much to him. He dips
into dusty account books and the ancient, gaping-open safe. (Its emptiness is another
intriguing 'negative' – it *also* means '$40,000 not here'.)

PRIVATE EYE AS PROWLER

Arbogast's car, returning, irrupts more fully into shot: this time he's *intruding*. Norman
having *forbidden* access to his mother, one would expect Arbogast to walk quickly to
the house. Maybe Norman going the other way inspired the sleuth to detour into
the office (with zilch narrative consequence). Perhaps it makes Arbogast more businesslike, more money-centred, than if his only interest had been the 'house of incest'.
Thus it strengthens the 'private eye' theme against 'sexual voyeurism' – a wise precaution, given the widespread impression that the detective work in *Rear Window* is
'really' and 'mainly' about voyeurism as a sexual pursuit.

　Arbogast enters the hallway respectfully, hat held low, revealing his baldness:
humility and baldness make him more vulnerable. Décor-wise, his entry recaps
Norman's but everything is changed. The camera entered with Norman; Arbogast
confronts the camera. Norman balked at the first few stairs, the carpet of which
made a flat 'wall', and walked through to a bare, sad kitchen. Arbogast takes a quick
look down the passage (this shot stresses its Victorian plushness) and, for him, the
staircase stretches upwards.

　Saul Bass having made a storyboard of the scene, Hitchcock, being ill, let him film
it, but dismissed the result as all wrong. Bass, it seems, shot close-ups of Arbogast's
hands, feet, etc. ascending the stairs, in what might have seemed a dynamic montage,
Soviet-style. Hitchcock thought this made Arbogast seem like a *threatening* intruder,
whereas he's a vulnerable intruder, approaching danger ahead.

　In Hitchcock's version, the ascending intruder confronts a high-angle camera,
which, to keep him in view, pulls backwards up the stairs (or seems to; it looks
more like a zoom lens on a camera *outside* the décor, in extra-diegetic space). The
'flattened-out' perspective then characteristic of zooms makes conspicuous the hallway space below him (into which he will indeed fall). The one detail shot shows
Arbogast's legs *from the back*: this sharply switched angle, on an apparently 'unmoti-
vated' detail, is a little 'dislocation', thus enhancing our anxiety (while 'preparing' the

backward fall). It's no-one's POV, of course. (Hitchcock doesn't use the subsequent slasher cliché – the victim watched from a lurking assailant's POV, perhaps because it would confirm impending attack too early, too heavily. Here, we musn't be *too* certain of imminent attack.)

The close-ups of the upstairs door's lower corner opening are carefully misleading. Their 'front-on' angle, cut in on Arbogast's look ahead, suggests it's more or less in front of him, but Mrs Bates will emerge from a door on his flank. Another little 'disorientation'.

SEVEN GOOD REASONS FOR ONE GREAT SHOT

1. As discussed in connection with 134, Hitchcock's main reason for the trio of plan views was to hide Mrs Bates being her son (here) and her own mummy (188).

2. The highly unusual angle lyricises the action. Suddenly introduced, it disorients us.

3. The plan shot has a 'diagrammatic' quality, the unseen faces depersonalise it slightly. It's a *cruel* shot.

4. As Arbogast ascended, the camera steadily backed up; now, it makes a sudden 'jump', which is both the climax of, and contrast to, the gradual ascent.

5. The floor plan climaxes the 'flat floor' perspectives. They were unstable and slanting, but this is composed to be strongly parallel to the edges of the screen – it 'locks in'.

6. Religious spectators may think of this shot as 'God's-eye view', Hitchcock-watchers may think of it as a bird's-eye view. (Same form, very different meanings.)

7. It's part of the switch from violins to brass. (One form, many functions, multiple spin-off: that's formal elegance.)

Logically, there's every reason why this formal effect should have multiple 'motivations'. Nothing is imposed by some code or convention which would *demand* such a shot; it's Hitchcock's free, optional and unique assemblage, and it's bio-ergonomic (it gears in with spectators' visual perceptions). The 'overhead viewpoint' has no specific meaning. Sometimes it distances us from the action, or depersonalises it, or grants us God-like objectivity: here, the disorientation is highly *lyrical*; and though it 'makes strange', Brechtian alienation it sure ain't. Every 'plan shot' is different (depending on other variables: what it shows, the film so far, style, etc.). An expressive face, in close-up, is neither a 'subjective' shot, nor a POV shot. But, as the medium's

excitement over close-ups reminds us, they're natural, direct and powerfully expressive in conveying a character's subjective state. In other words, it's not *point* of view,
but *field* of view, that determines the richness of a shot, as description and as information.[51]

A 'concrete' film-maker might 'see' Arbogast's ascent of the stairs, as the camera
backs up and away from him, as Arbogast approaching *the plane of the screen*, but
never quite getting there. Earlier, we remember, Arbogast did indeed seem to step
through the plane of the screen (and the camera). If Hitchcock didn't *plan* this 'echo',
it's serendipitous — a result of playing on Martin Balsam's forceful face and his two
narrative 'intrusions'.

SHOCKS WITHIN SHOCK

The script says the knife slashes Arbogast's cheek and neck, though reviewer esti-
mates range from its entering his eye to blood splashing up from somewhere round
his lapels. This shock is immediately capped by another, that of Arbogast toppling
backwards in space, arms flailing madly (like would-be wings). He lands flat on his
back, and Mrs Bates flies down on top of him (like a bird of prey?); and as she kneels
over him, the camera rises to her knife up in the air. This highly gymnastic finale
recaps ideas about the super-strength of the insane, some of which, I'm reliably
informed, are true, and not just folklore or inspired by vulgar Freudian rhetoric about
our titanic libidos.

Arbogast's fall was a special effect, a close view of Martin Balsam (actually leaning
back in a chair and waving his arms) superimposed on a fast track-forward down the
staircase. Physically, it looks unconvincing to me; Arbogast loses his footing so early
that he'd have slithered down half the stairs flat on his back. The effect is geared to
a quasi-hysteric, crowded audience, not to close formal inspection. The long-
sustained close-up evokes his subjective experience, while the 'exaggerated duration'
of terror, and its sustained presentation gives the surprised audience time to 'catch
the infection'. Also, Hitchcock liked depicting long 'aerial' falls (*Vertigo*, *Saboteur*, *North
by Northwest*).

ON THE CARPET

After the dark, cramped, neglected office comes the bright, plush, spacious, impec-
cably preserved house. Its carpets are conspicuous: even the slyly opening door displays a chink of carpet, the highly intricate pattern of which briefly impinges upon
our attention. As carpets stress floors, they help prepare the plan view, and Arbogast

sprawling flat, while also contributing to the hushed, feminine, smothering atmosphere of the house. (They're a big improvement on the script, which has creaking
stair stuff.) In *Murder*, Hitchcock renders the luxurious thickness of aristocratic car-
peting by an 'impressionist' shot of a humble commoner's feet sinking up above the
ankles into billows of stuffed fabric.

SPACE AFTER SPACE

Both script and film follow Arbogast's walk, on screen all the way, from his car parked
discreetly away from the motel porch to Mrs Bates' upstairs landing, via office, parlour and the hill between motel and house. What the script calls Scenes 158–74 are
actually shots with only seven scene headings. The film uses many more shots as
Arbogast traverses four 'spatial complexes' (car to porch, porch/office/parlour, the hill
up to the house, the house interior). They'd normally be described as eight or nine
scenes. But Arbogast's walk is one long continuous line, i.e. space. As he's visible to
us pretty well all the way, all these scenes should be only *one* scene! Clearly, our standard vocabulary needs re-inspection, and theories of 'scenes' as 'basic' units of 'film
language' come under question.

FREUDIAN FANCIES

My stress on carpets appearing behind Arbogast makes the house a feminine
symbol, a sort of sterile womb. The tall, stiff, wooden post on the banister turnaround
may seem to some a phallic symbol, but I think it links to the stiff, tense alertness
which makes ears prick up. It also strengthens depth in the shot.

Discussion of *Psycho* naturally concentrates on Marion's murder, with its obvious
sexual interest (including the women's puritanism which is imitated by 'Mrs Bates').
Killing Arbogast gets overlooked, partly because it has no evident sexual motivation
and fits no Freudian pattern. Though plausibles might well ask, for instance, 'To kill
Arbogast, why dress up as Mrs Bates?' However, a common-sense answer is available:
'Because Norman when himself is too sensitive, too timid.'

Dressing up apart, killing Arbogast is perfectly rational, as rationality goes. (People
sometimes talk as if murders are *ipso facto* irrational, like violence, crime, illegality and
immorality; however, theory of praxis confirms the nagging suspicion that the most
rational course of action is to cheat wherever possible but never get caught out.
Since that's a high-risk strategy, honesty is often the best policy. But murder itself can
be entirely rational. This I suspect is what Hitchcock feared, except when he felt religious.) At the same time, Mrs Bates plays like madness in old melodramas, with their

dangerous lunatics in upper storeys, like *Jane Eyre* and that merry little old man in *The Old Dark House*. So this act is half-rational, half-melodramatic, with no Method in its madness. Hence diehard Freudians can feel free to suppose that sexual madness must be involved, with Arbogast as with Marion. Perhaps Arbogast reminds Norman of the 'intruding stepfather'. I wouldn't call such interpretations wrong, in the sense of being somehow incorrect, but neither are they right, in the sense of *settling* anything. Nor are they started or developed or 'necessary' to the film. They're hiked in by whichever school of Freudian theory wants them, and relevant only to that. Psychoanalysis, although a *potential* science, remains, alas, an art, with all the erratic vagaries to which art is heir.

VISIONS AND REVISIONS

As already suggested, a story is more than a succession of events: it's a *progression* of events. Each scene inherits ideas from all its predecessors, does something to them and passes that to its successors. The two shock deaths weigh on following scenes so heavily that they're effectively *part of them*, although invisible. To replenish their gradually fading power, Hitchcock will deploy reminders and re-echoes, which new developments will both challenge and reinforce. The exact relation of 'continuing invisibles' and 'new images' can be difficult to preconceive, especially with *Psycho*, which heavily depends on 'the reverberations of shocks', and it's not really very surprising that Hitchcock, though famous for pre-preparation, so often shot differently from the script and, after shooting, excised whole sequences and pages (but added none). As often said, writing and editing are one: preparing a screenplay is already editing, and editing is rewriting.

◆

SCENES 175–83 SAM AND LILA WORRY ABOUT ARBOGAST'S LONG ABSENCE

Lila and Sam, together in the dark store, have waited not one but three hours for Arbogast, in vain. Now they worry whether to wait here longer, as Sam thinks wisest, or to go to the Bates Motel to find out what has happened, as Lila strains at the leash to do. When, by way of compromise, Sam reaches for the phone, Lila, irritated, sets off to go alone. He too gets up to go, but insists she remain here, since Arbogast, if merely delayed, would come back here. Sam, standing by an old

pick-up truck, finds no one in the motel office, and looks around, calling Arbogast's
name (180). Norman, standing by the swamp, hears, and starts thinking hard.
Having returned to the store, Sam, now as worried as Lila, suggests they consult his
friend, Deputy Sheriff Al Chambers (181–3).

A 'LEAST WORST' PROCEDURE

So far the film's scenes have fallen into well-defined 'groups', broadly matching places
with phases of the action, conveniently for analysis. But from here on, characters
move so rapidly around that grouping scenes together becomes problematic.
However, some sort of grouping, even if more rough than ready, is more convenient
than the alternatives. The next 80 scenes don't make one single, undivided unit; and
working 'scene by scene' would overly fragment the flow. Whatever grouping one
settles for risks over-emphasising certain 'breaks' and over-skimming others.
However, to note the problem should minimise its effects. Though 175–83 comprise
three quite separate scenes, they constitute one dramatic 'phase': worry about
Arbogast directs our protagonists to Sheriff Chambers.

THE WAITING GAME

After Arbogast's death, we need another little rest, or, at least, a different kind of unease. Here, Sam and Lila are bogged down in fretful indecision between two poss- ible courses of action. Sam's is prudent but passive, Lila's is alert but riskier. This risks the problem which undermined *The Wrong Man*, passive, baffled 'worry worry' anxiety, nagging helplessness. Without digressing too far into theory of box office, it's reasonable to attribute the earlier film's commercial failure partly to its long, heavy evocation of anxieties all too common and oppressive in 'real life', whereas escapist drama forms and topics allow more 'refreshment of the spirit'. Here, however, the couple's fretting and arguing maintains their energy flow, through a limited dose of 'everyday miserabilism' within a diversely electric film.

There's a 'to and fro' of standard gender roles. She's the decisive, active force, he's the sensitive prevaricator. His mind strays from the subject into sentimental inertia. 'Sometimes Saturday night has a lonely sound' might fit a torch song, or a ballad for lonely bachelors, and encapsulates his dispirited existence, but it sure wanders off the point. He quickly, roughly, adds: 'Ever notice that, Lila?' – as if preparing a pass, or just to hide his self-pity, or to restore an underlying toughness, though it sounds clumsily rough, even aggressive. (Which fits, for shortly his weapon against Norman will be pseudo-friendly bullying.) Meanwhile, as with Marion, he's the big tease, the great frustrator. Lila wants to make a move, so he says to keep waiting. When she makes her move, his counter-ploy is picking up the phone. When she gets him to go, she thinks they'll go together, but he makes her stay there. (Is this just his usual per- versity, or is it patriarchal 'Stay-here-woman-while-I-sally-forth'? In the end it's a 'criss- cross' of frustration: who wanted to stay, goes; who wanted to go, stays.)

As in the best-constructed dramas, their argument isn't 'right versus wrong': it's 'partly right versus partly wrong'. Lila's wish to explore together is consistent; Sam's successive ideas are uncomfortably close to inertia (waiting around indefinitely and then just telephoning in are still frustration). Even turning to the sheriff smacks of yet another 'detour' (with a touch of 'weak man abdicates responsibility to strong man in authority'?). Sam's every move so far gives way to, yet frustrates, Lila. Will some 'law-and-patriarchy network' fatally squelch her activism?

Quite a few *Psycho* spectators would judge Sam and Lila's 'intuitions' in the light of what they, the audience, know about the story, and what Sam and Lila don't. But here, that sort of pragmatico-moral logic lets us down: Uncertainty Rules OK. Any sort of intervention, even just phoning Norman, might find out nothing and give Sam and Lila away to Norman. As for Lila going alone, that might be *very* foolhardy. If, from Sam's night visit, Norman didn't suss out where Lila was, that was pure luck. Thus Sam and Lila blunder and argue and muddle through, *not* like smart heroes, but like two ordinary 'little people', invincibility *not* guaranteed (thanks to Marion's death). They're two small shopkeepers together – American equivalents of Hitchcock's own class, and of little Alice White, the girl behind the shop counter.

TAR-PIT LIGHTING

The new mood, of 'impulse' bogged down by rational indecision and inertia, brings a new lighting style. Sam and Lila are strong white shapes, but wrapped around by heavy shadow. Lila, sitting tense and heavy in Sam's office chair (his politeness, or 'she's boss'?), swivels nervously, tightly; his arms move from a strongly settled fold to fidget with a watch. At first, they're two white 'slabs' in a noir mass. Though stuck in the black substance, their movements get steadily stronger, and, as they move towards the door, they move back and forth across each other. At the risk of over-writing, one might say the scene starts as a sort of 'locked knot', which 'unwinds' like a spring, releasing them into the night. More exactly, Lila's restless twitches of the swivel chair 'launch' a stronger movement towards Sam (a forward slant of her back is particularly active: the freeze-frame shows its *direction*, though not, alas, the *thrust*); he makes a bigger movement round her, she rises with it; they step quickly down the shop's dark, narrow 'tube', till their impetus is blocked by their pause in black silhou-ette. On their way, they encounter *visual events*, notably the glass screen between Sam's office and the shop acts as a mirror, in which Lila sees herself, transparent to the forks and rakes associated with death, though the glass-diffused light adds a soft, pseudo-romantic patina. Sam's return starts as a reprise of this movement. Its obvi-ous beginning would have been Lila's POV of Sam entering the shop. Hitchcock reverses that: he starts on a long shot, from the front door, of Lila, seated heavily far back in the brightly lit office; then she runs towards the camera from brightness into silhouette. Her impetus is 'climaxed' when her quasi-POV shows Sam entering the door, in a stronger, because closer, movement. Both in silhouette, they talk across the bright, distant emptiness. The two shots have two conspicuous 'emptinesses': first, the foreground space, into which Sam is due to enter, then the bright background space, which Lila has just vacated. They're visual equivalents of 'a lonely sound', made extra desolate by the context.

As Sam leaves Lila, the camera dwells on her silhouetted face, haloed by the black hooks of tall, stacked rakes. Norman, likewise shadow-shrouded, stands brooding beside the swamp, a white tree behind him like a jerkily poised skeleton. Hearing Sam's voice, his head, sunk in silhouette, turns and looks, and leaves no doubt he's thinking hard. A cross-fade from his dark, alertly lifted head to Lila alone in the store hints, in this anxiety-saturated movie, at a possible plot development. Might he come to the store, where Lila is alone, much as 'immobile' Mrs Bates suddenly appeared in Marion's shower? That won't actually transpire but the cross-fade which links them makes a premonition, in this anxiously unpredictable movie. … A colleague takes this 'dotted line' connection more seriously, and reckons that the shot of Lila running towards camera as Sam returns plays on our subliminal fear that the man who comes in the door will turn out to be Norman, and that Gavin resembles Perkins just enough for the clarifying POV to *mix* shock with relief. (It's an interesting idea, and Lila's run towards camera is indeed a common shock trope: the victim runs hopefully into camera and gets her shock in big close-up.) Another possible 'echo': two white bodies in and out of tar-pit lighting 'echo' a white car sinking in a black swamp. Sam and Lila are so depressed, so bogged down, they feel like shit. But – they don't lie down in it …

SCRIPT VERSUS FILM (4)

The final cut omits about 30 per cent of the script. Most importantly, Sam and Lila talk much longer. She says she appreciates his calming influence (hint of a possible romance?), and they both seem softer than Gavin and Miles play them. (That different actors could make *different persons* of them is a useful reminder that dialogue, character and narrative role don't need to structure one another; as long as one or two simple story-points are satisfied, all the rest is effectively autonomous.) It's obviously true in Shakespeare; but even in 'modern' psychological dramas, where character and action are supposedly tightly geared, the differences between equally fine acting interpretations are often startling. Hence, in drama, authors, actors, and directors, function as co-auteurs. Otherwise, Sam spends rather longer snooping about the Bates house, and sees Mrs Bates' silhouette at the window. Lila, alone in the hardware store, knocks a shower nozzle to the floor, and things around her assume grotesque shapes. Minor changes. The script wraps Sam and Lila in thick cigarette smoke (without specifying whether it's a fug that hangs and veils, or clouds that roll around, or directional thrusts and spirals as per *The Last Laugh*, or …). The film has a brief little floating drift of smoke, at the start, but thereafter nothing softens the hard pitch-black/white forms, except pale gleams through dusty panes of glass as if from weak light bulbs (which will 'star' in the Bates house basement).

◆

SCENES 184–5 SAM AND LILA SEE DEPUTY SHERIFF CHAMBERS

In their night-clothes, in their hallway, Sheriff Al Chambers (John McIntire) and his wife come down to hear out Sam's and Lila's tale. The sheriff's surmise is that Arbogast caught up with Marion, went off with the $40,000, and telephoned Lila to put them off the track. Chambers telephones Norman who, although reclusive, is an old acquaintance, and now repeats his thoroughly credible tale, that Arbogast came, asked questions and went. Sam protests that he saw Mrs Bates at the window; a claim contradicted by the older couple's knowledge of local history. Mrs Bates died about ten years ago, after poisoning her lover, and then herself, with strychnine: a notorious case, the quiet town's only murder-followed-by-suicide. Sam and Lila are bewildered and silenced.

NON-NARRATIVE FUNCTIONS OF THIS SCENE

Whenever a 'plausible' asked Hitchcock why, when characters in his films were in danger of being murdered, they didn't go to the police, he testily replied, 'They don't go to the police, because it's dull', or 'This scene shows what happens when you go to the police' (here, as in *Rear Window*, the police are complacent, unlike the watchful citizen). This scene leaves Sam and Lila precisely where they were before, and they will go on to search the Bates domain, just as Lila urged. Narrative event-wise, this detour is completely unnecessary to the plot. If we expected action, it ends in yet another anti-climax. But then again, maybe Sam and Lila's redoubled bewilderment qualifies as a new climax, of a different kind. Even more important is the bewilderment, by new information, *of the spectator.*

A CASE OF NARRATIVE INDETERMINACY

Had Hitchcock wanted Sam and Lila to steer clear of the sheriff there's a good enough reason: Marion is a thief and may be still alive, so they might just betray her to The Law. (However shifty Arbogast's clients may be, and however unconnected federal, Arizonian and Californian laws may be, The Law, and law officers, can be unpredictable.) Luckily, Sam knows *this* sheriff of old, as a friend and neighbour, and Chambers will behave as Sam might have hoped. But few are the plausibles, and fewer still the ordinary spectators who want to think back to all that, now the story is closing in on Norman. Still, fear of The Law was an *available possibility*, and Hitchcock's spurning it illustrates how *weakly* some logic 'intrinsic' to the story governs its developments, and how new twists and turns are always possible, till the very last moment of the film.

Another peculiarity is Sam's claim to have seen Mrs Bates at her window. He does in the script, but not in the film. Maybe Hitchcock reckoned that we've seen her there twice already so a repetition might smack of *déjà vu*, and anyway, spectators would mentally substitute the earlier sightings while omitting a reconfirmation would help us empathise with Sam's loss of confidence. (Witness suggestibility is a major problem in real-life courtrooms; it's even stronger at the cinema.)

The scene starts with a cross-fade to the sheriff descending the stairs and centres on his thoughts. His face looms large but *within* the context of the foursome, which is felt 'within' all the closer shots. The dramatic design of the conversation might be called 'the biter bit': the bringers of shocking news get more shocked in return by very old news.

Phase 1: Sam and Lila talk, the sheriff listens silently. Their synopsis shows just how thin their story is. They look to each other for spiritual support.

Phase 2: the sheriff's brief, terse questions fill his visitors with shame – silent, but clear to see. Marion was bringing her unmarried lover stolen money, and both were covering up her crime.

Phase 3: the sheriff's theory, of Arbogast the thief, is another 'possible story' (and the only likely one we've heard all night).

Phase 4: The sheriff's prompt action, ringing Norman, is positive action at last, but also paradoxical (since we know it'll forewarn him) – dismaying too is the sheriff's neighbourly knowledge of Norman's insomnia and his friendly bit of business advice (which may prompt Lila's later ideas).

Phase 5: Sam's last-ditch claim to have seen Mrs Bates provokes the old couple's local history, and culminates in the killer question, 'Well, if the woman up there is Mrs Bates … who's that woman buried out at Greenlawn Cemetery?'

The sheriff's sarcasm is a touch thoughtful, however: he delivers the line with eyes enquiringly wide open and face half-turned to camera, as if intimating direct address to the audience, and we're just as bewildered as Sam, for we've seen or heard Mrs Bates four times, once unforgettably. Here's a new dimension, of grue-some confusions … teetering on the edge of a ghost story … like *Vertigo*.[52] (And after all, the detective story genre developed from ghost stories – spawning hybrids along the way.)

SCRIPTWRITING AS DOUBLE-ENTRY BOOK-KEEPING (2)

Time and again we've seen the film work on the differences between what the spec-tator knows and what the characters don't, and the differences between what *one* character knows and *other* characters and the spectator don't. This sort of thing helps explain why Jean-Claude Carrière kept his 'account books', enabling him to see at a glance exactly what each character, and the spectator, knows or doesn't know at each point in a script. These things can get intricately different, and handy reference helps authors out (the spectator does it in his head). Watching the film is easier than constructing it.

GUILT OR SHAME?

Sam's and Lila's discomfiture is the sort of thing that quickly gets called 'guilt' – partly through Christian influence (Catholic or puritanical) and especially because Freud, for whatever reason, also emphasised it. Too rarely invoked are guilt's less introverted cousins: 'shame', 'embarrassment' and 'humiliation'. Though often linked, and easily confused, these powerful emotions are nonetheless distinct.[53] 'Guilt' derives from a self-judgment, 'shame' is fear of others' judgment; it belongs with honour, moral status, fear of mockery and 'What'll the neighbours say?'. 'Guilt' is inner-directed, and sup-poses an 'inner voice' of conscience; 'shame' is outer-directed and supposes no such thing. 'Guilt' is to do with obedience to laws; 'shame' is about living up to standards of performance. 'Guilt' gears into moral obligations; 'shame' need not. Unfortunately, 'guilt' sounds 'deep and soulful', while 'shame' sounds 'superficial and merely 'social'. 'Guilt' is a Judaeo-Christian specialty, though rooted in 'fear', which, like 'shame' is the more worldly, universal and, perhaps, powerful emotion. What Sam and Lila feel, here, is 'shame', since they already knew all about the guilt; what upsets them is that it's known. No doubt it's mixed with fear, of what the sheriff might decide to do, and with guilt, which shame makes more vivid to them. Emotions are like troubles: they rarely come singly; what we experience, and label often too briskly, is more often a mixture of attitudes, emotions and considerations, in subtly different proportions.

Although, as suggested earlier, *Psycho* mixes melodrama with drama, the mixture is uneven. Sam's and Lila's story is more melodramatic than 'psychological', and they don't, quite, or for long, go on to doubt their reality-sense, or fear they're going a bit schizo (whereas James Stewart in *Vertigo* gets into deep hallucination, self-doubt and mental alienation). All the same, their dismayed faces and Sam's head sunk in shame again verge on the theme of *crazy thinking*, or fear of it. (A more 'psychological' film might have studied their thoughts about that, through a sleepless night, before they turn up with a completely changed attitude in the next scene – which would take place in a church.)

HERE COMES THE JUDGE

John McIntire was a 'character star' of countless American movies, especially Westerns and TV series (*The Virginian*, *Wagon Train*). The sheriff's rugged face – griz-zled, with cowcatcher eyebrows – contrasts with the rather suburban house. If, through cowpoke ignorance or small-town complacency, he'd sent Sam and Lila packing, we wouldn't have been surprised. But he listens patiently, his questions are short and shrewd, his Arbogast scenario makes excellent sense and he has a nicely impassive acceptance of his wife's interventions, which either anticipate his, or decide them, in the strange manner of some old married couples. He lets questions like Marion's theft slide, whether because he's Sam's friend or because they'd be outside his jurisdiction – either way, his version of law and order is mellow, man-of-the-worldly. He's not 'patriarchal', just paternal – a rock-solid man. Listening judicially, he's like a homelier, wrinklier version of the founding fathers in *North by Northwest*. (I feared I'd just free-associated that, till I looked at the script, and it said: 'a face des-tined for Mount Rushmore'.) However, the script saw the sheriff's face rather differ-ently from the film: more lean and narrow (which after 'Mount Rushmore' hints, perhaps, at Abraham Lincoln?).[54] In the film, he's less lofty, more earthy, less the pres-idential spirit devolved than a pioneer cowboy uplifted – which may be a touch less ironic (since the sheriff, though a good guy, gets things about as wrong as everybody else), but I like it a lot better.

THE SHERIFF'S WIFE

Mrs Chambers is there to confirm the sheriff's recollections of the Bates and to counterpoint them from her different angle – the rose-tinted complacency which Hitchcock really disliked, and often allocated to old ladies. Her round, sweet face is a touch blotched and doleful – is it only the residue of sleep and face-cream, or is she one of the sad, frustrated people, living in false sentimentality about life? She helped Norman choose the dress in which Mrs Bates' body was laid out: the dress was 'periwinkle blue' – the colour of American optimism. Jumping to conclusions about Sam's story, she interjects – 'Norman took a wife?' – her little shriek of unselfish joy encapsulating years of neighbourly goodwill. (And the 'every man should be married' tradition, which by the 1950s was combining Momism with the feminine mystique.) Her husband having shaken his head over the gruesome details of Mrs Bates' death, she tries to sweeten it, with a sexual scandal titbit, especially for Lila, in a 'woman-to-woman' confidence.

'LOVE THY NEIGHBOUR AS THYSELF': NEIGHBOURLINESS IS NEXT TO GODLINESS

As the scene opens, she has already admitted the visitors; the sheriff is still descending the stairs. He scarcely looks at her, or speaks to her, or acknowledges her quick suggestions, which he follows. The film gives her no name, and puts her furthest from the camera: she's 'merely' a quietly comic character. Patriarchal male effaces wife? Could be, but it could also be a mutual accommodation, between a traditionally undemonstrative couple. She's always a mediating presence, a welcome to the visitors, a pressure *upon* the sheriff. Though furthest from the camera, she's in the centre of the picture. For her, neighbourliness is all. Little does she know …. It's 'the fantasy of goodwill' (Richard Griffith's term for Frank Capra's vision of small towns, already subverted by Hitchcock in *Shadow of a Doubt*, long his favourite among his own films).

SPIRITUAL ARCHITECTURE

The sheriff's hall is graced with two sets of twin columns; disarmingly pretentious, they nonetheless insert a sort of legal idealism: 'Washington classicism meets Southern aristocracy.' Behind Lila's fraught face, parlour furnishings have the dead, secretive air of living rooms re-entered while everyone should be in bed. The sheriff puts his killer question in front of shadowy stairs, like the start of an uptwisting maze. The script's first sentence specifies wallpaper with roses, thus echoing the Bates house (as does the setting: hall and stairs). Instead of intruders going upstairs, towards mother's bedroom, The Law comes down (everything in its Oedipal place?). Are the Campbells and the Bates the 'light' and 'dark' sides of this community – of a certain Middle America? Of middle humanity, and its laws – very imperfect, but not malevolent?

TELEPHONE ETIQUETTE

The sheriff's wife suggests they ring Norman, then follows her husband's direction to do so, lifts the handset and, instead of dialling a number, asks 'Florrie' to connect her to the Bates Motel. There follows another telephone monodrama: from one side of the conversation, we deduce Norman's usual patter. The sheriff concludes by giving him good business advice (to relocate nearer town).

'THE CRAFT SO LONG TO LEARN'

Back-story as New Twist

This sudden new back-story could risk diluting the ongoing suspense, and delaying imminent action a couple of scenes too long. However, it immediately transforms the situation. It feels alive, thanks to the Chambers' vivid memory and continuing response to their personal feelings. As Janet Leigh remarked, 'periwinkle blue' makes a strangely brilliant colour-splash, though only a mental one; eloquent, too, its connotations – sentimentality, optimistically denying the fact of death). (It's a 'telegram' summary of Nancy Mitford, *The American Way of Death* [1963], and Evelyn Waugh, *The Loved One* [1945, filmed 1965]. It mixes 'modern optimism' with Gothic overtones of 'life-versus-the-cemetery', another genre fusion, which the new teenagers will make mainstream fare.)

Mise-en-scène

This *mise-en-scène* is unusually inelegant. The group of people make a static line across the screen, in a rather shallow vee, in a sort of tight sprawl, of mostly light greys. This has some resemblance to what some theorists think is 'Hollywood grammar and syntax' but Sharff calls 'master-scene discipline' (i.e. not a pre-specified syntax but a freely chosen procedure of discourse). It's much used for fast, low-budget shooting. The entire scene is first filmed in long shot; its start provides the opening establishing shot, after which it can be interrupted, as desired, by closer shots, filmed subsequently. Hitchcock starts on the sheriff descending the stairs, as befits his 'decision' role. Thereafter his power gets him some low angles, but they're shallow ones, and his face is briefly sprinkled with film noir-type shadows, but not for long;

his 'dominance' is subordinate to the scene's real action. Hitchcock's style is more lightly, subtly balanced.

'Tennis-match Alternation'

This has the visitors serving left to right against the sheriff returning right to left. However, the sheriff's wife stands on both sides of the net! In several shots of the sheriff, she's there as his partner; in several visitors' shots, she's there too! As diegetic space goes, it's entirely rational; but craft convention-wise, it's a bit unusual, as, in theory, it risks suggesting that there's two of her, sometimes looking at herself both ways! Luckily, in this case, no confusion arises, as other information *overrides* film form. (The power of spatial information to override 'grammar and syntax', which is also the power of *semantics* to override *semiotic* form, poses theoretical problems too complex, although fruitful, to recap here.)

Cheating Space

The parlour furniture makes tense, unsettling angles to the faces in front of them. And lovers of film-craft can find subtle delight in the plethora of discontinuities and cheats (e.g. how those columns shift around).

An Obscene Idea

Mrs Chambers brightly suggests that the figure Sam saw was not Mrs Bates but Marion. Oh! Ugh!

Twice-told tale

' —She ain't missing so much as she's run away?' 'Yes.' 'From what?' 'She stole some money.' 'A lot?' 'Forty thousand dollars.' Lila's answers, though tersely factual, are increasingly reluctant: as she speaks, she realises how each answer makes Marion's being in danger sound less improbable and increasingly shameful. The emotionless words, and their hard, deliberate speed, possess a sharp emotional subtext (improbability plus shame – an unusual combination). It's a subtext, derived from dialogue and context, in a sort of 'dialectical synthesis' (not especially Marxist). These *unwritten*, and in that sense *formless*, meanings are strongly emotional and explain Howard Hawks' observation, that 'If I can understand a script the first time I read it, it's no damn good.' Such meanings are often called 'hidden', 'inner' or 'deep' and the very word *subtext* suggests something underneath something – as if a text had a 'surface' with 'layers'. Curious metaphor. For texts are all on the surface of a blank sheet of paper, nothing is hidden; it's all in plain view. (Like a purloined letter, hidden in plain sight. Purloined from where? Might a mirror hold a clue? Dear Reader, you and only you, right now, are bringing meaning to this text … even more than it's suggesting meanings to you …)

SCRIPT VERSUS FILM (5)
A Lost Scene
A scene, thankfully deleted, has Sam and Lila spend half a page discussing whether they dare disturb the sheriff so late at night; until Sam acknowledges his own pro-crastination (a gain in self-knowledge, after his slick jargons). When they do ring, a clangorous doorbell makes them jump. Opening the door, Mrs Chambers confides her dislike of 'Tinkerbell', installed by her husband to catapult his brain out of sleep. Vaunting his 'mechanical brain' (a new angle on the 'thinking' theme), she invites them in, and the scene resumes as in the final edit. Clearly Hitchcock is continuing the 'hes-itational suspense', 'fear of embarrassment in everyday situations', and indulging at last in 'comic relief', though maybe audiences would have jumped at a loud ring (a sound absent from entries into the Bates house). If we add Marion kept waiting, it's actually the fourth of five 'threshold scenes'. All super correct, formally, yet risky. Hesitation here risked being one anti-heroism too many (though it's hard to be sure. Andrew and Virginia Stone had a cheap, surprise hit in 1955 with *The Night Holds Terror*, where a middle-class man, held hostage, with his family, by three gunmen, is realistically unsure what to do).

Lightening the Moral Touch
The film spares Sam and Lila a heavy moral homily from the sheriff (hardly necessary).

Vive la différance!
The script specifies roses on the wallpaper and carpets and, a detail lost in the film, sheriff and wife wearing identically patterned nightwear, as if to underline their 'his'n'hers' 'togetherness' (a 1950s theme). Perhaps, too, it's a kind of 'thinking alike', which, whether you think it's a bit over-sentimental, or, especially in an older couple, rather nice, keeps within the range of 'normal' a 'unisex' tendency which in Norman is macabre and incestuous. Mirror-theorists could pursue further reflections on 'sim-ilarity and difference'. Have their years together brought them so close they're like mirror-images – though, like all the mirror images in *Psycho*, originals and reflections are always different (the mirror shows the other side, or a partial fragment, or, light

and background are changed). Extreme Formalists might link this 'mirroring' with Mrs Chambers' tennis-match 'doubling'; I like it. Why, one wonders, did Hitchcock drop this happy detail?

SCENES 186–8 NORMAN HIDES HIS MOTHER

Norman puts down his office telephone and, crossing to the house, and going up the stairs and into the bedroom, urges his mother to let him carry her down to the fruit cellar, where she won't be found by the now inevitable enquirers after Marion's and Arbogast's disappearances. Despite her insulting protests, he carries her bodily down the stairs.

STRUCTURE AS STRATEGY

This scene exists to 'reassert strong suspense', which might otherwise fade as Sam and Lila get bogged down in their peripheral orbit. The sheriff having 'volatilised' Mrs Bates' existence, this scene reasserts her (while still denying us a close look at her).

It restores a little sympathy to, and distracts suspicion away from, Norman. Though he lets his mother ruin his happiness, for her sake, he can now override her wishes: the 'weak son' behaves like a 'wise father'. Though nothing decisive happens in this scene, its 'trail away' ending harmonises with the Uncertainty Principle, and makes another kind of ellipsis. These five reasons for the scene are to do with narration (sustaining suspense), not with narrative logic – with respect to which it's far from 'necessary': without this scene, the spectator will share Lila's shock when, entering Mrs Bates' bedroom, she finds no one there. (However, this point of the plot needs a 'stiffener', and the later scene does not.) This scene continues the series of staircase ascents. Back at 112: Good Norman stops at the bottom stair. Back at 134: Complicit Norman reached the door, but found no mother, only her bloody laundry. Then, at 174: Arbogast got to the landing, and mother found him. Now at last, Norman enters her room – but, the camera is kept out.

'AS I WAS GOING UP THE STAIR/ I MET A MAN WHO WASN'T THERE'
Scene 187 repeats the plan views of the landing of 134 (deleted) and 174, but within a different continuity. Norman enters the hallway, the camera staying close on him, but, as he starts to ascend the stairs, it stays where it is and, from behind and below him, watches him walk up and turn across the landing and disappear into his mother's room. As their conversation begins, the camera starts a trek up the empty stairs, but halfway up slants off towards the banisters, rises up and over the banisters, now clearly flying and, climbing fast, in a corner-cutting diagonal, closes over the top corner of the bedroom door, which Norman seemed to have left ajar. The camera continues through dark, indecipherable corner space, during which it must have all but looped the loop, for when we can reorient ourselves we're looking down on another plan shot of landing and the stairs we've just ascended. The mother–son conversation has been continuing (another sound-only scene, in off-screen space). Then, below us, the son emerges, carrying across his arms (as once he carried Marion), a frail night-gowned figure. Before he's halfway down those stairs, the scene fast-fades to black.

Far simpler ways existed of concealing Mrs Bates' mummified condition (e.g. concentrating on Norman and leaving her only just below the frame), but most of them display 'concealment'. This aerial looping is so spectacular it distracts us from what we're not seeing. It's a 'conjurer's gesture' (and by no means breaks the illusion, as Hollywood theory had been over-fearful – and neo-Brechtians too hopeful – showy figures of form might do). It's practically an *anti*-POV. It disorients us again, but in new,

space-thrust terms. First it hangs back but then its movement takes off and we perceive we're flying, by magic, but then it's shut out, but then – is it a bird? Or a bat?
Or a fly too high on the wall? Perhaps it's voyeuristic (and écoutist), but I think it's
more generally emotional than that, about the maternal realm, and mother/son sep-
aration/symbiosis/argument/shifted dominance, in love and crime.

TWO FLY'S-EYE VIEWS

That moment of indecipherable space has a precedent: when the camera enters the
hotel window after an 'indecipherable' space, it finds Marion satisfied on the bed and
Sam's thigh beside her. Are the two 'entries' opposite extremes – one *normally*
immoral, the other *morbidly* immoral? One, sexual indulgence, in a too-loose relationship, the other, pure, incestuous emotion, in a too-tight relationship? One 'low', cynical view, the other 'high', excluded, hysterico-neurotic.

But then again, it's our POV, it's our eye, not a neurotic fly's. Climbing the stairs
and then flying may indicate sexual excitement, but any excitement is Norman's, not
ours. The excitement of flying is also to do with *sheer anxiety*, and fear of what we'll
find out – it's not a sexual fear, it's an adult approach to some nasty, squalid crime
(like Brady–Hindley, Fred and Rosemary West – if they morbidly fascinate us, is that
really explicable, in everybody, in terms of sexual desires, or are our gut-feelings more
to do with cruelty and pain, that is to say, our fear/survival/power instincts, and our
'herd instincts', like morality and social responsibility, and the structures of these
desires?). Here, we're frightened of *what we may find out*, but, *we need to know the
worst*. It's not voyeuristic (which implies sexual pleasure); it's horrified, as decent
humanity should be. It's how Lila might enter this dread house: to hang back, then go
on, then feel her stomach lift and mind flutter … her head spinning like a bird
trapped near the ceiling.

This is not to say that no sexual 'prompt' nudges us to thoughts of incest (not
desired by us – few first-time viewers want to embrace Mrs Bates, and fewer still
second-timers). On our previous ascension of these stairs, with Arbogast, we looked
back and down upon him. Now, following Norman up, we see ahead of us a Victorian
painting of an extremely voluptuous young woman and an ornate frame implying
another such picture. (Who bought them, and put them there? Mrs Bates, narcissis-
tic about her youth, and seducing her poor son? Norman's real mother, long ago?
Norman, collecting, since?) This camera-movement is both sexually morbid (by
association with Norman) and normal (it's our POV). They're opposite states of mind
and the tension between them is dramatically interesting – like many kinds of 'mixed

feelings', 'conflicting emotions', 'ambivalence'. Norman regains some sympathy for his quiet reasoning, his patient firmness, despite his mother's corncrake jeers. So velvety, so vivid is the colour of Perkins' voice, we almost don't notice that this conversation is off-screen and 'invisible', and another 'monodrama' (Norman speaks both voices).

How thin and frail is Mrs Bates, cradled against her son, her little feet quivering (very noticeably, since they're held just over the wooden banisters). Not exactly that big, strapping, knife-plunging Amazon, towering over Marion, is she? Quite a clue, especially after the 'cemetery', to observant plausibles, who, like detective mystery novel-readers, love to pit their wits against the text, and half-guess, half-deduce the malefactor's identity before the narrative reveals it.

A quietly odd trope is the cross-fade from Lila's anxious face, in the previous scene, to a masculine hand slamming a telephone, hand-set and base-unit together, down on a desk. The double-slam hits us like a shock-cut, which may qualify this trope as that paradoxical thing, a shock cross-fade. The sheriff having hung up three pages back, this slam-bang scene-start is either a time-cheat or Norman has remained transfixed, thinking hard, the phone still in his hand. (The script hints at the latter view: it has Norman sit 'in the dimness, one lamp alight, the phone next to him, his hand still near it as if he had not been able to move his hand after hanging up' – but that moment has been cut.) His next bit of business, with light switch and window, recaps his first decisive acts after seeing Marion's corpse. Then a shot of the house, and Norman hurrying over there, recaps Arbogast's journey, though Norman moves more quickly. Norman ascending the stairs is another recap (albeit the camera reverse and loop). Such recaps, entirely unnecessary to the narrative, blend 'memory' with a renewal of Norman's perspective, 'changed' by harder resolve.

LESSER MOTIFS

Mrs Bates' dislike of the dank fruit cellar echoes Norman's references to damp, unaired linen (and the desert/swamp dryness). Does her bitter pun on 'fruity', meaning 'mad', echo Arbogast's disrespectful pun on 'nuts'? (Or is the 'fruit and nut' link smuggled in by me, inappropriately, from the well-known kind of chocolate?)

'Mother, please just for a few days': thus time is ever on the agenda, not as an abstract concept, but as apprehension, impatience, an agitation of duration and tempo – as in the shrill rhythms of Bernard Herrmann's music, and as in Bergson's distinction between 'duration' (time as human minds experience it) and 'clock time'. In this dramatic narrative, time is variously 'distorted' between 'action agitation', 'suspense', 'apprehension', 'dread' and, in this scene, a 'counterpoint' of movements towards uncertain possibility.

In the script, Norman accidentally knocks to the floor, not a *picture*, this time, but his own work of art, a stuffed shrike (title of a Pulitzer Prize stage hit filmed in 1955, with June Allyson, normally Hollywood's pleasantest wife, as a husband-impaling female).

Above and beyond the stairs to Mother's bedroom, a second, less grand flight leads to mysterious realms above: spectators may briefly notice its 'atmosphere', of 'melancholy infinity'. It's also a plant for Lila's explorations later.

◆

SCENE 189 THE CHAMBERS LEAVE CHURCH

As Sheriff and Mrs Chambers leave Sunday morning church, Sam and Lila approach them to offer a lift to the Bates Motel. Chambers replies that he's been already, and found nothing amiss. He advises Sam to report a missing person; Mrs Chambers invites them to Sunday lunch. Disheartened, the young couple almost give up, and go their separate ways, but narrowly decide to drive out there themselves.

A FOURFOLD TWIST

1. Sam and Lila, last seen distraught, have returned to the attack (well done); offering a lift makes things easy for the sheriff (good thinking).
2. But, he's made the move already (an admirable response). Thus, good qualities and right actions only pile on the frustrations, and the temptation to give up becomes ever more right and reasonable. (The narrative has jumped two scenes: Sam and Lila thinking through this overnight and the sheriff's early morning.)
3. Here's another 'between-scenes ellipsis' with 'retrospective surprises'.
4. It's a nice sunny day, near a church; so near the climax, it's the calm before the storm.

THE LAST TEMPTATION

The sheriff plus the church, traditional centres of small-town peacefulness plus a sunny morning plus Sunday dinner with neighbours plus responsibility transferred to the appropriate social agency – in the eyes of God, The Law, and community, Sam and Lila giving up would be beyond reproach. But, as T. S. Eliot almost said, 'The last temptation is the greatest treason/ To do the wrong deed for the right reason.' Nagging intuition – conscience – drives the extra mile.

Sam, weak as ever, briefly doubts his own eyes: 'Maybe I am the seeing-illusions type.' 'You're not', retorts Lila (the American woman tells her man who he is). This puts some lead in his pencil and he agrees that he, too, is dissatisfied. (Moral leadership helps others be who they really are.) Also 'the female's intuition is stronger than the male's, even when he's not wrong'. It's a corollary of the more familiar proposition, 'female intuition is right, male rationality is wrong'. But the gender divide is not so simple: the sheriff's wife, though a valuable neighbour and intimately knowledgeable, is a rose-tinted 'counter-realist'.

AESTHETIC AND SOCIAL NICETIES

1. Sam's squat pick-up contrasts with the slim church spire.
2. Mrs Chambers looks smarter, sprucer and happier than in the middle of last night. She's quietly proud of her husband's swift efficiency.
3. When she invites the couple to lunch, her husband says nothing, but she knows he'll agree, and his gaze follows hers around.
4. She says it to Lila, and then adds, 'And you too, Sam' (Sam, last as if least).
5. Chambers dismisses ghosts (right). He concedes Sam is not the 'the seeing-illusions type'; but we know Sam can be too suggestible (by lifestyle magazines), and the sheriff's form of words suggests a subtext like, 'You're a good friend, Sam, and we all understand the tricks night shadows can play, but you were too imaginative last night.'
6. The sheriff says 'drop this in the lap of the law': what he doesn't say is, 'put this in the *hands* of the law'. 'Drop in the lap of' hints at irresponsibility, and 'in the lap of' usually implies 'the gods', and their amoral whims.
7. Chambers suggests they step aside, so as not to block the path. It's *community* niceness, but *distracts* from what matters. It deserves respect, *but* . . . .

SCRIPT VERSUS FILM (6)

In the film, the church is traditional small-town WASP, of no particular denomination. In the script, it's Presbyterian. By tradition, Presbyterianism came not from WASPs but from Scottish Calvinism, and was more community autonomous (instead of hierarchical bishops, local presbyters). It was neither snob-class (unlike Episcopalians) nor Bible-punching fundamentalist (in the modern sense). The script refers to the churchgoers' complacency, but in the film it's evident only via the Chambers' good neighbourliness. Ethically, the Chambers look, if anything, Germanic or 'western Eastern European'.

SCENES 190–1 SAM AND LILA DRIVE TO THE BATES MOTEL

Sam and Lila, driving to the Bates Motel, decide to book in as man and wife and search the whole place.

INTO THE HOME STRAIGHT

Sam, driving, wonders what they should do when they get there; Lila tells him. They both leave their thinking rather late – another 'impulsion'? But Marion, alone at the wheel, never had a plan. Back at the store, Sam and Lila were all at sixes and sevens – now Sam consults her and, once prompted, she produces their plan (as befits the Victorian idea of woman as 'the quicker-witted sex').

Their 'man and wife' masquerade is a favourite situation in comedy and farce (it echoes Marion's intentions and presages a Sam–Lila romance). But no hint of genre mood is here; it's severely chaste, severely goal-directed. The light looks scruffy, between chalky and grey, but it's clear. The camera resumes its 'Marion's drive' position, again with a strong 'rear window-scape'. But now the road is straight and level, its long, converging perspective suggests hard, calm purpose.

SCRIPT VERSUS FILM (7)

In the film this scene has three of the 43 speeches written in the script. This speeds things along, but loses Lila's interesting back-story. When their parents died, Marion quit college and got a job, in order to put Lila through college. Lila, feeling guilty, renounced her chance of college and took her store job instead. So neither sister went to college, and now Lila wonders if her renunciation hurt Marion, as a rejection of her sacrifice. Sam, to console her, recalls Marion offering to 'lick the stamps'. They wonder if Marion unconsciously liked to suffer. Sam reassures Lila that they truly intended marriage. Lila says she came across a letter from Sam to Marion and approved the feeling it showed. She believes Marion was keeping him a secret from her only until all was above-board and respectable. Sam chides her for speaking of Marion in the past tense.

Two orphan sisters, reciprocal sacrifice ending sadly for both, pride in respectability – it's almost Victorian, but it's still modern – and in that respect, akin to Norman. Norman, a self-made orphan, won't relinquish his mother; the sisters mother each other. As Lila had tried to support Marion, so Marion had tried to support Sam. Marion was keeping Sam hidden, until she could present him respectably – with, on the mantel, a picture of her dead mother. The small pictures of her parents were the modest, decent equivalent of Norman's large-as-life, disgusting memorials (stuffed birds, stuffed mother). It's surprising that Hitchcock should have thought of putting such retro-thoughtfulness so close to an imminent climax. It's entirely irrelevant to any narrative event, as its very deletion proves. However, that's a traditional device – a thoughtful, melancholy 'pause' before action – much as Shakespeare's Henry V is thoughtful before the battle. However, the sisters' reciprocal sacrifice might have altered our ideas about Marion's drive, making it less *simply* sexual, but weaving the sexual thread in with family and moral emotions and obligations.

How instructive would a DVD be, if the additional material included such deleted scenes as were shot, or Hitchcock's preliminary sketches, maybe in some provisional assemblage, like *The Red Shoes Ballet Sketches*.

◆

SCENES 191–214 SAM AND LILA ENTER THE BATES DOMAIN

In the grounds of the Bates Motel, Sam and Lila emerge from Sam's pick-up truck and look uncertainly about. Norman watches from a lace-curtained window, sensing their purpose; sharp-eyed Lila sees a curtain twitch. Norman approaches them with friendly jauntiness. He's casual about the formalities, but Sam insists, pretending that his mean-minded boss grudges all expenses claims. When he admits he and Lila have no baggage, Norman smiles as if with worldly tolerance. But from his office doorway he watches them walk all the way along the porch (which is like a verandah) to their allocated cabin, 10. Here they plan their next move. Lila believes Norman stole the money, to start a better-located business elsewhere, and that Arbogast was stopped because he'd found out something. Sneaking along to Cabin 1, they find in its toilet bowl a scrap of paper with a fragment of a calculation involving '40,000'. Lila resolves to talk to Mrs Bates, shrugging off Sam's note of caution: 'I can handle a sick old woman.' To keep Norman busy while Lila sneaks around to Mrs Bates, Sam goes to Norman's office and strikes up a conversation. Lila, having gained the cover of an old shed in a yard, climbs a grassy bank towards the house, opens the door and looks in at the hallway.

THE TOPOGRAPHY OF SUSPENSE

Sam and Lila emerge into the motel space, which we've often seen before. But new camera angles and broad daylight transform it into an arena-cum-maze. The long porch has a right-angle turn in it, which brings Cabin 10 much closer to Norman's normal viewpoint, the office, and makes a more 'active picture' than a long straight line. The series of cabins and pathways between buildings make a 'warren' of little hiding places and long sight-lines.

Both men are falsely friendly. Norman, first seen in a new, high vantage-point, senses danger from the start, and sallies forth to face it, hands jauntily deep in his trouser pockets, broad shoulders swinging merrily. A joke turns him sharply cautious, then he relaxes, or does he? He keeps trying to skimp the signing-in – is he trying to minimise any trace of them, in case he has to dump them too in the swamp? Is nervousness making him frantically absent-minded? Or can he just not stand Sam's heavy presence? Facing him, Norman's supple body seems almost girlish.

The 'half-right, half-wrong' game goes on. Shrewd Lila shifts between a vague 'something wrong' and an astute, though provisional theory (overlooked by Arbogast and the sheriff), that Norman killed Marion for the money. Sam's worry about Lila meeting Mrs Bates is, as first-time spectators think they know, absolutely right; but Lila understandably dismisses it as more procrastination (reasonably, but wrongly). Sam worries about everything, but gives a piece of modest, self-effacing advice: that if she comes across anything suspicious, she should go straight back to town, not hang around to tell him (a salutory reminder that danger *is everywhere here*).

Against the prevailing colour, pallid grey, Sam's dark suit has heavy import. In Marion's cabin, it briefly 'configurates' with dark embroidery on the bedcover and makes a moment of visual mourning. Otherwise, his dark suit gives him a brutally solid, square-ish body presence.

VIEWS, LOOKS, LINES OF SIGHT AND TOPOGRAPHY

The drama now plays on spatial manoeuvrings. Movements around sight-lines, are a major theme – whether outdoors and indoors, much as in Western gunfights – and even when surprises aren't happening, we are on half-alert for them. The opening 'vista' resembles an establishing shot, though wider than it needs to be, and what it establishes is more a general sense of 'space as vulnerability to being seen' than necessary information about spatial relations (that's presented, as needed, in subsequent shots). Sam and Lila go from truck to empty office in a wide, open space which emphasises their 'exposure', while Norman appears in a high-up window: this unprecedented viewpoint is a touch mysterious, for we're so close to it that we only know where it is by deduction (as it's high up and has lace curtains it's probably in the house). Norman 'ambushes' Sam by suddenly popping out of his office doorway, whereupon Sam, by standing in the doorway, blocks his view of Lila sneaking up. Also, Sam is a head taller than Norman, reversing the Arbogast relation. Closer looks, too, play their part. Talking to Norman, Lila shoots a quick look at solid Sam, as if for reassurance, and a quickly observant one at Norman; there's considerable suspense of looks – will Norman notice Lila's look at him? Here, no doubt, the voyeurism theme encounters the more delicate plays of looks in social life, where a frank straight look denotes honesty, and yet 'it's rude to stare'. Sometimes eye-play in conversations can become little 'ballets' of eye-patrolling, of mutual acknowledgment and polite avoidance, and 'having something to do with your fingers' is also about 'giving you something to look away at'. (There surely are long treatises on eye movements in discourse semantics.) In Cabin 1, a very stylish shot has Sam looking up at the shower rail and noticing no shower curtain (it's the sort of thing a hardware man might notice), while Lila looks down in the toilet bowl (most of which Sam's body tactfully conceals, especially as she picks white scraps out of it). It's a remarkable combination of two 'cinematographic angles', one up, one down – to celebrate the crucial discovery.

REPRISE-EN-SCÈNE

Director Joseph Losey used selected objects in his films to work as 'markers'. Whether or not 'symbolic' in themselves, they were quietly emphasised, to aid the identification of scenes without resort to establishing shots, which Losey disliked, as their 'general' views are often irrelevant and weaken the dramatic grip. It may be only a doorknob or a banister-rail, meaningless in itself, and valid in this film only. Yet still our fourth 'visit' to the Bates domain is a virtual maze of markers – a zone of terrifying memories – but changed, by (first) daylight and (second) the intruders' mixture of wrong and right ideas, with their new pattern of fears and hopes. The delicate picture of the bird is back in its place, Sam will enter the office mirror, presage of death. Now, by day, we see the dark wooden frame, carved like a funeral wreath. But the guests' reflection within seems less 'trapped', partly because, by daylight, it's less separate from everything around, partly because Sam's dark bulk is stronger than every previous occupant's, and his dark veiled gaze has more brute power in reserve.

Lila approaching the house door is our fifth eye fixation on that space, from various distances and angles. (Norman involved it in three very long shots: dashing down to Marion's car, flying down to her cabin and then hurrying the other way, towards it from the motel office. Arbogast moved smartly towards it, and Sam's midnight scouting was 'compressed' within a tighter, closer, more static shot.) Lila's approach is quite different. It's in broad daylight, she starts from closer, from another direction (ascending not steps, but a wavering path up a steep bank) and via a camera which is not only 'inside the action' but emulates 'hand-held', akin to Lila's walking POV. More exactly, the editing alternates between Lila's approximate POVs of the ever-nearer doorway, and back-tracking shots of her, full face, advancing anxiously but with swift determination. Diegesis-wise, all the shots move in one direction towards the house, but graphic form-wise, shots pulling backwards alternate with shots pushing forwards – a push-and-pull contradiction, and therefore dynamic. Her POVs are slightly unsteady, like someone walking; the back-trackings too have a slight unsteadiness. Another 'instability': some shots of Lila are figure shots, others close-ups, others somewhere between. The alternation of track-back and track-forward breaks a Hollywood continuity rule, 'Never cut camera movements directly against each other' (mainly to avoid the disjunction which here is appropriate). It corresponds to a favourite Hitchcock trope (alternation of character near-POV., to aid spectator identification, with a 'reaction shot' of her face (to re-emphasise her face, whose expressive power character POVs sadly lack). Near-POVs are a standard Hollywood procedure, especially well adapted to the *immediate physical predicaments* of suspense–melodrama (hence Hitchcock's frequent recourse to them). In drama proper, it's less advantageous, since 'tennis-match syntax', in all its various forms (the camera between the characters, as described above, or alternating over-the-shoulder shots, or switching 'asymmetrically', etc.), gives both faces equal weight, while conveying a sufficient degree of character POV.

SCRIPT VERSUS FILM (8)

While Sam and Lila talk in Cabin 1, the script has the camera pan very slowly away from them, and then move in on one wallpaper rosebud, to reveal Norman's peeping eye. So, Norman knows their stratagem exactly (Sam is to keep him talking while Lila hunts for Mother). His eye moves away, and a brief flash of light precedes the hole being covered up again. This ingenious idea was carefully prepared, and suspense-wise it would seem an effectively ingenious boost, albeit no narrative consequence ensues, for the script will rejoin the film, in which Norman's special knowledge plays no role. It's not, I think, an inconsistency, for Sam hasn't stopped pressuring Norman – whose resultant mental absence fits this moment well. By now, Lila's general peril is firmly established, and the film can rev up speed for her (literal) ascent to a climax, of fear. (That spectator and villain share information which the heroes lack doesn't confuse spectator identification; on the contrary; it *intensifies* our identification with and concern for those who know too little.)

The script's numbering of scenes breaks down again. As Lila approaches the house, every shot gets a new scene number, and a shot headed 'Close-Up' somehow includes a general view of the hallway.

◆

SCENES 215–43 LILA FINDS MRS BATES

As Lila enters the hallway, Sam keeps Norman chatting in the office. Lila enters and explores Mrs Bates' bedroom, with its heavy, immaculate Victorian furnishing – and the imprint of a body on the coverlet. In the office, Sam's remarks to Norman become steadily more insulting. Lila reaches a higher landing and ventures into Norman's room, where a child-size bed is rumpled as if slept in. As Sam accuses Norman of having $40,000 to start a new business elsewhere, Norman worries about Lila and, backing into the parlour, stuns Sam with a heavy ornament. Lila, descending the stairs, sees him come running, and hides on a staircase to the basement. As Norman rushes up to his mother's room, Lila, instead of leaving the house, spots a light beyond the lower door, and discovers an old woman, who turns out to be mummified. Lila screams and turns to see another old woman loom with upraised knife, screaming 'I am Norma Bates!' – and, behind her, Sam, who, wrestling with her, reveals she's Norman himself.

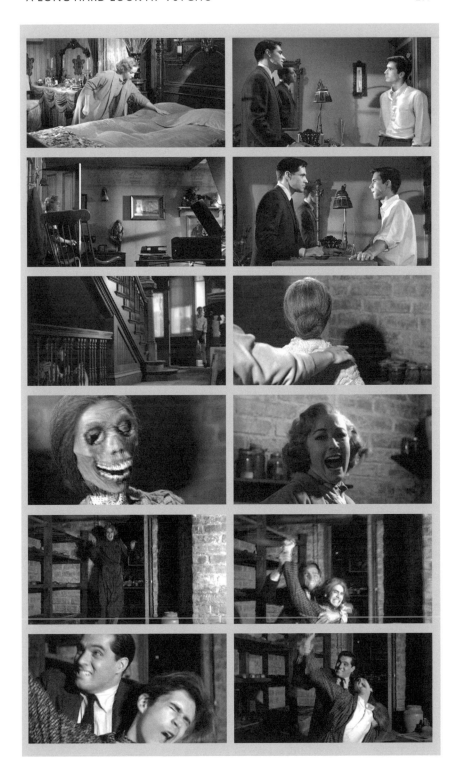

TURNABOUTS

Norman doesn't notice Lila's disappearance, until Sam mentions Mrs Bates (an Oedipal association maybe). Sam seeks him out for a friendly chat and, determined at last, becomes a remorseless bully. His previously butterfly mind now lies inventively, but, out of his own experience (as a stingy shopkeeper tied to miserly expenses). Hitherto dumb Sam proves the more cunning, while skinny, tricksy Norman wins the physical fight. As conversation turns to action, and Norman chases Lila, her exploration turns to evasion. He's even more bewildered than the intruders.

THE CROSSWAYS OF SUSPENSE

At last this strangely constructed narrative goes into a normal gear: two parallel actions (Sam's and Lila's) which finally converge. The interior of the house is almost shadowless and infested, not with cliché shadows, but with memories and ambushes – hallway, staircase and landings are surrounded by rooms, from any of which Mrs Bates may sally forth. Thanks to three earlier staircase scenes, Lila, approaching the bedroom, approaches a zone of maximum danger. It's not entirely logical, since we think we know Mrs Bates is down in the fruit cellar. However, we know she gets around (from her sudden appearance in Marion's shower), and is she ascending the stairs to attack Lila from the rear? Lila emphasises the imminence of danger, from any and all directions, when, in the hallway, she casts a look in each direction, and, turning right around, ends with her back to the fatal stairs, to close the door behind her (and in the camera's face).

THE DESK SET

Sam and Norman stand and talk across a desk, until a 'break-up and shift', into their back parlour scuffle. Having told Lila he'd engage Norman in chat, Sam starts friendly, claiming to seek company, but soon becomes the bully, or his true determined self, unleashed at last. It seems not a conscious decision (which normally we would be shown). Perhaps it's another 'impulsion': persuaded by Lila that Norman may have killed Marion, he can't control his feelings; maybe Norman's timid response to the first mild insults enabled Sam to suss his guilty conscience, with masculine intuition, and redouble his attack. Some spectators will think that since Sam gets himself knocked out, the moral is, that bullying people is always a culpable mistake, that the guilty should be treated as innocent until their guilt is proven, and that Sam, like Marion, shouldn't be 'impulsionist'. Other spectators, like me, will be easier going: nobody's perfect and Sam and Lila do not do too badly, 'muddling through'. Also, there are times when you *should* bully villains, just as sometimes your moral duty is to kill them.

Nonetheless, it reminds me of a scene in *Blackmail*, where well-meant bullying by the forces of good goes awry. The burly young Scotland Yard detective saves his girl-friend from very nasty legal proceedings, public humiliation, and a possible miscar-riage of justice, by bullying her blackmailer into flight. But then, carried away by punitive zeal, he calls up the flying squad, and the pathetic though malicious fugitive falls through a glass roof to his death. It's an accident, but he seems to some to be partly responsible, since he's perverting the course of justice, which is extremely wicked of him. Or is it?

Norman, by contrast, keeps his patience rather well, and his eventual anger at Sam's accusations is so justifiable that, from this scene alone, you might well think Sam the persecuting heavy and Norman the slim, boyish hero. But then again, Norman's answers, like 'I had a very happy childhood. My mother and I were more than happy', are *too* reasonable, *too* intimate. (It was also the sort of thing pre-Freudian people said, in rebuttal of 1940s *Rear Window* Freud.) As Sam rants about the $40,000, Norman genuinely has not the faintest idea what he's talking about. It's another 'mental absence', but entirely sane!

The character battle is expressed in postures. Gavin fakes relaxedness by a back-ward slouch-cum-forward crouch, bang in front of that mirror (entirely blocking it out – maleness obliterates ominousness?). Norman, also pseudo-relaxed, is a willowy, hands-in-pockets figure. They shape up like two boxers – an oncoming upper-cutter against a leaning-backwards long-range fighter – thuggery versus finesse. When Sam does appear in the mirror, he's so much taller than it and his gaze at Norman is so forceful, that the mirror can't frame him; all it can do is *redouble* him, thus reinforc-ing his power. Once Norman gets agitated, his jaw, then his fingers, then his body, twitch, as if that calmly spiteful chewing were now shaking him apart. (Hitchcock did something like that before, in *Young and Innocent* [1935], when the dance-band drummer with the nervous twitch fears that he's been seen and, by drumming con-vulsively and twitching more loudly, ensures that he will be.)

JOURNEY INTO THE INTERIOR

Each intruder gets a flight further than his predecessor – Norman stopped at the foot, Arbogast got to the landing, Norman stopped at the bedroom door, Lila enters and gets one flight higher to boot. But many things are different. The sepulchral hall-way now presents a black statuette, a baby Cupid on a lace mat (a colleague com-pares his uplifted bow to Norman's uplifted knife). Beyond is a window of stained glass (hints of Momist religiosity?). Lila, hesitating, darts looks every way before, riskily, turning her back on those stairs to close the door in the camera's face. Previous ascents of the stairs inspired mystical camera acrobatics; but almost all of her ascent is a 'deletion'. Climbing the last steps to the landing, she walks along it, across the screen to Mother's door, with the camera still fixed in the far-down position from which, earlier, it started its slow rise.

THE PULL OF THE PAST

Lila's ascent combines suspense with a voyage of discovery; and what she discovers is more back-story, silently told by *possessions*. Nothing has prepared us for Mrs Bates' bedroom, with its 'ornate damask-and-mahogany, thick and warm and ripe, an olla podrida of mismatched furnishings and bric-a-brac … with a white marble fire-place, its grate cold, but piled with ashes' – and looking chilly as a tomb. The belong-ings include, conspicuously, another black Cupid, this time grown into a boy, another wash-basin (this time a Victorian one) with a fresh cake of soap, a big heavy wardrobe with old-fashioned dresses (rather large, we may notice), another dark sculpture, of a woman's folded hands, presumably in the peace of death; and, sud-denly, three living presences – Lila standing startled between two reflections of her-self, one full face, the other from the back. (Explanation: she's standing between two mirrors, the mirror in front of her reflecting both her and the image behind her.) She extends a long arm to feel if the imprint of the body is still warm; her expression gives no clue either way.

A ROOM OF ONE'S OWN

Norman's bedroom is very different. On nursery furniture, against bare walls, rests a mixture of toys. Some are quite ancient (a 1900-type tin house looks like a toy of his mother's passed on, like the house we're in). Others are fairly modern. There's what I take to be a square-cut, modern-styled phonograph, though other critics reckon it's an ancient, 1920-style Victrola-era machine. Both fit, for they 'telescope' two kinds of time – historical time and growing-up time. On the turntable is an LP of the *Eroica*: adulthood, briefly attained, or pathetic aspiration or megalomania? Something draws Lila towards a tucked-away book; its sturdily bound cover is a blank, except for two emblems whose ambiguity as to 'up' and 'down' makes her flip the book confusedly, before studying its pages, with an expressionless expression. She's looking, not reading, for her eyes don't travel. It's held long enough to make us wonder what she's looking at and, if pornography is on our minds, as in 1960 it prob-ably wasn't, we expect her to show shock; but after a deadpan moment, we cut back to Sam in action. Why this non-commital moment? Such books were and still are sold in stationer's, and contain blank pages, to serve as diaries, the binding suggesting precious souvenirs. Perhaps it's Norman's diary, with nothing there, for an empty life. But when pornography was rarer and sometimes associated with rare, expensive books in neutral bindings (the sort Bogart pretends to want to buy in *The Big Sleep*), that's what this book might be, and in the script it is, for Lila's face twists in disgust. In that light, her long, blank look suggests the long moment *before* Lila's decent mind has *recognised* the entirely alien indecency. A well-observed point, and nothing to do with voyeurism *repressed*, scopophobia, sexual repression, etc. (Not that it couldn't be *pushed* that way, perhaps to link her sexual repression with her moral ferocity, her loyalty to her sister and her non-romance with Sam.)

THE SHAPES OF LILA'S WALKABOUTS

The rooms have different cinematic 'shapes'. Mother's bedroom is a square solid whole, often seen in wide shots: Lila's walk around it is a neat loop, around visual details and events. However, Norman's room is never a visual whole, just a succes-sion of tight details, few from Lila's POV. The basement is actually two cellars, with a door between, and steps down from it. The first is dark, dank and dingy, and presents a *hollow*, marked by brick walls and stairs around them, sideways on to camera. The second is the actual fruit cellar. Its stairs aren't seen, but deduced from Lila's upper body movements. Thus Lila, having ascended and descended through five successive doors, descends through two more. (For the mystically minded, seven doors like seven veils 'to truth' – not as in *Salome*, but as in *The Seventh Veil*.) The fruit cellar reads as a triangle, since Lila's POV points to the single figure of Mrs Bates, in a corner with her back to us.

MARKERS AND MOTIFS

Marion's dress closet was tiny, in a bare wall; Mrs Bates' is a sumptuous *armoire*; its door, a scary mirror, generates *two* 'false Lilas'. Marion placed the stolen money on her bed; now a body is imprinted *on the coverlet*. The body-moulded bed-linen recalls Norman's obsession with linen-changing – and Marion's body moulding the shroud. The cake of fresh soap evokes bodies in bathrooms. The fireplace, in cold, white marble (with, says the script, fresh ashes) picks up on Norman's phrase, 'The fire has gone out.' The boy-Cupid statues are 'mummies' of Norman's childhood. The folded hands echo Norman's hands folded beneath his candy-chewing mouth and, perhaps, Marion's soaping around her neck. We can almost smell the soap, the linen, the stone, the dry chill. All in all, this room is a total contrast to Lowery's un-airconditioned office.

Disorder – another kind of 'trace' – marks Norman's bed. His room is more 'modern' than his mother's, more modern than the dead birds have prepared us for (no dead bird is here). Most touching of all is the sailing ship. It echoes a ship on the warmly glowing lampshade by which Marion did her accounts – the act which set her free from her self-imprisoning escape. That was a galleon in full sail: this ship is more thinly sailed and isolated on a bare wall. Both ships are adjacent to the sisters' faces – as other mirrors have been adjacent to faces. Norman's ship suggests a boyish yearning for escape – to manly, bracing adventure.[55]

THE ART OF LOOKING

Instead of escaping while she can, Lila chooses to investigate the basement. Voyeurism theorists and punishment theorists might agree that she's a bad case of voyeuristic curiosity, no doubt explained by sexual morbidity, for which she's suitably punished, by God, or Alf, or poetic justice, by being scared half out of her wits. On the other hand, audacity is appropriate to modern heroines, and Lila proves worthy of her sister and Grace Kelly in *Rear Window*, who likewise pursues knowledge despite danger, though in her case there's also pleasure in the excitement of danger, suggesting a spoilt rich girl used to consumerist pleasure.

BODIES VERSUS MIRRORS

Sam's dark, solid, determined energy defeats the office mirror: his redoubled image expresses his new single-mindedness! Lila's strong nerves surmount her moment of panic at her two reflections (frontal and dorsal – the 'turnabout' theme, from the shower?). Mrs Bates' imprint on her coverlet is a reverse-mould, which is a sort of mirror, in 3D, sculptural form. Lila touches the mother's pillow, presumably checking for warmth; we don't know if she found it, but the gesture reminds us that imprints have what mirrors lack: *memory* for shape, and *warmth*. They're tactile, like one body against another, which mirrors are not – they're evanescent, cold, distanced – and schizo? On entering the house, Lila performed a 'turnabout'. In Mrs Bates' mirror, she appears behind herself. Her touch on Mrs Bates' shoulder turns the old woman round in her chair; promptly Lila turns too, to see behind her a second Mrs Bates, who herself is seized from behind, by Sam. The two men adopt the same body position, conspicuously, as both right arms are stretched up and out, grappling for the knife, which 'claws the air'. Their *tactile* 'mirroring' does *not* reverse. Finally, the second Mrs Bates disintegrates to reveal a *third* entity within its dress, Norman himself. Lila, too, had thrown one arm wildly up: startled, she deranged the light bulb, and set it swinging. A psychoanalyst might note that Mrs Bates' and Norman's rooms, though on different floors, are on *facing* sides of the stairs (a mirror position?). Sam's dark suit and Lila's stiffly swirling coat assert solid egos, though Lila eventually panics at the sight of the 'terrible mother', the Medusa. But who can blame her? And, before screaming, she holds her fear for a moment, as she surveys, in bewildered wonderment that parallels her deadpan look in the book, the skull-toothed matriarch before her.

The script specifies that the light of the swinging bulb shifts in the mummy's eye-sockets like eyes, as if enjoying the fight between the men (and, presumably, Lila's fright). Voyeurism, or just 'sado-*Schadenfreude*'? Does she 'mirror' us, the spectators, enjoying the film? But *are* we enjoying this fight, in her sardonic, satanic way? Or are we *in suspense*? (First-time viewers, as to the outcome, xth-time viewers, as to Hitchcock's fine details?) As Sam gets the upper hand, but before the grappling ends, Hitch fast-cross-fades us into the next scene, lest we enjoy this 'happy end': instead, we're bustled along from this unfinished, still mysterious situation, into something new.

As critics have noted, Sam's dark, strong look occasionally resembles Norman's. By a similar logic, Lila occasionally resembles Mrs Bates – both have tall, stiff figures, with pale, bony faces, and forceful, man-driving eyes. Lila too, is a fierce avenger. In the malicious face of Mrs Bates, does Lila confront her own Unconscious, her own Other? As short as her screaming is, I suspect it's just long enough to suggest hysteria, i.e. libidinal fear swamping her fine intelligence; from which she's saved by the physical strength of a weaker-minded man. And physical strength, as a force of nature, is worthy of respect. Brute, bullying force has its strategic place, in the materialistic scheme of things. And, perhaps, in the *moral* one – as Milton, for one, insists in *Paradise Lost*. Perhaps right *needs* might (and, providentially, is more conducive to it than egoism, which doesn't favour unity).

NATURE LORE

If *birds* are on your mind, Lila, looking through the basement banisters, could remind you of a caged bird. Round here, too, the music sounds like rooks, ravens, crows, shrieking triumphantly – death birds.

FRUITS AND NUTS

Is Mrs Bates' dried head like a coconut, or a dried-up fruit?

SCRIPT VERSUS FILM (9)

In myriad ways, the film tightens up the script: shortening Lila's hesitations, omitting her peek into a bathroom (too obvious an 'echo'), giving Norman a sailing ship picture (instead of kindergarten pictures all over the walls).

SCENES 244–8 THE PSYCHOLOGIST EXPLAINS IT ALL

Crowds and a TV truck have gathered outside the County Court House. In the DA's office Lila, Sam, Sheriff Chambers and various officials hear psychologist Dr Simon (Simon Oakland) recount his interview with Norman – or rather, with his mother, whom Norman now believes himself to be. Asked by Lila if Norman killed Marion, Dr Simon replies 'Yes. And no', and reassures the County Prosecutor that he's only trying to explain the crime, not to lay the groundwork for an insanity plea. He predicts that dragging the swamp will reveal the bodies of Marion, Arbogast and at least two other missing persons, probably young girls. Norman, as a child, was psychologically disturbed; after his father's death, he lived alone with his clinging, demanding mother, until she took a lover, whereupon, feeling betrayed, he poisoned them both. However, the pain of loss and matricide, rarest of crimes, drove the teenage boy to steal her corpse, weight her coffin for her burial, preserve her body as he did his birds and, since all that was still insufficient to conceal her loss, impersonate her and hold conversations in both their characters. Sometimes he seemed to, not just impersonate, but become, her.

He then projected his own jealousy onto the, already clinging, woman and, whenever a woman attracted his normal side, enacted the murderous rage he now attributed to his mother. While covering up the evidence of crime, he sincerely believed he was the good, loyally protective son, although, 'he was never all Norman, but he was often only Mother'. His dressing up was not, as a naïve official supposes, sexual transvestism, but a means of keeping his mother alive. The $40,000 will be in the swamp, for this was a crime of passion, not of property. A police guard asks if he should bring Norman a blanket, since he complains of a little chill; Dr Simon says yes, and the guard leads the camera through a corridor into the next scene.

THE SUSPENSE PATTERN

Immediately after the action climax, a few moments of media and police bustle allow a brief relaxation. But much remains to be explained – about this case and human nature – a powerful form of suspense, mixing emotional, moral, intellectual and ideological attitudes, and therefore issues. Sheriff Chambers, bringing Lila a cup of coffee, a considerate touch, sets this scene's agenda: 'If anybody gets any answers, it'll be the psychiatrist. Even I couldn't reach Norman, and he knows me.' The sheriff's remark concedes the limits of 'neighbourliness', of 'lived community', and he too becomes passive, before a modern, sophisticated, science, which bourgeois psychology, from the various behaviourisms (Eysenck, Skinner) through Freud to Laing or Lacan, claims to be. His deference, and the sharp response of the prosecutor, helps reconcile to it the many spectators who in the 1950s were still highly suspicious of psychology and psychiatrists.

Some commentators think this scene just tidies up a few loose ends. But the cinema audience, just like the on-screen audience, closely follows what in effect is a *second* climax – after the *action* climax, a *moral-intellectual* one. And it quietly prepares two more devastating 'codas' – for this pseudo-closure has two stings in the tale.

A STAND-UP TRAGEDY

After the whodunnit, the whydunnit. Dr Simon's exposition is yet another near-monologue, and instalment of back-story. It's not unlike a lecture to an audience, much of it delivered by an expert standing up, facing the camera, with an uninteresting wall behind. However, it's very much looser, and not 'talking head' but 'talking waist shot', with lively body swings as he addresses his on-screen audience (our friends to his left, officialdom to his right); he even contrives a short walk with his back to camera, talking sideways all the while. His listeners' brief, anxious questions and passive faces maintain and variegate a general mood. Though he usually faces the camera, he never addresses it, only the characters, whose brief questions and grim faces maintain the general mood.

BLANKET LIBERALISM

By 1960 the very word 'psychiatrist' had stock associations, in particular the humane, but just sufficiently tough, liberal urging us to understand that the really bad are pitiably mad and deserve a sympathetic cure, not punishment. Knife-wielding delinquents were victims of a poverty-stricken environment, or a broken home, or alienation, or fits of passion for which they couldn't be held responsible, since they're involuntary 'impulsions', and, 'Remember, Mr Complacent Spectator, that there but for the grace of God, go you'. Exhibit A: 'Inspector Ray' in *Rebel without a Cause*. Exhibit B: 'Gee, Officer Krupke, That's Why I'm a Mess' in *West Side Story* (1957, filmed in 1961). By 1959 'insanity pleas' were a hotter topic than ever, as in three box-office hits whose titles could have fitted *Psycho*: *Crack in the Mirror*, *Compulsion* (1959) and *Anatomy of a Murder* (Preminger, 1959, though *Murder of an Anatomy* suits *Psycho* better). *Compulsion* (whose penology is liberal) was inspired by the same case as *Rope* (whose penology is not). In *Anatomy*, the folksy-liberal lawyer (James Stewart) is rocked by a final hint that the client whose innocence we championed dunnit after all. The Zanuck films are challengingly liberal; Hitchcock and Preminger (always Austro-Teutonic, and inclined to *realpolitik*) are less trusting. (The idea of cultural debate *between* films, from within a broad consensus, which is itself a compromise between different positions, would fit Peter Biskind's thesis, in *Seeing Is Believing* [1983], of a 'liberal-conservative' consensus ruling Hollywood films through the 1950s.)

Dr Simon contrasts with your obvious WASP liberal, à la Peck or Fonda, with his nice combination of grey flannel humanism, careful scruples and quiet, crusading or obstinate, idealism. Simon's dark, greased hair, mobile eyes and aggressively slicing gestures suggest a tough city culture — closer, perhaps, to a prosecuting attorney, or that dark-eyed patrolman, or a David Mamet-type salesman. Ethnically, he might well be Italian, East European, or inner-city Jewish, or even Hispanic (like character actor Thomas Gomez, or the supporting cast in Orson Welles' *Touch of Evil* [1959], where Charlton Heston plays a Mexican). I could certainly imagine him as a Mafioso lawyer. So, ethno-culturally, we can't tell where he's coming from, which keeps us uncertain, and in suspense. In the end he okays Norman's blanket with a gesture implying 'oh, sure, who cares, why not go by the book', not a soggy liberal concern for the poor mad criminal (as per a late shot in *The Sniper* [Kramer–Dmytryk, 1952], of the serial killer's face bedewed with childlike tears, once he's arrested). Maybe Simon's unsentimentality gives his assent to liberal tenderness more weight. Maybe it detracts from it. Every spectator decides for himself – while *also* sussing ambiguity, as I think many will.

Hitchcock always insisted that *Psycho* was a roller-coaster thriller, not a case history and therefore not 'serious', psychologically. Dr Simon does something to repair that omission. It's geared to the upper level of popular sophistication then; as prepared by, notably, *The Three Faces of Eve*, which, though clunkily made, proved a box-office hit, thanks to its clinical air, and its source material, a bestseller upfronting case-history veracity. The same interest inspired *In Cold Blood* (Richard Brooks, 1966, from Truman Capote's bestseller, written 1959–65, published 1966). Technically, Simon's 'lecture-with-prompts' is admirably written – albeit *explanatory*, it's a succession of riddles, triggering curiosity. Its presentation of ideas combines a smooth, clear flow with leaps and paradoxes. It presents complex psychic processes in clear, concise, yet imagination-provoking synopsis. It's exemplary of language as a *spoken*, not a written, form. (The words on the page, read normally, i.e. with the eye, but without a conscious effort of silent articulation like 'inner speech' in the mind. It gives no idea of the *semantic* subtexts, which performance can bring out, or avoid.) As Simon Callow remarked, a proficient actor can give a text 20 different subtexts, which suggests they're not so much subtexts *belonging to the words*, and therefore spin-offs from language, but *new subtexts brought to them*, and so much less 'para-linguistic' than *a product of performance*.

THE ART OF RHETORIC

After shooting the scene, Hitch, notoriously slow to praise, said to the actor, 'Thank you. You have just saved my film.' As 'courtroom rhetoric' (an oral, not a written form), it's as electric as *The Paradine Case* was inert. Hitchcock knew this penultimate 'lecture' would need forceful 'acting', and for students of gesture – a visual medium, fusing psychology, kinaesthetics and a very general semantics – it's a rare treat, almost a demonstration reel, of how to do it. It follows *not* some conventionalised code of stereotypes, which you could look up in some dictionary with diagrams, but a mimetic expressiveness, improvised as the speaker goes along, perhaps involuntarily, perhaps instinct improved by conscious art. As the right hand flicks through the air, the forefinger warns of distinctions by switching to separate points in space. The phrase 'as if there was no one else in the world' is illustrated by the forearm swishing from side to side as if to 'illustrate' the idea of a very general, unbounded space. 'Giving oneself' cues two palms moving outwards, from stomach or heart. The pointing finger flips sideways over itself to indicate difference, contrast, opposition – to mean, indeed, 'on the other hand' (isn't verbal language itself saturated, even structured, by metaphors from body language?).[56] As Simon's right hand diagrams logical relations in the air, his left hand, stuck in its pocket, as if to leave the other a 'clear visual field', emerges to illustrate *heartfelt* attitudes. Attitudes heartfelt by Norman, not by the speaker, whose rhetorical demonstration combines empathy with the sincerity of madness, and a clinical objectivity. It's sympathetic yet it, almost coldly, refuses revulsion at murderous perversity. (It doesn't quite imply that Simon has a streak of Norman in him. Even if he does, and we all do, and we're all potential murderers, but for the grace of God, etc., Simon, can think madness at will, whereas Norman's madness thinks him.)

Dr Simon says he got the story from the mother: and our thrill of surprise may disguise the fact that she's not the mother at all; she's Norman and therefore not a reliable narrator (we need only recall her ideas about Marion). Nonetheless, Dr Simon seems sufficiently convinced by her testimony to assure us that the *real* Mrs Bates was a clinging, demanding, possessive woman. (But how can we know?) In an early draft of the script, Stefano wrote a flashback in which Mrs Bates, catching young Norman with an erection, gets angry, forces him into some of her clothes and smears lipstick on his mouth. It's a typical 'vulgar Freudian' manoeuvre: to seem to 'explain' something, you reiterate it as a scene in infancy, with a little twist: 'Cruel Mummy made me do it, and now I keep right on doing it.' Dr Simon's diagnosis is less pat: he stresses, not what Mrs Bates did to Norman, but what Norman did to himself. One may reasonably wonder if Hitchcock is challenging a general tendency, in bourgeois liberal psychology, to blame the parents. *Rebel without a Cause*, however, is more thoughtful than it looks, for it blames not only the cold, repressed, authoritarian father of Natalie Wood, but also James Dean's father, who's not patriarchal enough: he plays the friendly, smiling, buddy, like Arthur Miller's salesman but he lacks the moral principles for which the teenager pleads, and he meekly defers to his wife and *her* mother (matriarchy, as a function of the feminine mystique, and as in Caroline's marriage in *Psycho*). As Irish playwright Brendan Behan put it, around that time, 'Never throw stones at your mother/ You'll be sorry for it when she's dead;/ Never throw stones at your mother/ Throw bricks at your father instead.'

More quiet notes of unease: Dr Simon's confirmation, to Lila, of her vague aware-ness that Marion is dead is distinctly cursory (albeit correctly respectful); his superior smile, as he reassures the elderly DA, that his job is 'only' to understand, is rather smug; and almost before finishing his last sentence, he grabs his pack of smokes. All understandable, in this stressful situation, but, are these nuances a touch unfeeling? His indifference gets a notch more disconcerting, when a tall, grizzled veteran police-man, a kind, mild, 'grandfatherly' figure, has to fetch and carry for every comfort of the serial murderer (of women).[57]

WHAT DOESN'T HAPPEN IN PSYCHO

This scene is our last glimpse of Sam and Lila. How easily Hitchcock might have slipped in a quick exchange of looks, hinting at a sober friendship, which one day may become a little more – romance mellowed by shared uneasiness – as at the end of Blackmail? No such hint is given. However, spectators are free to invent their own little story, and I think Hitchcock reckons that those who wish to may reasonably suppose that after all Sam and Lila have been through together, they won't just walk away from each other, as outside the church they seemed about to do. Generally, Hitchcock rates trust and affection above romance (which, by itself, is infatuation – that is to say, the sane man's madness – and, in Vertigo, Promethean). As for sexuality, Hitch must be the only Hollywood director to have said outright that he's a celibate, with no interest in sex. (Some 'vulgar Freudians' may link celibacy with a morbid delight in contemplating murder and torturing spectators, but the enormous plea-sure which his films give a wide range of spectators reminds us how much more is going on, the delicate balances Hitchcock understands better than most – so that Robin Wood could consider him redolent with moral health. As for the correlation of celibacy with sexual repression and that with morbidity, it's a slapdash stereotype, just like 'all spinsters are embittered gossips'. There's no jot or shred of evidence that sexual repression leads to emotional meanness or violence – it's hardly even 'theory', just dogma. I'd rather admire Hitchcock's honesty, his indifference to a 'vulgar Freudian' prejudice and note the use of 'celibacy', a rather religious word.

A PSYCHO-MORAL AGENDA

So much Film Studies offers Freud as received wisdom, and overlooks other psy-chologies that it's worth noting that Dr Simon's analysis isn't really Freudian. By 1959 general psychiatry had subsumed into its wide range of eclectico-pragmatic theory all the Freudian ideas it would ever want; and most Freudian theory was, quite reasonably, rejected by the Behaviourists (Pavlov, Watson, Eysenck, Cattell, Skinner, etc.), who were at least as influential as Freudian theory was. To be sure, Dr Simon's diagnosis of Norman evokes the Oedipus complex, whence immediate appeal to 'layman's Freud'; but it makes scant reference to infantile sexuality, incest wishes, etc. Morbid closeness to a parent is hardly a Freudian discovery; and Simon's description of Norman's psychic plight stresses, not *unconscious* fantasies but, on the contrary, *real* guilt, *real* loss. The *progression* of Norman's psychosis (denial, projection, identification with the projection, etc.) is widely understood in general psychology and intuitively understood by ordinary people (hence Simon's ease with 'ordinary language'). His polite refusal of 'sexual transvestism' theory rather discourages 'pop Freudian' 'pansexualism', as indeed does *Some Like It Hot*, where Curtis and Lemmon sport drag not for sexual reasons but for fear/survival/power ones. The implied linkage with sex/gender behaviour (feminoid behaviour by male animals to show submission to more powerful males) derives from studies of animal psychology, not from Freudian theory. We may also note that Dr Simon's diagnosis takes the form of a *narrative*, that is to say, it's diachronic, a study of *change*, which exceeds the linguistic structuralists' self-limitation to synchrony and immobility. It describes Norman's denial in terms of a possibly *conscious* manoeuvre, which gradually overwrites the truth: if he's right, it corresponds to 'bad faith' in existentialist psychology, offered by Sartre as the Marxist *alternative* to Freudian theory; it also inspired R. D. Laing's radical *The Divided Self*, whose wide influence included David Mercer's and Ken Loach's *Family Life* (1970).[58]

Often, of course, existential psychoanalysis blamed 'bourgeois parents' (and mothers could be worse than fathers; as in *Family Life* the lower middle-class mother is more destructive than the rough-and-ready working-class dad). But for Hitchcock, the buck stops in Norman's head. Clinging and demanding his mother may have been, but 'Mrs Norma Bates' she never was – *he* was. Insofar as Hitchcock was something of a conservative (of a worldly, not a naïve kind), *Psycho* may well have expressed his scepticism about 'parentophobia'. Blame not the mother, but the son. The same shift is detectable in Transactional Analysis, and its PAC theory. To escape neurosis, don't blame your parents for it; accept responsibility, that is to say, be your own parent at last. In *Psycho* all three women 'mother' a man. Marion brings Sam money, and spots his unready feet, Lila tells him what he thinks. If, as I sometimes wonder, *Psycho* offers a 'cluster' of 'tall, straight woman' physiques – Marion, Lila, Mrs

Bates, the Insecticidal Lady (who's like someone in *Twin Peaks* already) – it might compose a 'mandala' of women: the modern-sensual, the dutiful, the haunted, the 'Blair Witch'. All lonely. Like all the men, young (Sam, his store assistant, Norman and even the patrolman, who gets a touch wistful) or old (even Cassidy, the pseudo-family man, gets down to a dismal drinking session with Lowery).

MATURITY OF THE COUPLE

In this film of lonely and split minds, their soliloquies and mental gaps, it's doubtless significant that Lila and Sam succeed by operating as a couple (whereas those who came alone – Marion, Arbogast, the sheriff – all failed). The couple work as a team; to do so, they must separate; and the film ends on a note of 'platonic separation' – with no romantic closure – and eventual romantic possibilities left strictly optional. We don't see them separate (as earlier, they seemed about to); but neither do we see them leave together. Apart or together, they're chastened: it's 'never glad confident morning again'. This, and the Preminger film, all but *close* the confident liberalism of the 1950s, and prefigure an often forgotten aspect of 'the greening of America': a *rediscovery*, by the liberal-conservative consensus, of the worst of human nature, lying doggo within itself.

SPANKING THE MONKEY

As if poor Norman hadn't sexual 'transgressions' enough already, a subsequent generation of critics loves piling others upon him: maybe actual incest with his mother went on; surely he was gay as well (getting bullied by Sam is latently homosexual, etc.); taxidermy and embalming imply unconscious necrophilia. Van Sant's remake has Norman beating his meat while admiring Marion, and, Sam baring his manly buns while standing by the window. Norman is credited with all these sins, not in a spirit of old-fashioned disapproval, but in the newer, 1970s spirit of complicity, with 'transgressivity' of all kinds – dope-taking, gay prostitution (*My Hustler* [1965]), incest (*Le Souffle au coeur/Murmur of the Heart* [1971], a new kind of Momism?), masturbation (*Spanking the Money* [1995]), gayness and its discontents (*My Own Private Idaho* [1991]) and the less sexual moral turnabouts (*The Godfather* [1972] *Prizzi's Honour* [1985], *Reservoir Dogs* [1991], *The Goodfellas* [1990], *Natural Born Killers* [1994]).

FURTHER REFLECTIONS

This scene is so 'retrospective' it needs no other 'echoes'. Though one might compare Simon's space-slashing gestures to Norman's knife 'clawing the air'. And, poss-

ibly, see them as 'equivalents' in power, one mad and destructive, the other constructive. (Whether or not knife and language are phallic performances.)

Though there's no screen prompt-back, one may think back to the two Mrs
Bateses in the window, seen by Marion, Arbogast and Sam. The first, since she moves
about, must be Norman dressed up. The second, which Arbogast sees while talking
to Norman, must be Mrs Bates herself, just propped up. Why, a plausible might ask,
would Norman put her in the window, for all the world to see, when supposedly
she's dead? Good question. Available answer: when Norman was in the motel, the
sight of her in the window soothed his uneasy mind.

SCRIPT VERSUS FILM (10)

In the script, the opening scenes brood longer on morbid crowds, callous TV crews
and stingy taxpayers. Its Dr Simon is a 'serious, frowning young man' who delivers his
spiel while sipping coffee from a plastic cup (this – *excessively* ironic? – 'cheapener' is
replaced in the film by the tactfully delayed cigarette). Chambers' giving coffee to Lila
is compassionate; Simon's sipping coffee is a touch disrespectful. (Young, serious,
frowning yet more casual – might this personify a rising generation, of more educated, more slovenly authorities?) The film deletes from Simon's spiel a paragraph
which, by half-preparing us for the following scene, might soften its shock.

SCENES 249–50 MRS BATES SPEAKS HER MIND

*The policeman carries the blanket through a corridor to a detention room. Here
Norman sits immobile, back to a blank wall, staring mostly into space, as his
mother speaks inside his head. How sad for a mother to have to condemn her
own son! But the wicked boy would have told them that she killed those girls. But
she'll prove to those who are always watching that she's as harmless as one of her
boy's stuffed birds. She'll not lift a finger, even to disturb the fly upon her hand.*

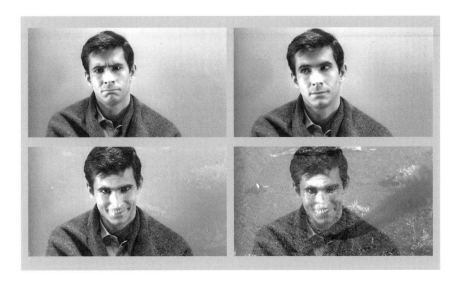

'AM I NORMAN DREAMING I'M MOTHER, OR AM I MOTHER DREAMING I'M NOT NORMAN?'

A brief corridor scene ensues in which several policemen, silently docile, manoeuvre around a doorway, from within which comes Norman's voice, now flat, neutered, void. In the bare room, Norman, wrapped in a blanket, like a feminoidal shroud, soliloquises to camera, which starts in long shot, moves very slowly forward, to hold in close-up the last half of the film's last, and most perverse, monologue. A close-up of the fly on his hand is inserted. His eyes move furtively, but with deep satisfaction, till a fast cross-fade brings, as if from beneath his face, the teeth of a smiling skull. Before the composite face disappears (for the skull alone would be crudely literal), it crossfades further, into 251, the final shot.

Mise-en-scène-wise, this is a starker, stripped-down 'variation' on the previous scene. It's another monodrama, from before a bare wall, largely to camera; but here the speaker is alone, immobile and his lips are sealed. I suspect this anticipated – and, perhaps, influenced – the main style of Bergman's *Persona* – a much less melodramatic meditation on a madwoman in white, clinical rooms, determinedly silent, but internally articulate, and a mother-and-son meditation and a two-psyche fusion.

HIMSELF AS HERSELF: 'OH WHAT A TANGLED WEB WE WEAVE,/ WHEN FIRST WE PRACTISE TO DECEIVE …'

Does Norman just *illustrate* Dr Simon's diagnosis? Even if that were all, the shift from Dr Simon's verbal back-story to Norman 'in the flesh' would hit us hard. But doesn't Norman's silence *subvert* the confident narrative of modern psychiatry. Dr Simon, like everybody else, is half-right, half-wrong. He understands that Mother had taken over Norman, who is now a subject abolished by his own bad faith, by his own post-modernist, schizo-fragmentation, that, just like Dr Simon, we need only shrug our shoulders and give him a blanket. But the scene hints at a further layer, not suspected by the good doctor. Mrs Bates thinks she grassed on her son, to stop him grassing on her. They're locked together, in pure treachery. It's a very Christian conception of 'pure evil' as an 'elementary particle' of pure egoism, paralytic and treacherous. Schizophrenia splits and divides Norman's mind, but it also multiplies the fragments into silent, obstinate, paralytic entities ('My name is Legion', the devil in scripture told Jesus). But, sure, Norman has triumphed over society, The Law, psychiatry: he's supreme, like the devil, in his little hell.

IF LOOKS COULD KILL

Formalists may think of Norman 'looking at the camera'. Voyeurism-ists can think he's looking at *us*, returning our stare, making us feel guilty for looking at him in particular, and at moving pictures in general. The script says Norman stares 'at nothing' (which is correct: neither camera nor audience exists in the diegesis or in the form).

The 'first-time' viewer, earlier cited, felt the shock of vicious meanness in Norman's stare (i.e. not identification, not guilt, but *confrontation*, and fear). Which was pretty well my reaction. In retrospect, I think of a nineteenth-century music-hall act, of which Hitchcock must have known. The performer, stage name Sam Hall, came on stage, sat staring at the audience and sang: 'Oh, my name is Samuel Hall, Samuel Hall/ And I stand before you all/ And I hate you one and all/ God damn your eyes.' It seems that his stare, and diction, chilled spectators to the bone.

Sometimes evil seeks to abolish the world, as in that capsule manifesto of sadism, from the early Victorian melodrama *Sweeney Todd* (1842): 'Oh that the whole wide world had but one throat, and I had the slitting of it!' Sometimes, to abolish the world, it will first abolish itself; and that's Hitchcock's *Psycho*.

THE BATES WITCH PROJECTION

In this flat, stark, clinical, modernistic composition, Norman's appearance is pure American Gothic – smirking like a gargoyle, enswathed and yet spire-like. He's not just Mummy, he's Mummy Mummy, self-embalmed in immobility. He's the great Momist nightmare, as in two Woody Allen pictures: *Everything You Always Wanted to*

Know about Sex but Were Afraid to Ask (1972), with the Monster Breast from Outer
Space, and its parasperm troops, and *New York Stories* (1989), with The Great Jewish
Momma in the Sky. Peter Biskind saw Perkins as a prototype of the feminists' new
man, in touch with his 'true' feelings – that is to say, his infantile all-destructiveness. To
merge with the mother, one's first love-object, one must disintegrate oneself (for
psychoanalytical theory: Melanie Klein and feminist psychoanalyst Christiane Olivier,
Les Enfants de Jocaste. [1980]). Insofar as Norman's 'fusion' with his mother exempli-
fies a dysfunctional identification, it's akin to 'negative identification empathy', the central idea of *The Disorderly Orderly* (Tashlin and Lewis, 1964), while in *Zelig* (1984),
Woody Allen's face behaves like an infant's mind – it's transformed into whatever cul-
tural/ethnic type he's been mixing with.

THE FEMINIST MYSTIQUE: I DISMEMBER MAMA

Mothers, some good, some bad, abound in Hitchcock films, for both artistic and
commercial reasons. In *The Man Who Knew Too Much*, Doris Day, like a singing Statue
of Liberty, saves her son from the enemy within and in *To Catch a Thief*, her mother
tells Grace Kelly, a spoiled brat now a spoiled grown-up, that she should have been
spanked more often (which in many countries today would criminalise the mother).
Psycho kicks in with its nightmare mother, as if adding a darker picture to the panel,
as 'the feminine mystique' of the 1950s begins to crack. But Mrs Norman Bates is a
figment of Norman's imagination, and of his private, conscious *symbolique*. She's
neither feminine nor maternal: she's a construct, rooted in hostility and loss, and,
more important, parent–child hostility (which though it *involves* sexual theory, can't
be explained within it). Is the Blair Witch a maternal part of the mind, disavowed by
the modern 'culture of narcissism' (Christopher Lasch)? And related thereby to
Shulamith Firestone's description of giving birth as 'shitting a pumpkin' (the 'feminist
mystique' displaced by an 'Excremental Vision')?

THE ETERNAL RETURN

The fly left undisturbed on the hand of Mrs Norman Bates would 'echo' the fly
which, in the script, disturbs Sam and Marion's kiss. Conceivably, these flies on the
wall are The Lords of the Flies whose aerial errancy could help explain some pecu-
liar camera positions, and especially if you've ever had metaphysical thoughts about
'the eternal return', and time bending around itself to end where it began. Though I
wouldn't compare it to movie-watching generally.

THE PARTING SHOT

A lesser director might have had the death's head completely replace Norman's. However, the composite face is scarier: a whole skull is too emblematic, too obvious, whereas the individual's face is more intimate, *responsible.* The 'half-skull' seems to have been a late thought: it's not in the script and some prints don't have it.

SCENES 250–1 RETRIEVING MARION'S WHITE AUTOMOBILE

The composite face is shattered by thick black chains from a tow-truck, rattling over the camera and hauling Marion's mud-caked white car, butt-first up out of the swamp. Then abstract bars, resuming the credit designs, traverse the screen, shattering this image also.

A MEMORIAL FOR MARION

Norman's triumphant malice disturbs our sense of 'case closure', and the image of Marion's car adds: 'Remember Marion.' The swamp will give up its secrets, and its $40,000, but the shot's brutality promises more horror (Marion's nude, multiply stabbed corpse jammed in the trunk, desecrating indignity). If the white car evokes Marion's white body, its trunk-up posture would rhyme with the buttocks-up shot decrypted by Van Sant, with black mud caked on it. It's less narrative than *summation.* For Marion's sake, spectators inclined to believe that some death sentences are just, will be fortified in their belief, which is not, as sometimes supposed, just 'primitive lust for revenge', or biblical 'eye for an eye'. Its wide public support engages *also* fear, compassion for victims, moral horror and awareness of the *differences* between murder and 'due process', between barbarism and deterrence.

Norman's calm, clinical isolation is followed by a cross-fade skein, of four images surging up, disrupting one another. The lateral bars recall the opening credits, whose menacing activity never died away – it only disappeared, beyond the veil of the midday sky over the city – and now closes over the midnight swamp – as if Marion's story belongs in the Book of Chaos.

Given Hitchcock's sometimes lavatorial humour, and Marion's face falling lower than the toilet seat, might these chains be his private joke about 'pulling the chain', in reverse … revealing the normally hidden …

If we dare run the risk of another over-interpretation, aren't those visually strong *chains* more than merely a realistic 'atmosphere' – are they a poetic (metaphor disguised as circumstantial detail, exactly as various realist theorists, e.g. Jean Mitry, advised)? As they grind away, like the due process of truth, and law, they're almost as grim as the swamp itself. The proposition might be that, since all our minds have their swamps of nasty secrets, we *need* the chains of truth and law to restrain the Caliban within us. It's a traditional view, and not Christian-pessimistic only; its outlines are obvious in Buñuel ('I find it easy to think sadistically'), in Bergman ('Whichever way you turn, your backside follows you'), Brecht (his belief that 'man is the wolf of man' would help explain his consent to Stalin the stern father), in the pessimistic kind of traditional conservatism ('Only Law and Order saves us from others and ourselves'), in certain nihilisms (Sade) and in certain myths (the *Götterdämmerung*). Hitchcock isn't nihilistic, but he understands what some nihilisms may mean, and says: 'Be afraid, be very afraid …' Very afraid even of The Law, which, although our defence against chaos, has chaos in itself. But it's the *lesser* chaos and certainly 'love' alone is not enough …

Matters Arising

PSYCHO STRUCTURE

Three Acts or Five Acts?

Hollywood scriptwriters, more than English ones, think in terms of three-act structures, roughly: Act I – Exposition up to first main conflict; Act II – Complications; Act III – Crisis and resolution. In some ways this fits *Psycho*: Act I is Marion's story; Act II brings the complication, Arbogast; and Act III brings the film's climax, with Sam and Lila. However, Marion's story is a very long and winding road, while Arbogast's act is short and sharp. So maybe *Psycho* is best treated as a *two-act* drama, in which Act I is Marion's story, and Act II is Sam's and Lila's (the latter subsuming Arbogast, the sheriff and Dr Simon). Or perhaps it's a five-act story, in which Acts I to III centre on Marion (I – Marion Leaves Phoenix; II – Marion on the road; III – Marion meets the Bates family), and Acts IV and V centre on Sam and Lila (IV – Their hesitations; V – In the Bates house). However, both formulations scant the last three scenes (Dr Simon, Mrs Norma Bates, Up from the swamp), which, action-wise, are the 'post-climax' resolution (traditionally called the 'falling action' and more recently, 'closure'). We notice also that *Psycho*, a well-constructed bourgeois narrative, approximates the Marxist-modernist shape of Antonioni's *L'Avventura*. Arguably, therefore, the structures are variations of one another. The *basic* structure of *any drama* is a two-act affair (Act I – The problem, Act II – The solution). But since *first* moves to a solution can *complicate* the problem, problems and solutions may shade into one another, so that 'Second Acts' have no clear demarcation. To put it another way, dramas trade not in *logical* problems, but in *human complications*.

Detecting some 'deep structure' in *Psycho* is hazardous, since, as suggested in *The Strange Case of Alfred Hitchcock*, the symmetries and variations in Hitchcock's story patterns accommodate a wide variety of ideas and idea-systems (especially if, as most aesthetic theories do, we admit *parts* of structures into story 'sub-themes'). The following came repeatedly to mind, while thinking the film over, but I've no desire to discourage other readings.

A 'Mythic' Structure

Literary criticism often appeals to 'mythic' or 'thematic' structuralisms (e.g. 'Cinderella' stories, or 'Oedipus' stories derived from Freud's simplification of Sophocles). *Psycho* fits the structure prioritised in *The Writer's Journey*, an application of Joseph Campbell's *The Hero with a Thousand Faces*, currently popular among writers seeking sure-fire narrative structures. In Campbellian terms, *Psycho* belongs with MGM's *The Wizard of Oz* (1939): 'a woman's journey'. Marion, like Dorothy, leaves a mundane, destructive world (Phoenix, Kansas), travels a winding road, encounters tests, thresholds, helpers and enemies (including a trickster – like the car dealer?) and 'approaches the inmost cave' (which in this case is a house) where dwells a 'wizard' (in *Oz*, a father figure, whom the daughter exposes, in *Psycho*, a mother-witch, who kills the daughter). Marion *doesn't* return from 'over the rainbow', she goes down the plughole, into the black swamp. The 'return journey', which in *Oz* provides the 'falling action' (!), is performed in *Psycho* by Marion's 'representatives', Lila and Sam. Topography and meteorology loom large in both films. Such structural similarities coexist with obvious and enormous differences – of genre, mood, morality, optimism/pessimism, etc. – which testify to the *inability* of any given structures to prescribe very much.

An Organic Structure

Many structuralisms concern themselves with narrative shapes. An 'organic structuralism' might start from thematic elements in a particular story. Marion, Lila and Mrs Bates are 'three faces of motherhood'. Mrs Bates, to be sure, is not a real woman, only a projection of Norman's sick, male, filial imagination, but her *apparent* presence overlaps with such 'terrible mothers' as Medea and Jocasta, the destructively jealous mother, especially as described by Christiane Olivier in *Les Enfants de Jocaste,* her enlightening riposte to Freudian Oedipal theory and Lacanian phallocracy. A fourth face of mother is Caroline's pill-providing mother, a fifth is Mrs Campbell's motherliness, and the script provides a sixth – for Marion and Lila are orphans mothering one another. This also establishes another 'mother' possibility – *no* mother – plus sisters as reciprocal mothers (which strictly speaking makes a seventh). 'Fatherliness' appears via Cassidy's spiel, Lowery's age, the Sam sheriff relation – and Norman's Oedipal jealousy of his stepfather and the PAC relations. The characters all pattern into one another. For instance, Marion forms one kind of pair with Sam (romance), another kind of pair with Lila (sisterhood), another kind of pair with Norman ('ships that pass in the night'), another with Caroline (needling workmate). Marion's journey sets up another 'group': Lowery at the crossing, the patrolman, the car dealer and the storm – their 'escalation' of 'confusions' gives her 'impulsion' its nasty twists. The office people make a *quartet* of contrasts. Sam–Lila–Arbogast make a *trio*. The useful paradigm is 'variations on a theme', and recombinatory structures, both very familiar in discussing musical structures. They're not formed by binary oppositions, and similarity as well as difference influences their meanings. The variations on all the set themes constitute the special agenda of the film. From this angle, *Psycho*, like *Hamlet*, is devoted, not to *one* theme, but to a combination of them – every theme is a thread, in a 'web' of attitudes, such as cultures constantly set up. Major psycho-moral themes here include impulsive/obsessive desire (Marion) versus treated stick-in-the-mud depressiveness (Sam), fierce loyalty (Lila) versus self-doubt (Sam), madness versus 'false lucidity' (the sheriff, the psychiatrist), and in particular the chaotic nature of thinking ('half-right, half-wrong').

A Genetic Structure

In his 'genetic structuralism', the Marxist Lucien Goldmann's relates texts or intellec-tual positions to the *alternative possibilities*, from which their *auteur* chooses. Along these lines, one could say that *Psycho* selects all its elements from the diversity of American cultural possibilities – including mythical and first discovered ones. Their similarities with other American films explain why 'difference' can't define meaning. Nonetheless, *Psycho* is a *unique* text *because* it's a unique structure; and it would also follow that the defining structure of *Psycho* is the 'moment by moment' flow, from one event to the next, through 90 minutes. From this angle, the three *Psychos* – Bloch's, Hitchcock's, Van Sant's – aren't 'variants on the same story', but 'three differ-ent structures (of ideas) using one narrative structure'.

In some respects, Marion's journey is loosely picaresque ('brief encounters along the way'). In other respects, its structure is very tight, though it's tied together, not by some 'logic' of events (for at any point the story could have developed differently), but by the recurrence of ideas and motifs (birds and birdlike traits, mirrors and rear windows, desert/swamp, two overhead shots, etc.). In its plays on *variable meaning within reiterated motifs*, one might posit a tension of classical and baroque, as in Racine.

A VISUAL THEMATIC

Strangers on a Train had a 'criss-cross' motif (the plot, tennis-court serves, tennis rack-ets on a lighter, railway tracks intersecting, like individual destinies). It integrates with other visual motifs (e.g. the fairground ride spinning out of orbit), thus avoiding monotony. *Psycho* makes much of a 'Janus-face' structure. In two bedrooms (the hotel, and at home), Marion U-turns round a bed. The cop drives in from the left, and then from the right. Mirrors are 'Janus faces' – the original looks one way, the image the other. Marion's relentless drive forward makes much of a rear window, i.e. looking backward. Marion turns about in the shower, while being attacked; but while dying, she turns back again, completing the turn. Lila, on entering the Bates house, also does a full turn (looking each of four ways, which, in folk tales, might symbolise *due* caution, against evil forces – unlike Marion's one-way rush). Other structures and themes abound, of course, as noted in the text.

SECRET STRUCTURES OF THE ANAL EYE

A psychoanalytical colleague makes a, to my mind, sensational suggestion, which I hesitate to put forward, lest it overshadow everything else. If, he says, a patient had conveyed to him, as if it were a dream, the story-space of *Psycho*, he might indeed suspect some 'A-N-L' theme. The turnabout motifs direct attention to what's *behind* Marion; the burly policeman approaches her from behind; a black car tries to over-take; a second black car bangs in bringing belongings on its back seat, and driven by another virile, lower-class male. Marion puts in the toilet papers bearing money cal-culations, thus evoking the Freudian equation, money equals gold equals shit. In Marion's case, the calculation expresses punctiliousness (another 'anal' characteristic), and the film separates her from the *other* Freudian association with anal, obsession with power. At this point, readers who are easily shocked (we know you're out there somewhere), please stop reading here now, skipping the next paragraph, which offends me too.

Marion, weakening under Norman's blows, turns about frenziedly in the shower, turning her back to her assailant; later, the eye-plughole cross-fade 'collapses' the 'looking' theme into *a black hole through which dirty things escape*. Simply put, a hidden theme of the dream is sodomy – though whether the dreamer wished to commit it, or feared it, or both, isn't clear. In Hitchcock's day this practice was strictly illegal, even between married couples, though differently regarded in different subcultures (*vide Lady Chatterley's Lover*). Hitchcock's 'root' culture deemed sodomy vile, and Hitchcock might have found it nastily intriguing. (He certainly knew tying up could have erotic vibes, though Truffaut, the innocent young Frenchman, seems to ignore Hitch's little nudge.) All this might go into a bin labelled 'Polymorphous Perversity', and we note that the story-as-dream successfully *disguises* the theme, which only surmise can propose. It converges, however, with power/survival/dominance themes, and with the 'Excremental Vision', as earlier proposed, and a psychoanalysis might diagnose 'anal' structures in the Hitchcock *oeuvre* (in *Psycho*, for example, the

date/time punctiliousness). As we go to press, I came across this note from the director of *WR – Mysteries of the Organism* (1971), a deeply thoughtful movie about psychoanalysis and America: 'the sphincter is the most authoritarian of muscles, that
which concentrates the greatest number of social pressures. Western society, which
is extremely anal, through its obsession with profit, work, leads to paranoia.'[59]
However, psychoanalysis insists that all adult psyches contain some infantile elements.
It's certainly not a 'master-key' to *Psycho*'s structure, or Hitchcock's films, it's just one
aspect among many others.

GENROLOGY *PSYCHO*

(To our gentler readers, welcome back.) *Psycho* posed problems for trade cate-
gorisation. It's both 'thriller' and 'horror'. It blends 'drama', 'suspense melodrama'
and, perhaps, 'woman's picture' (such as feminists prefer to call 'melodrama', thus
adding another sense to that overloaded signifier). It might now be categorised
with noir, though in 1960 Hollywood hardly knew the word. Does a word exist for
trade-offs of 'Gothic' and 'realism', in the sense of 'ordinary little people' films, à la
Chayefsky? If it does, does it denote a genre, or ungenrable exceptions? Since
'poetic realism' is a genre, would *Psycho*'s 'lyrical realism' qualify as its 'cousin' (with
a gothic tinge)? In terms of film genres, I'd plump for 'lyrical melodrama' – somewhere between Murnau's *Sunrise* (1927) and Laughton's *The Night of the Hunter*
(1955). Looking beyond movie genres, perhaps it's theatre of cruelty (a bourgeois
version of). Perhaps it qualifies as a tragedy – not, of course, 'pure tragedy', as per
I. A. Richards, but as 'impure tragedy' – a modern mutation, all the more interesting for its many forms, and for ending in 'inconsolable restitution', which Aristotle
would have called a 'mixed end'. All the genres proposed here are loose cat-
egories, and none prescribes stereotypical story elements (kinds of hero, story
shapes, 'attractions', etc.).

A STERILITY TRAGEDY

If comedy arose from 'satyr plays', and obscene fertility rituals, maybe tragedy con-
stitutes 'sterility ritual'. *Psycho* might testify to that. From a 'Golden Bough' perspective (as pursued through several Pasolini films), Marion's blood falling into the bath
would evoke menstruation (fertility falls on sterile soil), there's a desert theme, Mrs
Bates isn't *fruity* (an aspect of fertility), her coconut-head is dried, Norman's incestuous 'fusion' with his mother is a sterile one, and so on. It's not fully developed, but a
side-theme only – as 'fertility' is, in much modern life. Much modern sexual theory,

perhaps including Freud's, divorces sex and Eros from their 'right true end' in Mother (and Father) Nature, the reproduction of the species, and reduces sex to a source of individual, and if possible sterile, pleasure (a sort of narcissism). Does the strange aridity of *Psycho*, with its impulsions and empty surfaces, somehow reflect the fear of fertility, in modern society?

PROGENY

After Hitchcock's death, *Psycho* spawned three follow-ups, *Psycho II* (1983), *Psycho III* (directed by Anthony Perkins, 1986), and *Psycho IV: The Beginning* (written by Stefano, in 1990). They're essentially potboilers, with the odd smart touch, but nowhere near the first film's class.

Gus Van Sant remade the original in 1998 for a generation which takes as a norm both colour and more explicit sexuality. It follows the original pretty closely, often line for line, move for move, shot for shot. However, the fame of 'the shower murder' makes the shock of surprise near impossible, and Van Sant's forté is the description of drifters and wilful waifs; bourgeois marriage obsession seems way off his mental map. The leads behave more like fickle teenagers than frustrated adults (partly because cinema audiences are younger than in Hitchcock's days, partly because adults *are* less settled in their ways). Anne Heche relies on a sort of 'negative girl' baby-charm; the colour palette (soft pinks, orange, salmon) evokes '1970s road regionalism', not the weight and thrust of Hitchcock's visuals. (Their monochrome 'muscle' does have a colour equivalent: it's images using heavy shades of one or two strong colours.) Hitchcock's characters were all originals: Van Sant 'quotes' a lot (Dan Duryea, Red Skelton). The remake is not *insensitive*, but it's indecisive and *fey*. The two *Psycho*s have near-identical structure, narrative, dialogue and 'attractions', yet the world of difference between them demonstrates the power of *fine details* whose forms and meanings are so hard to describe in words that we're always tempted to think of them as 'mere style', or 'superficial detail'.

Perhaps the most interesting 'spin-off' is the art installation by Douglas Gordon, first presented at the Hayward Gallery in 1996, designed around a slow-motion showing of *Psycho* timed to last 24 hours. The extreme slow-motion 'expands' the film's micro-moments, and makes constructive use of the *best* elements of a meticulously crafted film. A welcome change, since high culture modernisms, like 'pop art', and post-modernism, rarely recognise what in the 'mass' and 'popular' arts is sensitive, careful, elaborated and traditional – whether or not bourgeois. Hitchcock's *Psycho* is deeply bourgeois – it's persuasive because it is *deeply* so.

'GUILTY! GUILTY! GUILTY!'

—exults the highway cop in *The Phantom Tollbooth*, as he hands its hero a ticket for moral incorrectness. In an admirable article in *Film Comment*, Professor James Griffith groups me with a monstrous regiment of critics, who want *Psycho* to make the spectator feel guilty (of voyeurism, misogyny, etc.). Griffith's shrewd point back-foots me, and, what's worse, jabs a nerve. On page 332 of *The Strange Case of Alfred Hitchcock* I do say, 'The film is a practical joke: it convicts all the spectators of Original Sin', and link it to 'a religious ritual, involving confession'. Alas, I didn't foresee the imminent takeover of Anglophone Film Studies by a combination of academic 'political correctness' and neo-Freudo-Marxist anti-humanism. *After* the deluge, any mention of guilt might seem to acquiesce with the later position. Instead, I'd have appealed to Aristotle's idea of catharsis, expanded from *only* 'pity and terror', to a more general 'shake-up' of ideas about 'the world one has to face'. It's a familiar reaction in the perform-ance arts. Cinema managers have testified that, after certain (popular) films, the audience leaves in sombre silence, *as if* plunged in solemn gloom, though later on, they'll talk about it with friends over coffee, and warmly recommend the film to others. Ingmar Bergman's films are famous for this effect, and I remember reacting like this to *The Seventh Seal*, to Fellini's *La Strada* (1954), Clement's *Gervaise* (1956) and other box-office stormers with long legs. Critically disliked films may also exert this effect (e.g. *Judgement at Nuremberg* [1961], *Ruby Gentry* [1952]).

Occasionally, I speak of an element of guilt in relation to Hitchcock's films but I never make it the *major* element, dominating identification. In general, I argue, exactly as Griffith does, that the hero's guilt does not trouble us much – as in the case of *Rear Window*.

DID HITCH CLIMB PARNASSUS?

Whether or not 'evaluation' is a primary task of criticism, people wax passionate about it. Unfortunately, it involves just about every controversy to do with art, cul-ture and honest witness to experience. Once upon a time, Parnassus accommo-dated *all* the Muses; today so many subcultures and specialisations thrive, that 'classic' status looks more like 'horses for courses' and 'for each art, its own (ever-quarrelling) gods'. Valuation-wise, these pointers spring to mind.

1. In the movie pantheon, the place of *Psycho* seems secure: the BFI's idea of devoting a book to it raised no eyebrows to my knowledge.

2. *Psycho* occupies a sort of 'inter-cultural' space, linking the formal-aesthetic refinement of traditional 'high culture', with middlebrow socio-moral thoughtfulness (as in, say, Orwell, Robert Louis Stevenson), some modernist characteristics, an emotionality (melodrama) verging on 'Theatre of Cruelty' and libidinal material which some modernists like to think is 'pulp'.

3. In high culture, interest in 'minor works' is thoroughly traditional.

4. In *The Strange Case of Alfred Hitchcock*, I argued that Hitchcock's films have such craftsmanship, such aesthetic elegance, that, as he said of *Strangers on a Train*, 'Isn't it a beautiful design? You could study it for ever.' Nonetheless, I thought his Hollywood showman prudence often clipped his artistic wings and kept most of his films on the foothills around Parnassus. *Psycho*, however, was one of the exceptions.

5. In the annals of 'mainstream movies', and of socio-cultural history, it marks a turning-point (the 'turn' from conservative-liberal consensus to 1960s 'liberation/alienation/uneasiness', and from humanism to post-humanism).

6. That impact is probably unrepeatable, and winning a place 'in the history books' isn't 'immortality'. Recently a young lady presenter on BBC2 introduced it with jokey-comfy comments about 'twitching curtains' and perhaps it's entering the category of 'films that don't actually scare you, but you like to think they do, for their other, quieter resonances' – a melancholy, yet honourable category, to which most 'horror' stories in fact belong.

7. In the course of studying it, I found things which had strong immediate impact (the shower sequence, the music) lost their power first, but the discovery of finer points *integrated* remembrance of the shock into a sensitising context.

8. In film culture, I'd place it alongside the best Powells, above the best Murnaus and within hailing distance of *Persona* – though perhaps it helps to see *Persona* first!

9. Thinking around for literary equivalents my free-association kept turning up *The Rime of the Ancient Mariner* and Books 1 and 2 of *Paradise Lost*, maybe because they're all 'spiritual journeys' – poetico-lyrical descriptions of twisted moral impulses – though more 'realistic' than, like Coleridge, romantico-transcendental, or, like Milton, 'worldly-puritanical-theological'. Though this free-association prioritises themes over 'cultural level', it might be a hint that Hitchcock's best films can lay claim to a small-holding on Parnassus.

10. Another possibility: much as D. H. Lawrence was a 'vitalist' of eroticism, whose 'genius' moments stem from his *lyrical* sense of Eros as a driving force,

Hitchcock's best films achieve a 'vitalism' of fearfulness, and of 'petty bourgeois prudence', as a 'transcendent' human drive.

11. Given the collapse of criteria across 'high post-modernist culture', the formidable powers of complex craftsmanship to work new 'inter-cultural' zones
(see point 2) of 'honest witness to human experience' require reassertion.

Notes

Publication details for works cited in the notes appear in the bibliography.

1. Usefully summarised in Eric Rayner, *The Independent Mind in British Psychoanalysis*.

2. Jacques Lacan and Vladimir Granoff, 'Fetishism: the Symbolic, The Imaginary and the Real', in Sandor Lorand and Michael Balint (eds), *Perversions, Psychodynamics and Therapy*.

3. It's often said that the scandal ended Powell's career, but this much-repeated story is entirely false, as a glance at his career makes obvious. Apart from anything else, film production circles are more tolerant than academic ideology chooses to suppose.

4. Spectator 'identification' is a highly problematic concept. Here at least, it's equivalent to 'passionate involvement based on affinity'. It's stronger than 'interest' or 'concern', and it does involve a certain shift of perspective, away from 'objective impartiality'; but it by no mean entails 'uncritical partisanship of one character only'. Here, many, or most, spectators would identify *primarily* with Marion, but also, and appreciably, with Sam.

5. On the female counterpart of the Oedipus complex, see, for instance, Christiane Olivier, *Les Enfants de Jocaste*.

6. 'Subliminal' is a weasel word, and its tricky ambiguities are beyond us here. Suffice it to say, that many effects and thoughts are subliminal in *some* respects (their exact mechanisms), but powerfully conscious in others. Similarly, evocative details which the ordinary spectator doesn't notice – 'can't see' – may be glaringly obvious to the eyes of film technicians. (Conversely, some film technicians can't see the film for the technicalities.) Continuity and its rules, which are more like rules of thumb, than like syntax and grammar in language, are famously problematic. Sometimes experienced craftsmen violently disagree about how a shot will or won't read when put near another.

7. Peter Bogdanovich, *The Cinema of Howard Hawks*.

8. Even Theodore Price omits it, from his 414 pages about *Hitchcock and Homosexuality: His 50-year Obsession with Jack the Ripper and the Superbitch Prostitute*. Some passages are spot on, but the problem remains, that if you headline certain streaks, and shrug off the wider sympathies and countervailing decencies, it all gets too lurid and inquisitorial, and risks traducing the whole person.

9. Shot dissection, aka scene dissection: the breakdown of scenes (and their actions) into

separate shots (cf Sharff; Salt). This aspect of Hitchcock's style owes less to Russian editing than to German editing (Murnau, Ruttmann, Pabst, Dupont), the pioneer importance of which film histories, mesmerised by Soviet theories, often overlook.

10. Surrealist or feminist spectators may regret Marion's capitulation to bourgeois resignation, or capitalism, or patriarchy, or all three, and reckon that as a triply oppressed woman she has every moral right to rob nasty men.

11. 'Deduction' is what detective stories call it, though it's sometimes called 'induction'; it's essentially empirical. It's a heuristic, not a rigorous, logic; but it's a logic nonetheless, a pragmatic logic, at the junction of praxis and what Marxists think is their rigorous theory. Medawar speaks of 'hypothetico-deductive empiricism', as the logic which understands the material world; whereas verbally rigorous logic has very restricted use.

12. In general principle, it's akin to the famous trope in *Stagecoach*, where the camera pulls back from the stage coach *far away down there* and reveals the Red Indians *back here* – waiting to attack … In theorising off-screen space, it's easy to overlook the fact that, even when the camera is 'in' the scene, it's almost always *back from the* shot: the edge of the frame is varying distances from the camera, with an 'apron' of hidden space between camera and picture.

13. The distinction between these two 'identities' ties in with David Reisman's very influential *The Lonely Crowd*. He distinguishes 'other-direction' – conformity to other people's ideas – as a newly prevalent American attitude – from 'inner direction' – conformity to one's own ideas – a more traditional, puritanical, American attitude. Inner-direction emphasises *conscience, guilt* and 'the lone moral stand'; as per *Twelve Angry Men* (1956). Outer-direction emphasises status, shame and going with the flow of 'community'. *Rebel without a Cause*, and its source, turns on the same distinction.

14. This scene reminds me of the strange car drive in Cocteau's *Orphée* (1950). A car stops at a level-crossing; on the other side, the landscape is in negative.

15. Why so few real-life problems are soluble by rigorous logic is a problem beyond our scope here.

16. In an earlier text I compared this cop to an Old Testament angel: the figure whose stern warning is very like a threat. The warning is also a test, and if you fail the test, the test destroys you. God, being God, knows in advance whether or not you will destroy yourself, so angelic visitations may result in your damnation. And perhaps that happens here: the cop's intervention pushes Marion further into folly. That God decides to damn you was heavily emphasised by traditional Calvinists (which the Puritans were), but Catholicism is uneasily aware of the logical problem (as of its more cheerful, but morally more dangerous, counterpart, the *felix culpa* paradox, whereby your very sins may bring you round to

God). *Psycho* is rather too secular for angels unawares; and in 1960 angels were an endangered species (though devils appeared in horror films). But from the late 1930s to around 1950, angels and other spirits made quite frequent screen appearances (e.g. Capra's *It's a Wonderful Life*, 1947), and since *Wings of Desire* (Wenders, 1987) they're suddenly all over the place again.

17. *How* short depends on composition, graphics, etc.; it could have been very roundabout; but that's another essay.

18. 'Opposition' is a popular term in film theory, but when are opposites 'binary', 'diametrical', 'complementary' or 'dialectical'?

19. By 'cultural' I don't mean 'ideological' in the now prevalent Marxist sense. Rather, I mean that cultural changes interacting with movie market changes plus technical changes etc. allowed many 'state of the art' minds to converge – but only *if* and *only insofar as* each of them, independently, made *different* choices which brought *different* positions together. (Just as two objects converge by moving in different directions.) Culture is far more diverse, far less *compulsory*, than most ideology theories suppose. The useful paradigm for 'a culture' is not 'linguistic structure' but 'ecological system', rich in extensively autonomous subsystems, cross-currents, niches, etc.

20. More on the dearth of tragedy in Hollywood, especially 1930–60, in Edgar Morin, *Les Stars/The Stars*.

21. Once set on a course, the primitive logic of the Unconscious is so rigorous, it doesn't notice differences, only similarities. (As in 'anything that's longer than it's wide signifies the phallus, anything that's not, signifies the vagina'.) Cf Ignacio Matte Blanco, *The Unconscious as Infinite Sets: An Essay in Bi-Logic*.

22. Cf, for example, Temple Grandin, *Thinking in Pictures and Other Reports from My Life with Autism*, and Julian Jaynes, *The Origin of Consciousness in the Breakdown of the Bicameral Mind*. Respectable evidence for 'full sensory replay' of memories and/or imaginings, under electric stimulation of the brain, first appeared in the 1930s (cf Richard L. Gregory, *The Mind in Science*, and Gordon Rattray Taylor, *The Natural History of the Mind*).

23. An early 'manifesto' of the flowing style is the 'railway-scape' in Renoir's *La Bête humaine* (1938). Maybe *Bullitt* (1968) kick-started the 'cataclysmic' driving school. If *Psycho* works on driving as 'nowherelessness', *Un Homme et une femme* (Lelouch, 1986) achieves, in modern equivalent, Dr Johnson's definition of happiness, as rapid movement in a carriage, with a beautiful female who can add something to the conversation (Anouk Aimée).

24. Did Ivens' film inspire the assassination scene in Hitchcock's *Foreign Correspondent* (1940), with its mêlée of rain, umbrellas, crowds, trams? Perhaps, but artists don't just imitate other texts; sometimes, 'great minds meet', and maybe Hitchcock was inspired, not by *Rain*, but by rain.

25. A keen sense of multiple symmetries, jigsawing in and out of each other, might link with volatile ambivalence: 'All relations are swiftly reversible'. And obsessions with relations might be a coefficient of splits. Schizos would be obsessive as a coefficient of the splits which limit mental movements, and paranoid because they're looking in the wrong place – 'the wrong way'. But all that risks Freudian hypochondria, whereby all turns of mind derive from some deep disease, and good health has no advantages – as if 'Only cripples can walk fast,' 'Only the nearly deaf know how to listen' and so on.

26. Cinema scares are often attributed to our Unconscious, but maybe that's too simple. For one thing, fear at a film is neither unconscious nor irrational. It fulfils all the criteria for conscious experience: we expected it, we paid for it, we know we're feeling it, we gently mock ourselves for doing so, we remember it well, we discuss it with other people and we theorise it by introspection. It also fulfils all the criteria for rationality: it's adaptive (to our situation, being in a cinema); it's socially sanctioned, and it's appropriate (lively response to *description* is a function of being *sapiens*). To be sure, our conscious, rational responses are mixed in with Unconscious and irrational ones, but nothing suggests that they dominate, since our behaviour is appropriate.

27. 'Deletion' and 'ellipsis' are different things. An ellipsis omits a *major narrative* event; and it's a *positive* figure of narration (often, indeed, a way of *emphasising* the event, or its relation to other matters). A deletion omits *irrelevant* details, for a *negative* function to *clear the way* for *positive* detail. The ellipsis is an *exceptional* omission within whatever continuity system the narration has set up. Deletions are *part* of a continuity system.

28. Coleridge's formulation predates the cinema of course, and was directed against those who confused response to *reading* fiction with belief in their truth. It's even more relevant today, given three ideas held even in seriously intended theory:

    1. That moving images induce 'belief'.
    2. That this is because they're 'illusionistic' and
    3. That 'illusionism' follows from 'realism'.

    None of these is true. Moving images may be phenomenally vivid, but that doesn't constitute an illusion, since, if we can recognise the subjects of the images, we must also recognise the images *as* images – as we do: we can see that a film is a film. Moreover, we see and know from our other senses, notably kinaesthesia, that we're in a cinema. Or if the images are on TV, we can see the set around the images, and the room around it. Our occasional feeling of an illusion arises when the moving images have concentrated our attention, thanks to their stream of interesting ideas, and thanks to a dearth of competitive interest from the immediate viewing environment. As for 'bourgeois illusionism', butt of Marxists, formalists and anti-realists, bourgeois art appreciation, like this book, depends on paying close attention to the forms of the medium *tel quel*. There also exists a 'popular aesthetic', to which all Hitchcock movies are geared. They rarely refer to forms or medium as such ('self-reflexivity', 'alienation effects';), for the very good reason that they've concentrated their rich meanings on a different level, that of an 'osmosis' of diegesis and style, from which level form and medium in themselves are irrelevant distractions. There is no fear of 'breaking an illusion'; most spectators of *Psycho* have already recognised Marion as Janet Leigh, Norman as Tony Perkins, and so on; they may be admiring their acting; and, in a general way, assessing the film ('It's okay, but there's not very much happening'). When some good reason exists to upfront film *qua* film, popular audiences have no problem with it: consider, for example, *Hellzapoppin!* (1941), *Our Town*, *La Ronde* (1950), *La Fête à Henriette* (1952). As for 'illusionism' depending on 'realism', consider *Bambi* (1942) and *Dumbo* (1941). Adult spectators shed tears over the talking cartoon deer, and the cartoon elephant who not only talks but flies by flapping his ears, but who would call these characters 'realistic'? (Why they're so *vivid* requires another term, another analysis, altogether.) And in just what sense in Herrmann's powerful *Psycho* music 'illusionistic' and 'realistic'?

29. Love/hate, as a consciously running theme, had irrupted earlier, notably in *Gone with the Wind* (1939), and in melodrama, as in *The Outlaw* (1940–3), *Duel in the Sun* and *Gilda* (both 1946). Especially thoughtful is *Ruby Gentry*. But *Psycho* found a new, quiet tone: 'I don't hate her. I hate what she's become. The illness.'

30. And even about very simple things – optical illusions, mirror-reversals….

31. I don't mean to rule out the feminine, and female desire to be desired, admired and envied, which may find covert satisfaction in 'peeping Tom' situations (Perkins' Norman seems attractive, soulful, safe and respectful). Perhaps it's the high point of her superiority to Norman, for which her naked death, in the shower, is an entirely undeserved payback. But I'd have thought protected modesty the main 'woman's angle' here.

32. One writes 'the camera closes on it', and some spectators will register this happening, but the phrase is really a form of words for a less definable effect: our gaze approaches the enlarging object, which, filling our field of vision, monopolises our attention (and, perhaps, presents new aspects). Before it was a, maybe poignant, *detail*, now it, and *its* details, acquires a new *poetic force*. The rule of thumb would be, that, whether or not we briefly think about what the invisible, irrationally present camera is doing, it's what's on screen that predominates in our perceptions and our minds. It's to do, not with 'illusionism', 'mystification'; it's a case of 'out of sight, out of mind' (and it's reversible, depending on context and other factors). The mention of the camera in this popular form of words reminds us how aware spectators are that a film is 'only' a film, a 'construction' and that they don't normally confuse diegesis with reality. A special interest in camera movements is entirely justified, but it

can get out of hand, as when formalists suppose that spectators 'think' scenes as if they were being watched by a camera, or that the camera corresponds to an invisible watcher-narrator (who may even verge on being an 'unacknowledged character in the drama'). Moreover, no camera observes a scene; it only records it. But all that's another essay.

33. *Epitaph* ... by William Camden, c. 1600, here misquoted, as that's usual.

34. Hitchcock must have known that ex-Victorian music-: hall-cum-urban-folksong: 'Your baby has gone down the plughole.' (An angel advises the poor bereaved mother: 'The poor little thing was so skinny and thin/It shoulda been bathed in a jug ...').

35. Russian montage is routinely described in terms of 'collisions' between 'hard cuts', a simplification which for brevity's sake we've followed here. In fact *Strike, Mother* and *Earth* make considerable use of cross-fades, whose juxtapositions are formally quite different from cuts (though less congenial to a Communist cult of decisive hardness in all things).

36. The continuity rule is usually given in shorthand form: 'Always cut on movement'.

37. My acknowledgments to David Cairns (University of Edinburgh) and Benjamin Halligan (University of Aberystwyth).

38. It's so convenient to write that the camera, or the film or the audience, were *in* the scene – taking a shower with Marion! And that the shower was constantly expanding, now in one direction, now in another, enough to accommodate, not only the camera, but the space between it and Marion. But that's hardly spectator experience. Rather, the diegesis and the film apparatus meet *outside* the diegesis, not *within* it. The camera is no more 'there', in the film, than the shower is 'here', in the cinema. The diegesis exists in a sort of Utopia – that is to say, a 'no-place', to which the imagination has access (a sort of metaphysical space, which sometimes manifests as space, though that's probably its metaphor for a system of relations). The movie *tel quel* is real, visible and concrete, but interest concentrates in the diegesis, as filtered by descriptive style, and to this we pay most of our attention, in the form of a 'willing suspension of disbelief', which we withdraw if it's boring, offensive or otherwise fails to meet our requirements. The medium looks like a seamless illusion, only because and insofar as we don't want pointless distractions. (In fact the impossibilities, intellectual and phenomenological, are too glaring and many to list.)

39. Audience *relief* when the car sinks seems to me a step beyond what, normally, 'sympathy' with a criminal in this predicament would connote, and this would justify the stronger term, 'identification'. 'Identification' is a weasel word, with many, tricky meanings, alas. In the meaning used here, which in my experience is the most widespread one, it doesn't entail 'total, uncritical, identification, restricted to heroes only'. That is but one type of identification (identification with an 'idealised ego'). Most character-spectator identification involves juggling several variables, notably, 'life-predicaments', desiderata and values (some

moral, some immoral; some official, some vernacular). Routinely overlooked in discussions of 'spectator identification' is its opposite, rejection, though it's obviously involved in the construction of a villain, which depends on spectator *repudiation* of attitudes on offer in the film. 'Goodies and baddies' is, after all, a familiar structure, often vehemently maintained (though it quite rarely coincides with the moral codes of the bureaucratic apparatus of the bourgeois state). Some melodramas maintain a simple 'soot and whitewash' polarity: the hero has no serious faults, the villain no redeeming virtues (not even amoral ones, like courage). It's a 'binary opposition', and, like most such 'oppositions', exists on a fairly low, even primitive, level of thought. Many melodramas strongly nuance it: the hero has serious temptations, even vices, amounting to villainous tendencies, and commits actions which seriously incriminate him (though they don't define him), while the villain has many powerful virtues, partial justifications, extenuating circumstances, etc. In many such cases, spectator identification shifts, as the story proceeds, and is frequently split – the splits may shift as the story proceeds, and a 'binary' frame may accommodate several changing and competing sub-conflicts. One distinction between melodrama and drama may be, that melodrama upfronts some such moral dichotomy (even when it nuances or troubles it), while in drama it's not a basic polarity – the conflict may *happen* upon it, e.g. as a character frequently 'does wrong', but heroism/villainy is a *description of a character*, or his actions, not a *shaping structure* of the narrative. In drama and melodrama alike, all identifications are open to challenge from other characters, even minor ones – our degree of sympathy with Marion partly depends on Lowery and Cassidy being 'unidentifiable-with' – one spiteful, the other mean. Our identifications with Marion, Norman, and Sam, have all along been *partial*, *ambivalent* and counter-balanceable. A problem with any terminology is that no clear line divides 'sympathy', which is 'feeling-with', from 'conditional identification'. In movies, and art generally, both relate to what anthropologist Lévy-Bruhl called 'la participation mystique' and to Edgar Morin's sophisticated version of identification theory in *Le Cinéma ou l'homme imaginaire*.

40. 'Superego' is a confusing name, since it's not 'above' the ego, but below it, and part of the Unconscious. The name hints at an entity which is *above* and *outside* the ego. A position which, oddly enough, would correspond with *social constraints* – which Freud might have thought worked on the Unconscious mostly *through* the Conscious mind. But if we think of them working on the Unconscious 'directly' (without modification by the Conscious, as Freud conceived it [moral, rational, respectable, adult, etc., etc.]) it would have some affinity with Lacan's 'The Other' (social constraints built into Conscious and Unconscious alike) – just as that has some affinity with Sartre's 'the others' ('Hell is other people' – because their minds, merely by looking at us, make us make ourselves unconscious of our real selves).

41. Freud emphasised 'castration', but some non-sexual punishments – disembowelling, boiling in oil, pulling apart by wild horses – are at least as frightening, and if psychoanalysis made more of power/survival, as radical/instinctual drives, they might be seen as not 'substitutes' for phallic disempowerment, but as even more unpleasant, in their own right.

42. Whence many problems about 'scenes' for theory, but that's another essay.

43. A few years later, crime fiction will dwell on morbid sexual goings-on of every stripe and hue. In his attitude to all this, Hitchcock was, I suspect, less morbid, or complaisant towards morbidity, than our cultural climate since. He was closer to Victorianism, to the Jesuits, and to Freud, than to post-modernism, in assuming that repression was a precondition of being human, and that even though all men are naturally wicked, they were naturally moral also, and that natural morality should be reinforced, by social discipline, into 'second nature'. Maybe he had suffered an overdose, but that didn't alter the principle. He never claimed to be some sort of saint: on the contrary, he was uniquely frank (in his canny and controlling way) about certain moral, emotional and sexual shortcomings.

44. Insofar as they *attract attention*, if briefly only, as the film goes on, they're different from still smaller details (the preconscious, the subliminal, etc.) which contribute as much, or more, to what Leavis called 'the texture' of a work of art. But that's another can of worms-within-worms …

45. As awful as this seems to have turned out, it's easy to imagine how a mild prank, in an era when practical jokes were more common and acceptable than now, might have inadvertently gone wrong.

46. Craft terminology is often very approximate, and what 'natural' really meant was, I think, more like 'consistent with the procedures of this world and its style'. But that's another problem.

47. And not only in narrative. In some paradoxical formulations of information theory, information *is* surprise. Consistency is tautology and redundancy, except where *some* surprise *or other* is expected, so that 'no surprise' becomes significant.

48. Does anyone market 'Bates Hotel' notepaper, perhaps around Hallowe'en?

49. It's arguable, though not provable, that Cassidy, Lowery, the dealer, Arbogast (and later Sheriff Chambers) are all father figures, by age, authority, power and a theme of trust. The cop and (later) the psychiatrist would be young father figures (an unusual, but intriguing, category). Hollywood 'character stars' whose roles would represent covert 'father figures' (with varying degrees of ambivalence) include Emil Jannings, Edward G. Robinson, Pat O'Brien, Paul Muni, Charles Laughton, Karl Malden (in two Brando films), Marlon Brando in his turn (in *The Godfather*) and, through his last two decades, John Wayne. In *Movies: A Psychological Study*, psychoanalysts Martha Wolfenstein and Nathan Leites note that 1940s'

villains are regularly covert father figures; this would link with sociological theory about American rejection of the immigrant father (Geoffrey Gorer, *The Americans.*

50. Ronald Bergan, *Anthony Perkins – A Haunted Life.*

51. 'Subjective' shots and 'point of view' shots can be confusing terms. In traditional trade parlance, a 'subjective' shot is what the audience would see if it were in some obvious position in the scene depicted, and excluces POVs, for which 'character's POV.' might be clearer. 'Point of view' has another confusion. Sometimes it means 'the point from which a view is seen', sometimes it means that view itself; the latter view applies in 'point of view shot'. Arbogast's face is his point of view in the first sense, but not in the second.

52. Detective stories evolved fron ghost stories, via Wilkie Collins and the Gothic (romantic or urban), and have negligible trouble evolving back, as desired.

53. Piers Gerhart and Milton B. Singer, *Guilt and Shame: A Psychoanalytic and Cultural Study*, and Daniel L. Nathanson (ed.), *The Many Faces of Shame.*

54. Hollywood films occasionally made characters mini-clones of political figures. In *The Grapes of Wrath* (Ford, 1940), the worker-friendly director of a Federal project camp is a 'mini' FDR.

55. Perhaps it echoes Hitchcock's boyish dreams of escape, expressed through drawing up meticulously real(istic) timetables of long foreign journeys. But that's 'control freak' escape, where 'sailing ship' escape implies manly adventure. The two attitudes fight it out in *Rich and Strange. East of Shanghai* (1932), whose depressing conclusion is, that *real* adventure can get *really* nasty; but, safe return is spiritually blinkered. Heads you lose, tails you lose; but it's better to only lose your tail, than your head as well …

56. Piaget attributes basic structures of meaning to 'sensori-motor operations' in *Main Trends in Inter-disciplinary Research*, while Lakoff and Johnson root verbal language in metaphors of bodily experience (*Metaphors We Live By*).

57. *Psycho*, like many a good film, offers good topics for debate, a use which would challenge the false consensuses assumed by ideology theory, and the catalogues of 'stereotypes' which reduce the better films to the level of the worst. 'How should Norman be treated?' might set those feminists who demand the death penalty for rape, against liberals who deplore the American revival of the death penalty, and pose interesting questions, like, should Norman's violence, which proves that he's *very* mad, spare him the death penalty which the violence against women of more typical males deserves? Or is the very distinction between sanity and madness a legal fiction, related to nothing *real* in human psychology, as radical liberals against conservative ones? But then again, if, as Laing, for the radical liberals, argues, we who seem sane are also mad, though less obviously, should the sane and the mad be equal before the law? Would Norman's execution be any great loss

to society, or to himself? Might it, indeed, count as euthanasia – saving his *real* self, from a hideous fantasy? There's nothing like a real madman – saint or sinner – to prompt rich, unmanageable debate.

58. The extent to which psychoanalysis in the US was departing from, or rather, refusing to rejoin, conservative Freudian orthodoxies, is spelt out in Marie-Claire Durieux and Alain Fine, (eds), *Sur les controverses américaines dans la psychanalyse*.

59. Julien Suaudeau, 'Dusan Makavejev, The Childhood of Art'.

Credits

Psycho
USA
1960

Directed by
Alfred Hitchcock
[Producer
Alfred Hitchcock]
Screenplay by
Joseph Stefano
Based on the novel by Robert Bloch
Director of Photography
John L. Russell
Edited by
George Tomasini
Art Direction
Joseph Hurley, Robert Clatworthy
Music by
Bernard Herrmann

© Shamley Productions, Inc.
Production Company
a Paramount release
Unit Manager
Lew Leary
Assistant Director
Hilton A. Green
[2nd Assistant Director
Les Berke]
[Script Supervisor
Marshall Schlom]

[Camera Assistant
Jim Sloan]
[Key Grip
Frank Harper]
[Gaffer
George Meerhoff]
Special Effects
Clarence Champagne
Set Decorator
George Milo
Costume Supervisor
Helen Colvig
[Costumes
Rita Riggs]
Make-up Supervision
Jack Barron, Robert Dawn
Hairstylist
Florence Bush
Titles Designed by/Pictorial Consultant
Saul Bass
[Title Animation
William T. Hurtz]
[Bird Handler
John 'Bud' Cardos]
Sound Recording by
Waldon O. Watson, William Russell
[Body Doubles
Janet Leigh in Shower Scene:
Marli Renfro
Anthony Perkins in Shower Scene:
Anne Dore]

Cast

Anthony Perkins
Norman Bates

Vera Miles
Lila Crane

John Gavin
Sam Loomis

Martin Balsam
Milton Arbogast

John McIntire
Sheriff Al Chambers

Simon Oakland
Dr Richmond

Vaughn Taylor
George Lowery

Frank Albertson
Tom Cassidy

Lurene Tuttle
Mrs Chambers

Pat Hitchcock
Caroline

John Anderson
California Charlie, car salesman

Mort Mills
highway patrolman

Janet Leigh
Marion Crane

[uncredited]

Alfred Hitchcock
man in cowboy hat outside realty office

Virginia Gregg
voice of Mother

Helen Wallace
customer in Sam's store

Frank Killmond
Bob Summerfield, Sam's assistant

George Eldredge
Chief of Police James Mitchell

Francis De Sales
district attorney

Sam Flint
official

Ted Knight
prison guard

Paul Jasmin
voice of Mother in prison

Black & White
9,767 feet
109 minutes

Credits compiled by Markku Salmi, BFI
Filmographic Unit

Bibliography

This bibliography relates to works cited in the text, and issues and approaches there, which the reader may wish to follow up.

ON *PSYCHO* IN PARTICULAR

Bergan, Ronald, *Anthony Perkins – A Haunted Life* (New York: Little, Brown, 1995).

Durgnat, Raymond, *The Strange Case of Alfred Hitchcock: or, The Plain Man's Hitchcock* (London/Cambridge, MA: Faber/MIT, 1974). (Some embarrassing errors of detail but see Andrew Sarris's quote on jacket.)

—— 'If the Punishment Fits', *Film Comment*, January–February 1997 (response to James Griffith).

'Gene', '*Psycho*', *Variety*, 22 June 1960.

Griffith, James, '*Psycho*: Not Guilty as Charged', *Film Comment*, July–August 1996.

Leigh, Janet and Christopher Nickens, *Psycho: Behind the Scenes of the Classic Thriller* (New York: Harmony, 1995).

Perkins, V. F., '*Psycho*: Charm and Blood', *Oxford Opinion*, 25 October 1960.

Psycho – The First Time, produced and directed by Martina Hall, Executive Producer Tim Kirby, BBC2, 29 May 1999.

Rebello, Stephen, *Alfred Hitchcock and the Making of Psycho* (New York: Dembner Books, 1990, New York: Harper Perennial, 1991).

Sharff, Stefan, *The Elements of Cinema: Towards a Theory of Cinesthetic Impact* (New York: Columbia University Press, 1982).

THE RAW MATERIALS

Bloch, Robert, *Psycho* (New York: Simon and Schuster, 1959; London: Robert Hale, 1960).

—— *Once Around the Bloch: An Unauthorized Biography* (New York: Tor, 1993).

Schechter, Harold, *Deviant: The Shocking True Story of Ed Gein, the Original 'Psycho'* (New York: Pocket Books, Simon and Schuster, 1989).

HITCHCOCK STUDIES

Bogdanovich, Peter (interview), *The Cinema of Alfred Hitchcock* (New York: Museum of Modern Art–Doubleday, 1963).

Chabrol, Claude and Eric Rohmer, *Alfred Hitchcock* (Paris: Editions Universitaires, 1957).

Douchet, Jean, *Alfred Hitchcock* (Paris: Editions de L'Herne, 1967).

Durgnat, Raymond, 'To Catch A Hitch', *Quarterly Review of Film Studies*, vol. 1 no. 8, Winter 1983.

—— 'The Business of Fear', in Nick James (ed.), *Sight and Sound Hitchcock Supplement*, July 1999.

Gottlieb, Sidney (ed.), *Hitchcock on Hitchcock: Selected Writings and Interviews* (Berkeley: University of California Press, 1995).

Kapsis, Robert, *Hitchcock: The Making of a Reputation* (Chicago: University of Chicago Press, 1992).

Paini, Dominique and Guy Cogeval, *Hitchcock and Art: Fatales Coincidences* (Montreal: Montreal Museum of Fine Arts, 2001).

Price, Theodore, *Hitchcock and Homosexuality: His 50-year Obsession with Jack the Ripper and the Superbitch Prostitute – A Psychoanalytic View* (New York: Scarecrow, 1992).

Rothman, William, *Hitchcock: The Murderous Gaze* (Cambridge, MA Harvard University Press, 1982).

Sharff, Stefan, *The Art of Looking in Hitchcock's Rear Window* (New York: Limelight Editions, 1997).

Spoto, Donald, *The Dark Side of Genius: The Life of Alfred Hitchcock*, (New York: Little, Brown, 1983; New York: Ballantine, 1984).

Truffaut, François, *Hitchcock* (New York: Simon and Schuster, 1967; London: Secker and Warburg, 1968; revised edn London: Collins, 1986).

Wood, Robin, *Hitchcock's Film. Revisited*, (London: Faber and Faber, 1991).

Žižek, Slavoj (ed.), *Everything You Always Wanted to Know about Lacan (But Were Afraid to Ask Hitchcock)* (London: Verso, 1992).

FILM STUDIES AND FILM THEORY

Biskind, Peter, *Seeing Is Believing: How Hollywood Taught Us to Stop Worrying and Love the Fifties* (New York: Pantheon, 1983).

Bogdanovich, Peter, *The Cinema of Howard Hawks* (New York: Museum of Modern Art, 1962).

Campbell, Joseph, *The Hero with a Thousand Faces* (Princeton, NJ: Princeton University Press, 1973).

Dickinson, H. Thorold, *Slade School of Fine Arts Lectures*, University College London, 1960–4.

Durgnat, Raymond, *Films and Feelings* (London/Cambridge, MA: Faber/ MI., 1967). (See chapters 14–24, and appendix, on plot structures.)

—— 'On Semantic Complexity', *Poetics Today*, University of Tel Aviv, Spring 1982.

—— 'From Narrative to Description', *Quarterly Review of Film Studies*, vol. 7 no. 2, Winter 1982.

—— 'Towards Practical Criticism', *American Film Institute Education Newsletter*, March–April 1984.

Griffith, Richard, Arthur Mayer and Eileen Bowser, *The Movies* (New York: Simon and Schuster, 2nd edn, 1970). (A sound and perceptive outline, which, as its authors' names suggest, is more sophisticated than it may seem.)

McKee, Robert, *Story: Substance, Structure, Style, and the Principles of Screenwriting* (New York: Regan Books, 1997; London: Methuen, 1998).

Makavejev, Dusan, in Julien Suaudeau, 'The Childhood of Art', *Positif*, no. 490, December 2001.

Morin Edgar, *Les Stars/The Stars* (Paris: Editions du Seuil, 1957; New York: Grove Press/John Calder, 1960).

—— *Le Cinéma ou l'homme imaginaire: essai d'anthropologie sociologique* (Paris: Editions de Minuit, 1956, 1978).

Salt, Brian, *Film Style and Technology: History and Analysis* (London: Starword, 1983; 2nd edn, 1992). (It's the nearest thing Film Studies has to a Bible: rigorous theory, empirically derived, involving inside knowledge of studio pragmatics and change.)

Sharff, Stefan, *The Elements of Cinema: Towards a Theory of Cinesthetic Impact* (New York: Columbia University Press, 1982). (Develops Russian montage theory to apply to Hollywood continuity editing.)

Valkola, Jarmo, *Perceiving the Visual in Cinema* (Finland: Jyväskylä University, 1993). (A further step in the application to film theory of scientific visual perception theory.)

—— *Aesthetic & Cognitive Perceptualism* (Finland: Jyväskylä University, 2000). (Signs, symbols, and concepts in art educational context.)

Vogler, Christopher, *The Writer's Journey, Mythic Structure for Storytellers and Screenwriters* (Studio City, CA: Michael Wiese Productions, 1992, 1999).

Wolfenstein, Martha and Nathan Leites, *Movies: A Psychological Study* (1950; New York: Atheneum, 1970).

SOCIO-CULTURAL STUDIES

Bogue, Roland, *Deleuze and Guattari* (London: Routledge, 1989).

Dichter, Ernest, *The Strategy of Desire* (New York: Doubleday, 1960).

Dingwall, Eric, *The American Woman* (London: Duckworth, 1952).

Firestone, Shulamith, *The Dialectic of Sex: The Case for Feminist Revolution* (New York: Bantam Books, 1979).

Gorer, Geoffrey, *The Americans A Study in National Character* (London: Cresset Press, 1948; London Grey Arrow, 1959).

Kinsey, A. C., *et al.*, *Sexual Behaviour in the Human Male*. (Philadelphia: W. B. Saunders, 1948). (This and next based on the study of 10,000 Americans.)

—— *Sexual Behaviour in the Human Female* (Philadelphia: W. B. Saunders, 1953).

Lasch, Christopher, *The Culture of Narcissism: American Life in a Culture of Diminishing Expectations* (New York: Norton, 1978).

Marcuse, Herbert *One-Dimensional Man: Studies in the Ideology of Advanced Industrial Society* (London: Routledge and Kegan Paul, 1964).

Mead, Margaret, *And Keep Your Powder Dry: An Anthropologist Looks at the American Character* (New York: W. Morrow, 1942).

Mitford, Jessica, *The American Way of Death* (New York: Simon and Schuster, 1963).

Packard, Vance, *The Hidden Persuaders* (New York: D. Mckay, 1957).

Reisman, David, Nathan Glazer and Reuel Denney, *The Lonely Crowd: A Study of the Changing American Character* (New Haven, CT: Yale University Press, 1950).

Taylor, Gordon Rattray, *Sex in History* (London: Thames and Hudson, 1953). (See especially Appendix B on 'Theories of Matriarchy and Patriarchy'.)

—— *The Angel-Makers: A Study in the Psychological Origins of Historical Change 1750–1850* (London: Heinemann, 1958). ('Traditional' sexual behaviour.)

PSYCHOANALYTIC STUDIES

Balint, Michael, *Thrills and Regressions* (New York: International Universities Press, 1959).

Bergeret, Jean, *La Violence et la vie: la face cachée de l'Oedipe* (Paris: Payot, 1994).

Berne, Eric, *Games People Play: The Psychology of Human Relationships* (New York: Grove Press, 1964).

Blanco, Ignacio Matte, *The Unconscious as Infinite Sets: An Essay in Bi-Logic* (London: Duckworth, 1975).

Brown, Norman O., *Life Against Death: The Psychoanalytical Meaning of History* (London: Routledge and Kegan Paul, 1959).

Gerhart, Piers and Milton Singer, *Guilt and Shame: A Psychoanalytical and Cultural Study* (New York: Norton, 1953; 2nd edn, 1978).

Green, André, 'La Mère morte', in *Narcissisme de vie, narcissisme de mort* (Paris: Les Editions de Minuit, 1983).

Lacan, Jacques and Vladimir Granoff, 'Fetishism: the Symbolic, the Imaginary and the Real', in Sandor Lorand and Michael Balint (eds), *Perversion, Psychodynamics and Therapy* (New York: Random House–Gramercy, 1956).

Nathanson, Daniel (ed.), *The Many Faces of Shame* (New York: Guilford Press, 1987).

Olivier, Christiane, *Les Enfants de Jocaste* (Paris: Payot, 1980).

Rayner, Eric, *The Independent Mind in British Psychoanalysis* (Northvale, NJ: J. Aronson, 1991).

Rycroft, Charles, *The Innocence of Dreams* (London: Hogarth Press, 1979).

COGNITIVE STUDIES AND METATHEORY

Coulthard, Malcolm, *An Introduction to Discourse Analysis* (London: Longman, 1977).

Grandin, Temple, *Thinking in Pictures and Other Reports from My Life with Autism* (New York: Doubleday, 1995).

Gregory, Richard L., *The Mind in Science: A History of Explanations in Psychology and Physics* (Cambridge: CUP, 1981).

—— *Mirrors in Mind* (New York: W. H. Freeman, 1997).

Jaynes, Julian, *The Origin of Consciousness in the Breakdown of the Bicameral Mind* (Boston, MA: Houghton Mifflin, 1976).

Laing, R. D., *The Divided Self: A Study of Sanity and Madness* (London: Tavistock, 1960).

Lakoff, George and Mark Johnson, *Metaphors We Live By* (Chicago, IL: University of Chicago Press, 1980).

—— *Philosophy in the Flesh: The Embodied Mind and its Challenge to Western Thought* (New York: Basic Books, 1999).

Lévy-Bruhl, Lucien, *Les Fonctions mentales dans les sociétés primitives* (1910; as pursued in H. R. Hays, *From Ape to Angel* [London: Methuen, 1958], and in Jacques Havet (ed.), *Main Trends of Research in the Social and Human Sciences, vol. I* [The Hague: Mouton–UNESCO, 1978].

Medawar, P. B., *The Art of the Soluble* (London: Methuen, 1967).

Ogden, C. K., *Opposition: A Linguistic and Psychological Analysis* (London: Kegan Paul, 1932; Bloomington: Indiana University Press, 1967). Theory of Oppositions demonstrates 29 logically different types of 'opposition'. It's a valuable spin-off from Ogden and Richards, *The Meaning of Meaning: A study of the Influence of Language upon Thought* (New York: Harcourt, Brace, 1923), with its rejection of Saussure. It may seem strange that they didn't push semantic theory further and Fredric Jameson in *The Prison-House of Language* (Princeton, NJ: Princeton University Press, 1972) fantasises that their political unconscious must have feared some eventual encounter with the invincible dialectic of Marxism. A more likely possibility is that pre-war ideas of scientific rigour , too rigorous for the 'fuzzy-edged logic' which a general semantics absolutely requires, couldn't give their project due support; relevant sciences like cognitive psychology, cultural sociology, logically appropriate semantics, didn't start to blossom until the late 1950s. Richards' personal interest was complex 'poetic' meaning, as pursued in *Principles of Literary Criticism* (London: K. Paul, Trench, Tribner, 1924) and *Practical Criticism* (London: K. Paul, Trench, Tribner, 1929).

Piaget, Jean, *Structuralism* (London: Routledge and Kegan Paul, 1971).

—— *Main Trends in Inter-disciplinary Research* (London: Allen and Unwin/Harper Torchbooks, 1973.

—— Goldmann, Lucien and Maurice de Gandillac, *Entretiens sur la notion de genèse et de structure* (Paris: Mouton, 1965).

Taylor, Gordon Rattray, *The Natural History of the Mind* (London: Secker and Warburg, 1979).

Wilden, Anthony, *System and Structure: Essays in Communication and Exchange* (London: Tavistock Press, 1972).